THE CREEKS WILL RISE

THE CREEKS WILL RISE

People Coexisting with Floods

WILLIAM S. BECKER

CHICAGO
REVIEW
PRESS

Copyright © 2021 by William S. Becker
Foreword copyright © 2021 by Bill McKibben
All rights reserved
Published by Chicago Review Press Incorporated
814 North Franklin Street
Chicago, Illinois 60610
ISBN 978-1-68275-275-3

Library of Congress Control Number: 2021940931

Cover design: Kateri Kramer
Cover photograph: Pete Olsen, https://www.peteolsenphotography.com
Typesetting: Nord Compo

Printed in the United States of America
5 4 3 2 1

To Eileen Schoville and Joni Peterson

CONTENTS

GUIDE TO ACRONYMS

AP	Associated Press
ASCE	American Society of Civil Engineers
ASDSO	Association of State Dam Safety Officials
AWG	Anthropocene Working Group
BLS	Bureau of Labor Statistics
CBO	Congressional Budget Office
CCI	Center for Climate Integrity
CDBG	Community Development Block Grant Program
CDP	Carbon Disclosure Project
CEI	Competitive Enterprise Institute
CO_2	Carbon dioxide
CSCs	Climate sanctuary cities
CWSRF	EPA Clean Water State Revolving Fund
DEA	Drug Enforcement Administration
DOE	US Department of Energy
DOI	US Department of the Interior
EEG	Electroencephalography
EIA	US Energy Information Administration
EIS	Environmental impact statement
EPA	Environmental Protection Agency
EPRI	Electric Power Research Institute
FEMA	Federal Emergency Management Administration

FMA	Flood Mitigation Assistance Grant Program
FWS	US Fish and Wildlife Service
GAO	Government Accountability Office
GDH	Gross Domestic Happiness
GDP	Gross Domestic Product
GLRI	Great Lakes Restoration Initiative
HUD	Department of Housing and Urban Development
IPCC	Intergovernmental Panel on Climate Change
NASA	National Aeronautics and Space Administration
NASEM	National Academies of Science, Engineering, and Medicine
NIBS	National Institute of Building Sciences
NOAA	National Oceanic and Atmospheric Administration
NYU	New York University
OPEC	Organization of Petroleum Exporting Countries
PDM	Pre-Disaster Mitigation Grant Program
PMF	Probable Maximum Flood
PPM	Parts per million
ROW	Rights of Way
SRI	Superfund Redevelopment Initiative
TVA	Tennessee Valley Authority
UCLA	University of California, Los Angeles
UCF	USDA Urban and Community Forestry Program
UCS	Union of Concerned Scientists
UN	United Nations
UNFCCC	United Nations Framework Convention on Climate Change
USACE	US Army Corps of Engineers
USGCRP	United States Global Change Research Program
USGS	US Geological Survey
UWSG	Urban Waters Small Grants Program
Y2Y	Yellowstone-to-Yukon Conservation Initiative

FOREWORD

A DAY BEFORE THANKSGIVING A FEW YEARS AGO, scientists from thirteen federal agencies issued the latest of their quadrennial reports on how global climate change is affecting the United States. The Trump administration hoped the report would get little attention on a holiday weekend. Instead, the obvious attempt to bury it made the report even more newsworthy, and it received wide coverage.

However, one climate impact in particular has yet to receive the attention it deserves. The lives of tens of millions of Americans depend on aging and inadequate flood-control structures on our rivers and coasts. Few were built to handle the record rains and unprecedented storm surges we are experiencing today. In fact, they were not even built to handle the range in climate variability we've seen in the past five hundred years. They are a national disaster waiting to happen, and the risk grows greater with each passing year.

There are at least 30,000 miles of recorded levees and more than 91,000 dams in the United States. Many were built to protect crops, store water, or provide recreation. Many others are meant to protect people and property. The typical flood-control dam was built to be reliable for fifty years, but when the American Society of Civil Engineers issued the most recent of its periodic report cards on America's infrastructure, it found that the average dam is approaching sixty. About 15,600 of these structures are classified as likely to result in fatalities if they fail. Failure is more likely and more deadly as the dams get older, the weather gets more severe, and more people move into floodplains thinking they are protected.

Climate change produces floods that exceed the capacities of old dams and test whether their age has made them unable to do their jobs. There are no precise data on how many dams have failed, but we know of 173 failures and 587 near failures between January 2005 and June 2013. As Bill Becker points out in this book, nearly 140 million people live within reach of floods along the nation's 3.5 million miles of rivers and 95,000 miles of shoreline. Engineers estimate it would take $115 billion to repair the dams and levees whose failures could cost lives. The experts warn that these structures are inherently risky.

So, we face a tough decision. Will we spend the money to repair flood-control infrastructure and upgrade it to handle the much larger floods and storms that climate change produces? Or is there a better way? Bill argues that there is.

He traces the long history of the nation's attempt to subdue rivers and waves and explains why a toxic mix of special interests and greed has increased rather than decreased the risks of death and destruction from floods in America. Then he describes the deepest lesson of floods: We must change our relationship with nature and stop treating it like an enemy we can control and defeat. Instead, we have a great deal to gain by collaborating with it. In fact, the quality of our lives, and even our survival, depend on it. With greater urgency than ever, we must achieve what our most important environmental law calls the "conditions under which man and nature can exist in productive harmony."[1] There is no other sustainable way to meet the real needs of this and future generations.

—Bill McKibben

INTRODUCTION

I HAVE ENORMOUS RESPECT FOR WATER in its natural habitat. It has almost killed me three times. I have been caught in an ocean undertow and swept away twice while fly-fishing in rivers swollen by spring runoff. Water can be as deadly as it is beautiful. It is fundamental to life, but it can kill.

No one knows that better than people who have survived destructive floods—or whose loved ones have not. It is in the nature of rivers to pour over their banks and oceans to invade coasts. It is in the nature of humans to like living near water. That has caused conflicts since a human built the first fixed structure in a floodplain.

In the United States, it has been two hundred years since the Supreme Court decided that people had the right to live wherever they want, and when they make poor choices, the federal government should protect them. In the years that followed, and especially in the twentieth century, the government built dams and levees, channelized rivers, installed floodwalls, and tried to control water with a variety of other engineering projects.

Paradoxically, these structures both saved lives and put lives at risk. People moved below dams, behind levees, and near seawalls assuming they were safe. Some were attracted to the water, the views, and the growing property values. In other cases, low-income families have lived in floodplains because lots are less expensive, and they are all that is left due to urban growth.[1] As a result, many families with the fewest resources to protect themselves or recover from floods are hurt most by them.

Over the generations, we have learned, confirmed, forgotten, and learned again that rivers and oceans are not predictable, and flood-control structures are not infallible. By the 1960s, Congress realized that despite all the money it had spent on flood-control projects, damages kept rising. Today, floods remain the most frequent and most expensive type of weather disaster in the United States.

From nature's standpoint, however, floods are necessary. They replenish soils, build new lands, and create habitats. They are disasters only when people and property get in the way. It follows that the safest way to avoid flood disasters is to prohibit development in floodplains, relocate the people who are already there, and let rivers to their jobs.

That would not be easy, but it could be less expensive and would certainly be safer than building more flood-control structures or upgrading those built fifty, sixty, or one hundred years ago. About 165 million of us—half the nation's total population—were affected by floods in 2019 alone.[2] Flood disasters are getting more destructive because of climate change, because dam and levee failures are more likely, and because the population in flood-prone places keeps growing. Every year that passes without doing something about this perfect storm puts Americans at greater risk.

This qualifies as a national crisis that requires attention now. We shouldn't have to wait for more deaths and destruction to occur before leaders have the political will to act. Instead, we should assess flood risks and mitigate them before the inevitable disasters occur.

As 2020 began, the National Weather Service warned that twenty-three states and nearly 130 million Americans were at risk of flooding in the coming year.[3] Seas are already rising and jeopardizing coastal property. Extreme floods that used to be rare are becoming common. Yet our current federal policies irrationally encourage Americans to become flood victims.

Over the last century, our response has been to send in bull-dozers to tame rivers, yet that hasn't stopped floods from getting worse or federal spending on disaster recovery to keep rising. Now, the more than 90,000 dams around the country are getting old and less reliable. If they begin to fail, the damages and deaths will be catastrophic.

In addition to eliminating those risks, we must accept that floods are a symptom of a much deeper issue: our self-defeating attitudes about our relationship with nature. In part II, I will explore how we can begin collaborating with natural systems rather than trying to subdue and control them. In my view, and that of many others, changing that relationship is the most critical mission of this century.

People in the environmental, energy, and climate-action communities will be familiar with some of this book's information. Students of history and people in the above-fifty crowd will remember many of the developments I recount from the 1960s and 1970s. I included them here to benefit younger generations, hoping that the information will help them build on these foundations for the next phase of America's evolution, especially concerning our relationship with the natural world.

I wade deep into our history with rivers and natural resources, including the greed that has motivated our mishandling of them. And although humankind's dissonance with the natural world is a global issue, I focus on the United States. I consider it the most extreme example of the misguided assumption that prosperity and environmental stewardship are mutually exclusive goals.

There are priceless benefits—economic, psychological, and practical— in the natural world. Reacquainting ourselves with them and repairing the damage that industrialization has done will be an invaluable gift for generations to come. It also is the most pragmatic thing we can do to improve our health, safety, and general welfare today.

Finally, a word on the book's title. I first heard the phrase "Good Lord willing and the creeks don't rise" when I was a boy. Generations ever since have appropriated the phrase to express the more general recognition that our best-laid plans and intentions are vulnerable to forces over which we have little or no control. One of the most consequential is global climate change, a phenomenon that we, not other forces, set in motion. We must stop emitting the pollution that causes climate change and adapt to the disruptive and dangerous new reality we have created, including rising seas and record floods. Unless we better understand and respect the environmental systems we have altered, climate change will be immeasurably worse, and our efforts to adapt to it will be ineffective. I will begin with the story of a community that figured this out decades ago.

PART I

WATER

1

THE KICKAPOO VALLEY

We must begin thinking like a river if we are to leave a
legacy of beauty and life for future generations.

—David Brower, conservationist and mountaineer

THERE ARE STILL UNPROTECTED PLACES IN AMERICA that have not been
too discovered, which is to say, spoiled. In 1968, just back from a year
in the Vietnam War, I looked for a place like that to process the experience. I wanted somewhere peaceful and full of nature, far from media
and the antiwar protests that were growing more violent in cities and on
campuses around the country.

As fate would have it, I happened across a woman in Chicago who
owned a farm in Wisconsin. It was to be her retirement place someday,
and she was looking for a few people to care for it until she was ready.
I moved there a month after meeting her.

The farm consisted of 250 acres in a valley between forested hills. Its
old frame house had once been painted white and its barn was a faded
red. The outbuildings were a serviceable chicken coop and a springhouse
where cold water bubbled up through fine sand, as pure and constant
as water can be. The farmhouse was tucked against one of the hills at
the end of a long gravel driveway. The driveway was connected to a
narrow country road through our valley, which we learned was called
Sleepy Hollow. The country road connected to a state highway that led
back to the chaos of civilization.

Five other people were already living on the farm when I arrived, each recruited by the same woman. The oldest of us was in his early twenties. None of us had ever lived on a farm before or cared for an animal bigger than the ill-tempered Siamese cat that one of the married couples brought with them. He disappeared every night and reappeared in the mornings, often bleeding from a wound he suffered while fighting with a wild animal of some kind. One time, he went out and never came back.

Despite our lack of experience, the owner put us in charge of several dairy cows, four aggressive goats, a dozen sheep, a bunch of chickens, and a horse. When we expressed a little anxiety about being responsible for these living things, the woman, who was a bit of a mystic, simply told us, "Pick up your shovels and you'll know what to do." It was her metaphor for learning to trust our intuitions.

This was years before Google, so we relied on an antique animal husbandry manual whose cover had come unglued. Our backup was a local veterinarian who was kind enough to take our calls and give us free advice. We were nervous about caring for these animals. They all were likable—except for the goats, a mean chicken, and a ram that enjoyed charging and sometimes knocking down anybody who went into the pasture.

It was the type of place I'd hoped for. The owner's expectations were high, so we worked long days, often dawn to dusk, milking the cows, baling and stacking hay, putting up new fences, weeding the vegetable garden, and trying to figure out how to keep the chickens from cannibalizing each other. One of the other men, Stan, was in charge of the chickens, but the book said nothing about cannibalization. Stan tried various solutions. He gave the chickens more supplements. When that didn't work, he staked out the coop to see who the bully was so he could chop off its head. That didn't work either.

We learned as we went. We figured out that it was easier to toss a hay bale downhill than uphill when we heaved it onto the hay wagon. We wasted a lot of time trying to drive the sheep into the barn without a dog. They responded by scattering in all directions. We figured out that they would follow us obediently into the barn if we led them with a bucket of oats and shook it so they could hear that it contained food. It kept their undivided attention.

Work on the farm was hard, but I found it to be therapeutic. So was the absence of radio, television, and newspapers. But the best therapy came from the land. Because we were wedged between hills, the valley was cast in shadow by late afternoon. Every evening as dinnertime approached, the next farmer down the valley bellowed "BAWWWSSS" (boss), which echoed between the hills and called his herd home for milking. By sunset, the only sound was a single whip-poor-will that hung around the farm. We played guitars and sang a few evenings each week, but there was not much downtime. We grew lean and muscular. It was an excellent life.

I should tell you more about the farm's location. Sleepy Hollow is in the Kickapoo River Valley of southwest Wisconsin. Our farm was several miles from the Kickapoo River, which flowed for 130 miles between hills as tall as thirty-story buildings. The river is nourished by 500 miles of spring-fed streams that provide ideal habitat for brown trout. The valley itself is home to more than 300 species of plants and flowers, more than 100 species of birds, and all manner of mammals—muskrats, beavers, white-tailed deer, raccoons, woodchucks, minks, otters, and foxes. The Kickapoo ends at the Wisconsin River, a tributary of the Mississippi.

This is the driftless area of Wisconsin, a 24,000-square-mile region that includes parts of three states. The hills prove that the last ice age spared the region from the glaciers that flattened most other places before it ended about ten thousand years ago. Some geologists believe the Kickapoo Valley is one of the oldest river systems in the world, and it looked to be true. The place has an ancient feel. It remains largely undeveloped except for small family farms and villages every few miles. The forested hills that cradle the river and the ancient stone outcroppings that rise from its banks convey that the valley has gotten along quite well without humans, who after all are only squatters on a zeptosecond of geological history.

The Kickapoo meanders in so many directions along its course that it also is called the most crooked river in North America. In fact, *Kickapoo* is the Algonquian word for "one who goes here, then there." Geologists call it a misfit stream, meaning it isn't large enough to have shaped the valley through which it runs. In fact, the river is only 15 feet wide in some places. But *misfit* fits because the river is moody and it can turn violent. Its watershed is 500,000 acres of the hilly terrain, which sends runoff cascading into the river during heavy rains and thaws. The runoff carries silt, which settles on the bottom of the river's channel, reducing the amount of water it can contain.

The Kickapoo has a long history of going rogue. It picks up speed and volume from its tributaries and spills over its banks to inundate farms and villages. Most floods are inconvenient "anklet ticklers," but some are devastating.

Several other conditions in the valley make it ideal for floods. Wisconsin winters can freeze the ground well into spring so the soil is unable to absorb rain. Other times, the snows are so abundant that the spring melt causes floods. Year-round, sustained rainstorms can saturate the ground until it can hold no more, and the rainwaters rush down the hills and into the river. Floods have always been part of life in the valley, but the big ones are part of its lore. Everyone refers to them by the years they happened: 1907, 1912, 1917, 1935, 1951, 1956, 1978, 2007, 2008,

Kickapoo River in Wisconsin's driftless area. *Mark Mille*

2016, and 2017. Floods have been so frequent that two of the counties through which the river runs hold Wisconsin's record for flood-related emergency declarations. The Kickapoo River is always present, always flowing, and always dangerous.[1]

We ate well with vegetables from the garden, eggs from the chickens, whole milk from which we made cream and butter, and the world's best homemade bread. One of the women loved baking and kept yeast growing on a windowsill in the kitchen. Challah was a favorite. Sometimes we traded eggs for other foods, like the maple syrup that two old bachelor brothers down the road cooked every spring in their sugar bush. We helped them gather the sap and dump it into a long sheet-metal bin on top of a wood fire, where it would bubble and boil until it was thick and brown.

We didn't need much else, but I wanted a little spending money, so I went to work part-time for the weekly newspaper in the nearest river town, Soldiers Grove. The paper was called the *Kickapoo Scout*. It was the oldest in the valley.

The newspaper office was located on Main Street in the center of Soldiers Grove's modest and water-damaged business district. People wandered in and out all day with contributions for the paper, including pages of notes on who did what with whom, when, and where. Readers eagerly anticipated this information more than anything else in each week's newspaper. It was gossip the big daily papers didn't cover. I gradually met many of the villagers and learned more about the community's history. The flood that stood out most in people's memories occurred in 1951, a record-breaker at the time. Eight inches of rain fell during the last week of July. That flood took six lives. Some say ten.

Old black-and-white photos captured scenes as the river surged through town with enough force to send cars tumbling down Main Street side-over-side. All manner of debris, mud, animal wastes, and unidentifiable other things raced along with the current. I asked one elderly woman what the '51 flood was like. "Devilish things," she said, scrunching her nose. "Devilish things."

One photo shows dented cars piled on top of each other, as though the river had stacked them politely like a good guest before moving on. The most famous photo shows two elderly sisters in the second-story window of their house. The river pushed it off its foundation and carried it away with the sisters inside, but it lodged up against a large tree before it floated very far. A small aluminum motorboat fights the current as the pilot tries to talk the women into climbing through their window and into the boat.

The pilot turned out to be the banker from the next town downriver. The sisters finally agreed to let him help them into the boat. "With fear I stepped from the upstairs window into the swirling rescue boat," one of the sisters told a reporter. "It was then I resolved never again to complain about material things." The photo went viral, which in 1951 meant that readers clipped it from a city newspaper and passed it around for a while.

One might expect the people in Soldiers Grove to have post-traumatic stress disorder (PTSD) from their many floods, but they were

Elderly sisters are rescued during the 1951 flood in Soldiers Grove. *Compliments of Don Dennison Collection*

afflicted instead with what I called "floodplain amnesia." Years later, while working with flood victims in other communities, I found that this was typical. After each big flood subsided and a little time passed, people forgot about the bad parts but remembered how their community came together. Floods were bonding experiences. Farmers came down from the hills and out from the valleys to share milk, bread, fresh meat, and vegetables. People who needed help didn't have to ask. A reclusive farmer who was seldom seen in normal times might be found shoveling the muck out of a widow's home. Floods provided confirmation that neighbors still helped neighbors, that people were fundamentally good, and the community was what a community should be. Arguments were forgotten and grievances forgiven in the aftermath of a flood, and people rationalized that each one would be the last.

After a couple of seasons on the farm, tuned up physically and emotionally, I decided to go back to the city to find a full-time job. I moved to Madison, Wisconsin's capital, and began work as a reporter and photographer for the Associated Press.

Madison is home to the University of Wisconsin's main campus. In the 1960s and 1970s, it topped the list with Berkeley as the hottest hotbeds of violent protests against the Vietnam War. Kent State was known for the four students who were shot to death by members of the Ohio National Guard. Madison was known for a bombing that killed a researcher working in the middle of the night at the Army Mathematics Research Center on campus, a facility rumored to have something to do with Agent Orange. The four men responsible for the bombing thought the building would be empty at that time of night, but they were wrong.

I spent many nights running through the streets ahead of tear-gas clouds, stopping every half hour to pound on strangers' doors to telephone updates to the AP bureau in Milwaukee. It seems surprising now that almost everyone let me into their homes, but they did. Because I had a camera hanging from my neck, protestors mistook me for a cop, and police mistook me for a protestor. I managed to elude violence from either group until a policeman struck me in the head with his baton one afternoon, knocking me down and breaking my Nikon. I had managed to get through the Vietnam War without a significant injury, only to be knocked nearly unconscious by a peace officer at home. But war is war wherever it is fought, except that we weren't awarded Purple Hearts in the war at home.

Many of the demonstrations deteriorated into riots with students smashing the windows of office buildings and stores, staying just ahead of the police. Once, when a protestor leaned against a parked car to rest, its burly owner turned up and punched him in the face once or twice to express his opinion about kids he assumed were avoiding the draft.

The stress of those nights took its toll over time. We might expect real wars to desensitize soldiers to violence, but I came back from Vietnam hypersensitized to the point that I couldn't even watch movie violence without stress attacks where I felt on the edge of a bottomless pit. Nevertheless, I soldiered on with the AP until early one winter morning on the way to work. I felt I had to vomit, so I pulled over to the side of the road. I heaved up a mouthful of blood that was shockingly red against the fresh snow. It was a pretty clear signal that it was time to pull back from the job. Destiny came to my rescue again a day or two later when the *Kickapoo Scout*'s owners called to say they were ready to retire. They asked if I'd like to buy the newspaper.

2

GLORY DAYS

People in small towns, much more than in cities, share
a destiny.

—Richard Russo

SOLDIERS GROVE DID NOT CHOOSE to become what federal officials call a
"repetitive victim" of floods. The village began with a single lumber mill
built on the bank of the river in the 1800s. Flooding was not a problem
until later when logging and farming cleared trees and other vegetation
from the watershed's hills.

The sawmill attracted a trading post, the trading post attracted more
settlers, and soon it was a town. As the end of the 1800s approached,
the villagers installed waterworks and the first electric service in the
valley. People were afraid initially that light bulbs would cause fires, so
it took a while for electricity to catch on. But before long, the village's
Electric Light Company turned the power on at 6:00 PM and turned it
off at 11:00 PM. Customers paid one dollar per month. On nights there
were dances, the lights stayed on until 2:00 AM.

Soldiers Grove built its first school in 1898. Cement sidewalks and
the first telephone appeared in 1900. As the years went on, the community added an opera hall, funeral parlor, furniture store, barbershop,
jewelry store, grist and flour mill, movie theater, dance hall, several
banks, a tin shop, a blacksmith, a tailor, a tobacco warehouse, drug
stores, harness shops, a bootmaker and wagonmaker, various restaurants,

11

Main Street, Soldiers Grove, back in the day. *Photographer unknown*

and an ice-cream parlor, soda-pop factory, stockyard, barrel-stave maker, livery stable, and more taverns than any other town in the region on a per capita basis.

Traveling troupes of entertainers put the village on their circuits, performing in the opera house while the audience watched from three balconies. Medicine shows entertained during intermissions. When workers removed siding from a building many generations later, they found posters advertising Kickapoo Indian Sagwa. It was an elixir made from rhubarb, chili peppers, mandrake root, an antioxidant from a South American tree, a chemical commonly used as a water softener, and alcohol. It was supposed to cure "dyspepsia, sick headache, sour stomach, loss of appetite, heartburn, depression, neuralgia, female disorders, liver complaint, constipation, indigestions, rheumatism, impure blood, jaundice, bilious attacks, fever and ague, and all diseases of the stomach, liver, kidneys and the blood."

People were most proud of the Head Quarters Hotel, which offered the finest accommodations in the valley. It was three-stories tall with a lobby decorated in oak and walnut wainscoting and hand-painted murals of local scenery. But it wasn't until 1892 that Soldiers Grove felt it had

Kickapoo Indian Sagwa: The cure for whatever ails us. *Photographer unknown*

really arrived. That was the year the Kickapoo Stump Dodger came to town. To pay for the railroad's construction, each village along the route contributed $500, farmers donated rights-of-way across their lands, and people without property or money provided labor.

The train carried farm produce to market and transported people up and down the valley. It was not known for speed. At one point on its maiden trip, a woman driving a horse and buggy kept up with it. People figured the crew was cautious about the newly laid track. But in time, progress derailed the Stump Dodger. Highways improved, and trucks took over most of the freight business. The trucks spared farmers the inconvenience of herding their livestock to the railroad station in Soldiers Grove.

Automobiles took away much of the train's passenger business, the logging industry faded, and the valley abandoned the Stump Dodger. After World War II, the population drain began. Many young men moved to cities for jobs rather than going home to places like the Kickapoo Valley. Part of Soldiers Grove's vitality was due to a state highway that ran through the middle of the business district. Unfortunately, the

Stump Dodger

The Stump Dodger brought a boost to Kickapoo River villages until cars and trucks took over in the 1930s. *Courtesy of the Johnson family*

state later relocated the road to bypass the town. Many villagers considered it a death blow to their economy. The federal government eventually classified the entire region as "economically depressed." When I took over the newspaper in 1975, more than a third of the village's households earned less than $3,000 a year.

Now, most of the commercial enterprises fit onto a block-long section of Main Street. Only three or four of the buildings were less than a half-century old. They reminded me of boxers who had taken too many punches. But the old buildings were wooden monuments to endurance, still standing despite generations of abuse from the river. There was still a hardware store, a supermarket, a feed mill, a gas station, a lumberyard, a cheese factory, and a bank. The Kickapoo Valley Medical Clinic operated out of a prefabricated ranch house.

My newspaper office was one of the older buildings. Its original pressed-metal ceiling had survived, but the floor had not. A soft spot

Main Street, Soldiers Grove, across the Kickapoo River before relocation.
Kathy Fairchild

indicated where the joists underneath had rotted. I learned to avoid it. A long-abandoned remnant of the village's heyday, the Electric Movie Theatre, was next door, locked up for decades without electricity. Inside, its seats were scattered and covered in silt. The villagers didn't talk about it much, but everyone figured that one more severe flood would relocate Soldiers Grove to the Mississippi River.

Until that day arrived, life went on as usual. Farmers arrived after morning milking and joined their retired friends for breakfast at the Village Café. People came and went from the bank and the supermarket. A fire siren sounded every day at noon, setting off a chorus of howling dogs. On sunny days, old men sat on a bench outside one store, chatting, napping, and watching the world go by on Main Street. When the sun shifted to the opposite side of the street, they shifted, too, and settled on another bench that was permanently reserved for them.

Every June, Soldiers Grove celebrated Dairy Days, a big deal in Wisconsin. The annual Dairy Days parade moved proudly down Main

Street featuring John Deere tractors; huge draft horses; men, women, and children wearing Western finery on horseback; and the North Crawford High School Band, which was pretty good even though it played a little off-key. We cut it some slack because few of us had ever tried to play a tuba while marching.

Miss June Dairy Days waved to us in her prom dress from the back of a polished convertible. To seem more substantial, the parade always turned around at the end of Main Street and made a second pass. It was led enthusiastically every year by a young girl with Down syndrome who was loved as though she was the whole town's daughter.

The Kickapoo Valley was in the people's blood. When one old man couldn't work his farm anymore, he sold it and died a couple of weeks later, most likely because his life lost purpose when he didn't have to milk his cows twice a day. One afternoon, the sheriff came to my office and asked me to take a ride with him. A half-mile outside the village, we walked to a cluster of trees on the riverbank. An elderly man from the Soldiers Grove nursing home lay dead there, a pistol in his hand, his jacket neatly folded by his side with a note on top. He wrote that his life was not worth living anymore because his body wouldn't let him do what he loved most: fishing, hunting, and hiking along the river. I printed his obituary in the *Scout* that week without mentioning how he died. Suicide was not the kind of information that was welcome in a small-town paper.

3

THE DAM

A dam tears at all the interconnected webs of river valley life.

—Author Patrick McCully

THE FLOOD OF 1935 FINALLY CONVINCED PEOPLE UP and down the valley that the river was killing their communities. So, in 1937, they jointly petitioned Congress for a flood-control project. Dams and levees were the preferred solutions in those days because President Franklin Roosevelt's New Deal was funding public-works projects to create jobs.

Environmental regulations didn't exist yet, so except for Congress's approval of the money, dam building was not inhibited by government-mandated studies and approvals. As writer Marc Reisner noted in his book on dams in the American West:

> The astonishing thing about . . . the whole era—was that people just went out and built it, built anything without knowing exactly how to do it or whether it could even be done. There were no task forces, no special commissions, no proposed possible preliminary outlines of conceivable tentative recommendations. Tremendous environmental impacts, but no environmental impact statements.[1]

World War II, then the Korean War, delayed congressional action on the Kickapoo Valley's request. Meantime, the 1951 flood confirmed the valley's need for protection. In 1962, Congress finally gave the US Army Corps of Engineers (USACE or "corps") the go-ahead to build an earthen dam 71.5 feet high across the northern end of the Kickapoo River, a mile above the village of La Farge. The dam would impound an 800-acre recreational lake. Because it would be too far away to protect Soldiers Grove, the corps intended to build two levees there, one on each side of the river. The cost for the entire valley's flood-control project would be $15 million. It was to be the most ambitious public works undertaking in Wisconsin's history.

However, Congress gave the corps discretionary authority to alter the plan. So, the USACE expanded it to a 103-foot-high dam and an 1,800-acre lake surrounded by thirteen recreation areas. The lake was to cover 14 miles of the upper Kickapoo River at a cost of $26 million. The corps estimated that it would attract 735,000 tourists every year—a godsend for the businesses in La Farge. Like all the villages along the Kickapoo, La Farge was an economically depressed community surrounded by economically depressed farms. The lake promised tourist dollars, construction jobs, and opportunities for new businesses.

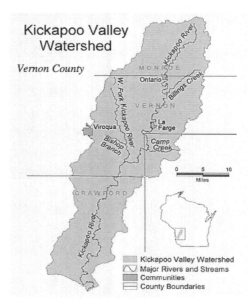

The Kickapoo River watershed and villages. *FEMA*

Whoever owned land around the lake would see their property values skyrocket.

The corps began buying more than one hundred farms in the project area at fair-market value, despite emotional opposition from some land-owners. Then in 1970, the National Environmental Policy Act became law and required that federal agencies assess the impacts of projects involving government funds. The La Farge dam was one of the first projects obligated to have such an assessment. It revealed issues about endangered plant species in the project area and potential problems with the lake's water quality. The corps tweaked its plans to address those problems, and Congress gave it the go-ahead.

By now, the cost had climbed to $38 million. Wisconsin senator William Proxmire, who was famous for uncovering wasteful government spending, asked the corps to reassess whether the benefits of the project still exceeded its costs.

The corps found that the project failed the new benefit-cost test, so it suspended work in 1975, the year I took over the *Scout*. The corps had completed half of the dam's embankment by then, stop-ping just short of blocking the river. It had spent more than $18 mil-lion and had dislocated more than a hundred families. La Farge lost property tax revenue, customers for its businesses, and students for its schools.

Although work stopped, the congressional authorization was still in effect, giving people in La Farge hope that the dam would be completed. In the meantime, the corps turned its attention to Soldiers Grove, per-haps hoping that the benefits of the levees there would help the project's benefit-cost ratio. The corps finally informed the village that it was ready to present its plan for protecting the community.

The Reveal

The corps scheduled its presentation for a Wednesday evening in the vil-lage's middle school gymnasium. Anticipating my first real news story at the *Kickapoo Scout*, I joined the stream of people filing into the gym and taking seats in folding chairs while two army officers taped charts to the walls. Soon there was standing room only.

The officers began by explaining that Soldiers Grove was 15 miles from the proposed dam. There were so many tributaries along that distance that the dam would not offer much protection. So, the corps would spend $3.5 million to build a levee on each side of the river as it wound through town. The village's share would be $220,000. Also, the community would have to set aside $10,000 every year to maintain and eventually replace pumps to remove water from the business district if there were unusually heavy rains or a levee failure.

When the officers mentioned the local costs, the crowd stirred. The corps dealt with projects that cost millions and even billions of dollars, so it might have assumed that a few hundred thousand dollars wouldn't be an issue, but it was. The villagers knew they couldn't afford the levees. The pump set-aside alone would double the community's property taxes, and $220,000 exceeded its statutory debt limit.

There were other reasons the plan didn't make sense. The $3.5 million project would protect a business district whose assessed value was only $1 million. And even if they were affordable and did their job, the levees would just turn Soldiers Grove from a dying town vulnerable to flooding into a dying town protected from flooding. Buildings would still be worth next to nothing. Levees might keep water out, but they wouldn't keep young people in. Most left the community and never came back after graduating high school.

Besides, the older villagers had seen the Kickapoo in full rampage. They were not confident that the two earthen berms would stand up to it. A flood three years earlier in Rapid City, South Dakota, was still fresh in mind. Two dams failed in the Black Hills, contributing to a flood that killed 238 people and injured 3,000.

The final blow to the villagers' expectations was a law Congress passed in 1968. It required that any new building in a floodplain had to be elevated 3 feet above the level necessary to protect it from 100-year floods. Existing buildings would have to be floodproofed if their repairs exceeded 50 percent of their value at the time of the flood. The law required at-risk communities to pass ordinances to this effect. If they didn't, no one could obtain any kind of federal funding, including loans or mortgages from federally insured banks. Soldiers Grove had enough trouble retaining businesses without requiring them to take on the additional costs of floodproofing. And most of its floodplain buildings were not worth the extra investment anyway. The villagers had hoped a levee would exempt them from these requirements, but it would not.

I wasn't sure what kind of flood protection the villagers had anticipated after waiting forty years, but this was not it. They were looking for a rebirth, not the same old life inside two walls. When the meeting was over, I walked out of the gym next to Pat Young, the owner of Grove's jukebox repair shop. "They should just pick this place up and move it out of here," he joked. We chuckled.

But I woke up in the middle of the night, thinking it was not such a bad idea.

4

THE SOFT PATH

People shouldn't be living in certain places—on earthquake faults or on flood plains. But they do, and there
are consequences.

—Czech Canadian scientist Vaclav Smil

THE NEXT MORNING, JERRY SCHOVILLE, who with his wife, Eileen, was
the *Scout*'s previous owner, met me at the newspaper office to brainstorm
about "picking this place up and moving it out of here." A move would
not have to involve the entire town; only the business district and about
25 percent of the village's homes were in the floodplain.

We weren't aware of the law Congress has recently passed obli-
gating the USACE to consider nonstructural alternatives. When I
read its environmental impact statement for the levees, I saw that
the USACE briefly mentioned relocation and dismissed it as "socially
unacceptable." However, it came to that conclusion without asking
the village. The first step, Jerry and I decided, would be to determine
whether the businesses and the village board would welcome a study
of relocation.

I visited with Cecil Turk, the village president and amiable owner
of the local supermarket. I asked whether he thought the village board
would support relocation as an alternative to the levee. "I think they'll go
along," Turk replied. "I've been thinking about the same idea for some
time. I wondered why it hadn't been given serious thought."

Back in my office, I drafted a short questionnaire to survey businesses on whether they'd agree to a study. Eileen Schoville took it up and down Main Street and returned an hour later with the results: nearly all of the business owners were willing to consider relocating.

The next day, I wrote a proposal titled "Relocation: An Alternative for the Village of Soldiers Grove." It happened that the village board was meeting that evening, so I showed up and passed the proposal around. After a short discussion, the board gave me the go-ahead to send it to the corps.

My write-up described how moving away from the river would free the community from repetitive flood disasters and free the federal government from paying for repetitive flood relief. I suggested that Soldiers Grove could become an example for other communities prone to floods. I pointed out that "when people come in conflict with a river, sometimes it's the people who should change."

With me looking on, Cecil Turk shows the relocation proposal that Soldiers Grove submitted to the USACE. *Wisconsin State Journal via AP*

I took the proposal to a printer the next day. Before the ink could dry, a member of the village board, Ron Swiggum, owner of the Village Meat Market, came to my office and asked for a dozen copies. He didn't say why he wanted them, and I didn't ask. He came back an hour later and put fifty dollars in small bills on my desk. He had distributed the proposals up and down Main Street in exchange for donations to reimburse me for the printing costs. I sent one copy to the USACE. Several days later, a representative called to say the corps was willing to substitute relocation for the levee in valley's overall flood-control plan.

Evacuating the old business district and rebuilding it on higher ground seemed implausible on the one hand and utterly sensible on the other. The old buildings could not be disturbed without collapsing, so transporting them to a new site was not an option. We'd have to build new. That was a good thing, though: it would give business owners a fresh start in safe and modern buildings. Soldiers Grove could use the Federal Emergency Management Agency's (FEMA's) buyout program to purchase the old buildings at fair market value.[1] The village would pay its share with bond revenues or other federal and state grants. Also, Wisconsin communities were allowed to keep their property-tax revenues for economic development rather than sending them to schools and counties—an arrangement called Tax Incremental Financing. I mailed the proposal to the members of Wisconsin's congressional delegation and the state's major media.

Two months later, the corps issued a revised plan with relocation substituted for levees in Soldiers Grove.

Before long, fleshing out a plan and investigating where we could obtain the funds to do it became a full-time job. I had a newspaper to publish, so the village secured a small federal grant to hire a full-time relocation coordinator. It chose Tom Hirsch, an architect from the Chicago area who had moved to the valley with his wife. He wasn't yet licensed to practice architecture in Wisconsin, so he drove a school bus. The grant was meant for hiring underemployed people, and Tom definitely qualified.

We heard that another town, Niobrara, Nebraska, was in the process of moving, so Cecil, Tom, and I made a road trip to have a look. Niobrara was flooding from underneath because of two dams and an

Tom Hirsch posts documents for the community to see on the village's relocation plans. *Courtesy of the author*

impoundment the corps built downriver. When we arrived, we had to stop at an intersection for a large Victorian house rolling slowly down the street, towed by a truck. As the house passed, we could see breakfast dishes still on the table, showing how careful the process was. Even though none of the business buildings were sound enough to be moved that way in Soldiers Grove, the spectacle confirmed for us that relocation was possible.

We recruited landscape-architect students from the University of Wisconsin to help us evaluate possible sites. They did the work for academic credit. The village board selected several acres of vacant land next to the same highway that had been moved from Main Street decades earlier. That helped persuade business owners that relocation would be good for business. The site was adjacent to one of the neighborhoods outside the floodplain, a half-mile from and 55 feet higher in elevation than the downtown.

It wasn't long before news media got word of the project. One weekend, a Chicago radio station interviewed Milfred Burkum, the owner of

The weekly newspaper in Soldiers Grove kept the village's residents abreast of developments. *Courtesy of the author*

the village's feed mill. With the second Arab oil embargo fresh in mind, Burkum mentioned casually that solar energy might be a good option in the new town. I had been tempted several times to suggest that, but I held back because I worried it would make the move seem even more radical. But since one of the old-timers brought it up, we added solar energy to the list of possibilities for the new business district. I was surprised by how quickly everyone embraced it. Maybe solar energy seems more practical in towns whose residents include retired farmers. They are accustomed to working with nature. Farming is an active partnership between people, land, sun, and rain.

Hirsch contacted two of the nation's best known "green" architects, the husband-and-wife team of Rodney and Sidney Wright, who specialized in designing "passive" solar buildings.[2] Heating was a significant expense in Wisconsin, so heating with the sun was attractive. Remarkably, the Wrights promised that solar-heated buildings would cost no more than comparable conventional buildings in the region. The village board hired the Wrights to design the municipal building. It did so with a strategy in mind. The municipal building would be the first to be constructed at the new location. Anyone hesitant about relying on solar heating during cold Wisconsin winters could visit the building to experience it in action. In addition, the Wrights' contract included a requirement that they set up a storefront office on Main Street where people could drop by to ask questions and see architectural drawings of how individual buildings and the business district in its entirety would look.

To give residents an opportunity for input at every stage, the village board created an advisory committee to help guide the project and identify opportunities for the move to achieve co-benefits—in other words, solutions to other problems that could be solved during relocation. The co-benefits for Soldiers Grove included:

- Moving the business district closer to a state highway where it was more visible to potential customers
- Using local materials in construction and hiring local labor
- Changing some of the businesses to provide missing goods and services so people didn't have to shop elsewhere
- Providing recreation facilities in the evacuated floodplain, including a campground and showers for canoeists, picnic shelters, tennis courts, horseshoe pits, a corral for equestrian events, a baseball diamond, and a memorial to the community's war heroes and veterans.[3]

Although Congress would not pass the Americans with Disabilities Act for another decade, Soldiers Grove made sure the entire business area was handicap accessible. One of the community's favorite sons was "Bullet" Bob Peterson. He earned the nickname as a high school track star before he fought in Vietnam and came home a paraplegic.

To make sure the new business district would demonstrate responsible energy use, the village board passed several innovative ordinances. One required each new building to comply with thermal performance standards at least twice as stringent as those in state law. Another, believed to be the first of its kind in the United States, required every new building to obtain at least half of its heating energy from the sun. A third ordinance prohibited any new construction from blocking another building's sunlight.

Hirsch and the Wrights also considered an often-overlooked factor in new construction: the influence of "microclimates" in the immediate areas of the buildings. Wherever possible, the buildings were oriented and landscaped to block winter winds and channel summer breezes.

But perhaps the most important co-benefit was the opportunity to replace the old buildings with new ones that were healthier and more comfortable for customers and owners and that kept energy bills low to help pay off any loans required to build anew. Relocation was an opportunity for building owners to capture some value from real estate that no one else was likely to buy.

Meanwhile, the community benefited from cleaner air and an increase in its tax base. The nation benefited from a little more energy independence, a little less of the carbon pollution responsible for climate change, and a demonstration of a more intelligent and ecological approach to disaster avoidance. Many years later, as climate change became a national issue, the project would be called an early example of mitigation (by reducing fossil energy pollution), adaptation (by anticipating and avoiding the larger floods that climate change would produce), and ecosystem restoration (by returning the floodplain to the river so it could slow and absorb floodwaters).

While buildings went up at the new site, they came down on Main Street. It was a bittersweet experience for many owners and their customers. One sunny day, I stood across the street from the Wonder Bar, a longtime watering hole. The bar's owner, Marie Herbst, was there along with a patron I'll call George. He wore striped overalls containing a beer belly that preceded him by a second wherever he went. He was a jovial, salt-of-the-earth man.

We watched as a bulldozer moved into position. "We had a lot of good times in there," George said wistfully. I avoided looking at Marie so she could shed a private tear or two. The bulldozer gave the Wonder Bar a nudge, and it collapsed into a cloud of dust and a pile of rubble. Before the dust even settled, the bulldozer operator moved his machine to the next building. He had a lot of work to do before the evidence of old times and floods was gone.

5

THE BATTLE OF LA FARGE

Choosing to save a river is more often an act of passion than of careful calculation. You make the choice because the river has touched your life in an intimate and irreversible way, because you are unwilling to accept its loss.

—David Bolling

THE HISTORY OF THE DRIFTLESS AREA includes a tragic war between Native Americans led by a sixty-five-year-old Sauk warrior named Black Hawk and more than a thousand US soldiers and Illinois militiamen. Between April and August 1832, the two sides fought brutal battles in northwest Illinois and southwest Wisconsin because of a treaty dispute about land. More than seventy soldiers and settlers and as many as six hundred Native Americans had been killed when it was over. Black Hawk did not want war. He tried at least twice to appeal to US soldiers for negotiations. In both instances, the soldiers didn't have interpreters and couldn't understand Black Hawk or his emissaries, and the war continued.

More than 140 years later, in the 1970s, the La Farge dam project triggered a new land battle. The corps now planned to build a dam that would create a lake by putting nearly 9,000 acres and 12 miles of river permanently underwater. It would destroy one of the driftless area's most scenic areas. While relocation inched along in Soldiers Grove, the dam escalated into a national controversy. Environmental groups such as the Sierra Club opposed its completion, as did Wisconsin senator Gaylord Nelson, the leading environmentalist in Congress and

Concept drawing of the La Farge dam. *USACE*

the founder of Earth Day. In the valley, the battle was between Kickapoogians who wanted to save the river and those who wanted to save
the region's economy.

While one side focused on what the upper Kickapoo Valley would
gain from the lake, the other side focused on what the valley would lose.
The La Farge dam project would do what the last ice age did not: It
would destroy features formed hundreds of millions of years ago, including sandstone bluffs that looked like they were nearly as old as God.

I followed the controversy and published articles about it in the
Kickapoo Scout. I was neutral at first because I appreciated both views,
food for the table versus food for the soul. Before long, however,
environmental groups produced credible studies showing that Lake La
Farge would not deliver what its supporters hoped. One study found
that most man-made lakes generated few local jobs because construction and hotel management were done mostly by outside companies.
Studies of other lakes in agricultural areas showed that runoff carried
fertilizers to the water and caused eutrophication, a condition where
high levels of nutrients result in algae blooms. The algae consumed
oxygen, killed fish, smelled bad, and gave people swimmer's itch.
Still other studies concluded that the lake would drown endangered
plant species.

One of the sandstone bluffs that line the upper Kickapoo River. They were formed near the shores of an ancient inland sea that covered part of the central United States from 700 million to 250 million years ago. Rivers eroded mountains in northern Wisconsin and carried sediment to the sea where it was deposited in the layers seen here. *Courtesy of John Toren*

These findings convinced me to begin editorializing against the dam. Before long, I found myself in a newspaper war with the *La Farge Epitaph*, the weekly newspaper in the village just below the proposed lake. Our editorial exchanges made lively reading, mostly because *Epitaph* editor Lonnie Muller had a flair for earthy rhetoric. I argued with facts. Lonnie returned fire with gritty metaphors, unapologetic hyperbole, and colorful insults that even I found entertaining. That was the thing about Lonnie. I usually disagreed with what he wrote, but I always got a kick out of the way he wrote it.

Veiled and not-so-veiled threats from elsewhere were more serious. One northern valley resident warned me that he'd make sure I lost my advertisers if I continued opposing the dam. Someone sent me an anonymous note warning that I should enjoy my house while it lasted. I raised my fire insurance coverage.

The People's Court

As the tensions grew, one of the dam's most vocal supporters, La Farge funeral director Arlen Johnson, invited me to come upriver and explain my views to farmers and business owners there. I considered it. The folks in La Farge could be the most hostile force I had faced since Vietnam. The Kickapoo Valley's farmers tended to be burly and muscular with pitchfork skills and the ability to castrate an animal before it knew what was happening. I wondered if it meant anything that a funeral director invited me.

Johnson probably didn't expect me to accept, so I did. On a Wednesday evening a week later, I drove the dark country roads to La Farge and parked in front of its bank, where the meeting was to be held. A sign taped to a wall told me to go to the basement. I opened the door to a windowless and sparsely appointed room with concrete block walls. Two dozen businessmen and farmers were there, waiting to begin. They grew quiet as Johnson escorted me to the table at the front of the room. Everybody appeared to be in a bad mood.

I took a seat next to Johnson and Bernard Smith, a big, weathered man who raised sheep and rented canoes on the river. Smith and I knew each other from past conversations. He was astute and usually friendly, but he was cool now when I said hello. Johnson began by introducing me and explaining why we were there. I looked at the faces in the room, some shaved and others stubbled, tanned farmers and pale shopkeepers, some dressed business-casual and others in overalls. The overalls gave off the sweet, earthy smell of cows.

Johnson gave me the floor to explain why the *Kickapoo Scout* was the only newspaper in the valley that opposed the dam. I was relieved that my voice was steady as I began. "I'm a newcomer in the valley, and you have lived here all your lives," I said. "I realize that. But I own a business and I live here now. I've made deep friendships. I consider this my home.

"I'm not a member of the Sierra Club, and I'm not on Senator Nelson's payroll. I'm not in cahoots with a bunch of environmentalists who only care about the valley so they can canoe once or twice a summer. I'm not opposed to economic development. But I am concerned about the future here, and I feel I have its best interests at heart.

"This dam project has developed into a situation where there's no simple solution. Whether or not it's built, somebody is going to get hurt. To me, the question is what kind of flood protection will do the most good with the least harm to the river. There's no question that we have to stop the flooding so we can build a better economy. But after some of the things we've learned about the dam and lake, I have to think there's a better way.

"I don't want the Corps of Engineers or the federal government to abandon the valley. I think the money should be spent to end these floods. But the cost is too high. I'm not talking about dollars; I'm talking about the cost of losing the best part of the river. The beauty of this place is its greatest asset. This is one of the few places that remains much as it was millions of years ago. It's where people can go when they are fed up with noise and pollution and want to experience clean air, quiet, and everything else the valley has to offer. There are a lot of lakes, but there are too few places left like the Kickapoo Valley. Once any part of the river is gone, it's gone forever. Maybe we should look harder at ecotourism to bring new jobs and business opportunities."

I went on a little longer, encouraging us to work together on a solution. When I was finished and sat down, it was Bernard Smith's turn. He rose from his chair and loomed over me. He barely controlled his anger. I was an agent of the devil, he actually said, one of the liberals from the city trying to take away the valley's only chance for survival. What did I know of the hard life here? Who the hell was I to interfere?

Smith sat down. I didn't respond. I'd said my piece and he'd said his. The room was silent for what seemed like several minutes, but I thought I sensed a different feeling now, as though the tension had dissipated a little. Smith's scolding apparently had been cathartic.

Johnson was even a little warm as he closed the meeting. "We're glad you agreed to come," he said. "We had you pictured as some kind of long-haired freak who'd show up with chains and knives." I thanked him, and he adjourned the gathering. I left while people lingered in the room talking. Nothing had been settled, but I drove back to Soldiers Grove glad that I had accepted Johnson's invitation.

Arguments over the valley's future continued at the state capital in Madison and in Congress. There was a good chance the dam and lake were inevitable now that farms had been bought, the land abandoned, and construction started. But Wisconsin's other US senator, Bill Proxmire, and Governor Patrick Lucey joined Gaylord Nelson in opposing completion. Lucey supported the project when it was first proposed, but now he issued a carefully worded statement that he hoped the experience would lead Congress and the corps to develop better policies in the years ahead.

The corps rarely proceeded without a governor's support, so it declared a formal moratorium on the project pending further studies. Probably at Nelson's urging, the US Department of the Interior (DOI) designated the upper Kickapoo as a National Landmark, making it even harder for the corps to cover it with a lake. But Congress's authorization of the dam was still in effect, which kept a flicker of hope alive in the valley that the project would be revived. Nelson knew that, so he began work in Washington to have the dam officially deauthorized.

Things in the valley got nastier. Rumors circulated that someone was planning to blow up the bluffs along the river to destroy the scenery and endangered plants. Somebody chain-sawed trees across the Kickapoo to send the message that there would be no canoeing whether or not the lake was completed. Since it was federal property now, the FBI was called in to investigate.

After two residents of the valley were quoted in a city newspaper that they opposed the dam, one reported that her fences had been cut and sugar poured into her farm equipment's gas tanks. The other, a motel owner, said his windows had been shot out, and his customers were being intimidated. He and his wife stuck to main roads now, he said, because they were afraid of what might happen if they drove on remote county roads. The district attorney looked into both sets of allegations and decided they were "figments of imagination."

Muller published a long, passionate letter from one of his readers. "Controversy and greed are beginning to rear up its ugly head," she wrote. "A so-called Sierra Club has suddenly become interested in a puny little weed that found its way into a rock formation along the riverbank. Now, ecology of this one small plant is being weighed against the progress and welfare of several thousand inhabitants along the Kickapoo River."

She continued: "Personally, I'd like to extend an invitation to every member of the Sierra Club and their political colleagues to don boots and bring their shovels to clean the flood debris from our farms and highways following one of our major floods. It might be a good idea if they went so far as to follow the Kickapoo to its mouth and bring back and spread on the farmers' land all the rich soil the river carried away. Maybe after a few days of backbreaking toil, that little weed wouldn't look so important compared to the problems of the farmers and inhabitants of our little valley."[1]

Back in Washington, Senator Nelson recommended that the land the corps had purchased be made a national park. Muller reacted with one of his inimitable editorials: "No doubt some damn environmentalist sent a suitcase of money out to Nelson and told him to stop the dam. The SOB sits back there in Washington collecting damn good monthly paychecks and forgets about the poor people back here struggling along on 50 bucks a week. The people who come to state and national parks want to do something besides sit around and scratch their poison ivy. People want to swim, they want to lay on sandy beaches, they want to fish. . . . I think Senator Nelson has completely been zonked out for eating so many Chesapeake Bay oysters in fancy eastern nightclubs."

The Silent War

At one point, the *New York Times* published an article that further aggravated the feeling in the valley that East Coast intellectuals and weekend tree huggers were trying to deprive Kickapoogians of their one path out of poverty. Louis Goth of the *Times* described the situation this way:

> The silent war that was waged [by the corps] devastated the 10 miles between La Farge and Ontario, the heart of the planned reservoir. Driving along [Highway] 131, the countryside suddenly becomes lifeless, no cattle dot the pastures, no dogs bark a greeting. Homes that had been occupied since the Civil War

stand empty, their windows shattered, their insides gutted. A mile or two north of La Farge, a gravel driveway curves sharply to the right. It ends at an abandoned farm and a sign that reads "Lake La Farge, Kickapoo River Flood Control, 13% complete, St. Paul District Corps of Engineers". Beyond that, a field surrendered to weeds offers mourners a grandstand view of the execution.

Across the Valley, through a filter of soft haze, a road grader has sliced down a hill inch by inch. A bulldozer has gouged into the riverbank on the near side. . . . Work would pause when a siren whined for one full minute; at the end, there was a dull, echoing thud, and a hundred tons of rock cascaded down a cliff. It's an agonizingly slow way to die.[2]

Muller did not disappoint. He responded:

All [the article's author] can see is the poor displaced persons and the wrecks of all those magnificent plantations. Most of those displaced persons are now fat and sassy. They used to run around munching on turnips, as emaciated as river rats. . . . [Now] they drive new pickup trucks and live in houses. An indication of their affection for the Kickapoo is the fact that most of them have moved to the highest hill they can find. They sleep securely each night with no fear of being awakened by a 40-foot wall of sewage coming down from Ontario. . . . [The *Times'* article should] be framed and hung on every wall. In case the dam is halted, we would have something to read while we starve to death.

In a last attempt to save the dam, the corps issued a report in January 1977 pointing out that it had already spent $18.5 million on the project and that the dam was only 600 feet short of completion. Nearly 9,500 acres of land had been bought and removed from local tax rolls. Eighty families had been evacuated from their homes and farms. The corps appealed for the go-ahead to finish the dam at a reduced cost of $16.3 million, with the savings achieved by eliminating flood control in Soldiers Grove. I assumed this was payback for my opposition to the dam.

Back in Washington, DC, Proxmire armed himself with the signatures of seventy-three other members of Congress and urged newly inaugurated President Jimmy Carter to order an end to the La Farge dam project. Carter had campaigned on a promise to "get the corps out of the dam-building business." In the spring of 1978, he issued a hit list of water resource projects, including the one in La Farge. At Nelson's urging, the president formed a special task force to make a final appraisal of alternatives to the dam. It concluded in the spring of 1979 that if another form of flood control were to ever happen along the Kickapoo, it could only be done village by village as each accepted that the dam would never be built.

Muller had seen the end coming. He published a weary and disheartened editorial. "I know in my own mind that we are the closest to losing the dam right now as we have ever been," he wrote. "If the dam is delayed any more whatsoever, the area dies. And when the area dies, the last trace of the stubborn Kickapoo people will slowly obscure themselves into oblivion. May the tears of the people then create the last great Kickapoo flood."

6

THE DEDICATION

Rather than leaving themselves at the mercy of unpredict-
able weather patterns, the relocation project has allowed
Soldiers Grove to determine its future, and it will reap
the benefits for years to come.

—*American Rivers*

SOLDIERS GROVE COMPLETED ITS RELOCATION IN 1983. The new business district consisted of thirty businesses, three municipal buildings,
twenty-four apartments, ten homes, and a large, modern nursing home.
Some homeowners on the fringe of the floodplain chose to stay there, so
earthmovers created mounds on which their houses were elevated above
the 100-year flood level.

The most symbolic building in regard to America's addiction to oil
was a solar-powered gas station, an oxymoron, on the side of the state
highway. The largest building was Cecil Turk's 7,000-square-foot supermarket. The Wrights designed it so well that the heat cast off by the
store's refrigeration motors combined with the body heat of customers
supplemented sunlight to warm the building in the winter. The state
required all buildings to have furnaces, but Turk didn't need to use
his. He had no heating bills for years, a significant accomplishment in
Wisconsin's northern climate. He eventually turned on the furnace just
to make sure it worked.

The Wrights kept their promise about the cost of the buildings. Most
of the passive solar heating systems consisted of a section of fiberglass

The passive solar heated business district. *Courtesy of Soldiers Grove Library*

panels on the roofs instead of plywood and shingles. Cost savings from less plywood and fewer shingles paid for the panels. One of the more expensive parts of a passive solar system is "thermal mass"—indoor concrete, stone, or water features that take advantage of the second law of thermodynamics: heat goes to cold. When the sun makes a room's air warmer than its thermal mass, the mass absorbs the warmth until the temperatures of the air and the mass are the same. At night when the interior temperature drops, heat transfers from the thermal mass back into the room. Thermal mass allows solar energy to keep a building heated evenly around the clock.

The Wrights demonstrated their creativity in the village's new fire hall. They calculated that water in two tanker trucks was sufficient for the building's thermal mass. The town did not need to spend money on more concrete or brick.

When all was said and done, the relocation cost was about $6 million in public money, including local tax dollars. About 40 percent came from federal funds. The village served as the project developer and paid for streets, sidewalks, and infrastructure. Business owners bought only the footprints of their buildings. It was clear that $6 million would be a bargain for the nation's taxpayers. They'd never again have to pay for disaster response and recovery in Soldiers Grove.

Villagers put up a solar energy sign outside of Soldiers Grove. *Courtesy of Eileen Schoville*

A common problem in floodplain relocations is that some people and businesses are likely to leave town. That happened with about a third of the businesses in Soldiers Grove. But it was important to look at the big picture. FEMA says that 40 percent of businesses do not reopen after floods, so relocation was a net gain. In addition, the community had a better chance of attracting new enterprises in a modern business district where floods were not a problem.

When the move was completed, Soldiers Grove became a celebrity for a while. Busloads of tourists and students stopped to see what a solar town looked like. Books and magazines featured the project. It became the subject of two documentary films, one of them broadcast on public television. PBS aired it again ten years later after the Great Mississippi River Flood of 1993. The mayors of several flooded communities saw it and tracked me down at the US Department of

Energy (DOE), where I was working then. They asked me to help them plan their own relocations.

Over the next few years at DOE, I assembled teams of renewable energy experts, architects, landscape architects, and urban designers—all well versed in sustainable development—to work with other communities on "sustainable disaster recovery." We required that mayors give us their blessings and that they ask all residents to attend two-day town meetings over a weekend. Before we arrived in town, we asked schoolteachers to have their students draw pictures of what they'd like the town's future to be. We taped the drawings to the meeting rooms to remind adults that they were engaged in recovery as much for their kids' futures as for their own.

Our routine was to arrive on Friday afternoons to tour the communities and their challenges. On Friday evenings, we held the first of the weekend sessions, introducing ourselves and briefing the communities on what was to come. We made clear that our team was not there to plan their recoveries or the new developments that would take place. The people who lived there would do that. Our role was to help them expand their menus of choices by telling them about possibilities that might be unfamiliar—renewable energy and energy efficiency options, for example. We encouraged people to think overnight about their hopes for the community.

Residents of small towns are typically suspicious of outsiders, so one or two of us would go to a local bar Friday night to have a few drinks and get to know some of the townspeople. If all went well, we would have a few new friends and allies on Saturdays when the real work began.

Many of the town meetings were vintage Midwest, held in school gyms with church ladies providing coffee and lunch. We began Saturday morning with a "treasures exercise." We put two large tablets at the front of the room, one labeled YES and the other NO. We coaxed people into identifying what they liked about their old towns and wanted to see replicated in new development. On the NO tablet we wrote down what people did not like about their towns and wanted to see improved. "See this," we said when the exercise was over, "you've started designing your recovery."

Over Saturday night, we drew architectural perspectives or created models of what the community might look like based on the YES tablet. We presented the drawings when the community assembled on Sunday. We spent the day getting feedback, sometimes by breaking into smaller groups. A week after we left, we sent the communities master-planning documents to carry out their vision.

Again, our role was not to design the new development; it was to expand the towns' menu of options for recovery. People often were not familiar with geothermal heating and cooling, passive and active solar systems, or how to maximize the energy efficiency of buildings. If the town was considering a relocation project, we went through how it could proceed. Then we sent communities master plans for how to achieve what they envisioned, including potential sources of finance.

Soldiers Grove had been a boot camp for this work. My experience there was formative. As you might be able to tell, I've never forgotten it.

7

MNÍ WIČHÓNI
(Water Is Life)

All water has a perfect memory and is forever trying to
get back to where it was.

—Toni Morrison

LET'S GO BACK TO FUNDAMENTALS. The first thing to acknowledge about
water is that we can't survive without it. No living thing can. It makes no
difference whether we are humans, cyanobacteria, or blue whales. Water
is life. Anyone who puts water at risk puts life at risk.

That's why the western United States have been famous for shooting
wars over water. More recently, water stress has moved east with population growth, reductions in groundwater supplies, declining rainfall, and
hotter temperatures. By one calculation, water-poor areas have shifted
east about 140 miles since 1979.[1]

That is a problem for agricultural and urban uses, of course, but
it's also a problem for electricity. The water used to operate and cool
nuclear and coal power plants accounts for more than 40 percent of
the nation's freshwater withdrawals. Power generation from these types
of plants has been curtailed scores of times around the nation because
cooling water or water discharges have been too hot, or because water
has simply been unavailable. The importance of water will become more
and more evident as the climate changes.[2]

The second thing to acknowledge about water is that a lot of us want to be near it. Some families have lived alongside rivers or on seacoasts for generations. Forty percent of us in the United States live near the oceans or the Gulf, 46 percent of our jobs are there, and 40 percent of our Gross Domestic Product (GDP) is generated there. Another 41 million people live in river floodplains, and the number is rising even as floods are becoming more extreme. Those data are indicative of water's pull on us, but the incontrovertible proof is that people are willing to pay more for hotel rooms that overlook the ocean. Case closed.

Maybe we feel a connection with water because it makes up 60 to 70 percent of our bodies, or because our species emerged from it, or because we each repeated that experience at birth. Everyone seems to agree, however, that water calms us and helps us feel renewed. Marine biologist Wallace Nichols calls this state the "blue mind."

"We are inspired by water," he says, "hearing it, smelling it in the air, playing in it, walking next to it, painting it, surfing, swimming, or fishing in it, writing about it, photographing it, and creating lasting memories along its edge."

To prove that the blue mind is real, Nichols put on a swim cap connected to electrodes and plugged himself into an electroencephalogram recorder. He jumped into the ocean to take readings on how his brain reacted. The test proved that we like being near, in, or under water because of "prefrontal cores, amygdala, evolutionary biology, neuroimaging, and neuro functioning."[3] Which is to say, we like water because our brains are wired that way.

The third thing to know is that our attraction to water is becoming more dangerous. We have spent generations and fortunes trying to domesticate rivers and oceans with only limited success. Water does not like and ultimately is not deterred by the stuff we put in its way. Rivers and oceans are wild, and climate change is making them wilder.

This is a worldwide problem. Nearly 2.4 million people, or about 40 percent of the global population, live within 60 miles of oceans, which can put them within reach of storm surges from today's stronger typhoons and hurricanes. More than 630 million people live less than 30 feet above sea level where they are at risk from rising seas.[4]

Our best engineers tried for much of the last century to resolve the conflict between rivers, waves, and people. They've had only limited success. As we will see later, the long battle may be coming to an end.

River Towns

Most development in America's floodplains began much like it did for Soldiers Grove. Many river towns were founded in the 1800s. Rivers were critical to moving goods and produce before there were railroads and roads. In the 1820s, the Mississippi River carried pork, cotton, and other farm products to New Orleans ports. By 1860, more than one thousand steamboats paddled up and down the river, guided by pilots who had to know every rock, sandbar, and depth reading. "A pilot in those days was the only unfettered and entirely independent human being that lived on the earth," Mark Twain wrote in 1883. Rivers helped pioneers move west, and their furs move to markets. Lumberjacks floated logs to sawmills. Towns used the currents not only to power those mills, but also to grind grain and eventually to generate electricity.

River towns had unique personalities then, and they still do, because all manner of people passed through them. Samuel Clemens lived in one, Hannibal, Missouri, in the 1840s and early 1850s. The city was a principal character in his writings as Mark Twain. It bustled with life. There were tobacco factories, two slaughterhouses, three blacksmith shops, and a distillery. Farmers herded pigs through the streets. "River towns attracted a special type of character—hard-working, fun-loving people who accepted the threat of flooding and other dangers of life along rivers as well as enjoy the inherent beauty and vitality of river life," one historian wrote.[5]

Most floods were minor nuisances. Big floods tested the toughness of river towns. The people who survived them enjoyed bragging rights by marking high-water levels on their buildings. It was proof that nature could not chase them away.

The problem was that towns stayed in place while rivers changed. Their levels went up and down; their flows went faster or slower; they wanted to cut new channels and change course from time to time. The more that communities and industries relied on rivers, the more they wanted them to be stable and predictable. And that's when the trouble begins.

The Mississippi River is probably the best known and most extreme example. It flows for 2,340 miles, from Lake Itasca in northern Minnesota to the Gulf of Mexico, descending 1,475 feet along the way. A drop of water that starts at the lake arrives at the Gulf ninety days later. It is the second-longest river in North America, but the longest—the Missouri River—and nearly twenty other significant rivers are part of the Mississippi River's drainage basin. The basin covers 1.2 million square miles, the largest in the United States and the third largest in the world.

Efforts to tame the river with levees go back to the early 1700s. By the time of its great flood of 1927, levees extended for 1,500 miles. Today, 3,500 levee miles try to contain the river, but they do so with only mixed success.

Engineers have deployed several other measures to tame the Mississippi and other rivers they want to control. The Mississippi River's

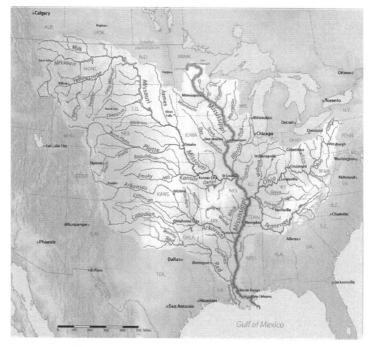

The Mississippi River watershed. *Wikipedia*

channel wants to flood, and it likes to wander away from the development on its banks, so the Corps of Engineers uses a toolbox that includes twenty-nine locks, dams, and slack water pools on the Upper Mississippi. Built in the 1930s, they were designed to last fifty years and are deteriorating now as they approach one hundred. At last report, they need more than $1 billion in repairs. From St. Louis to New Orleans, the USACE uses "river training structures" to deepen the channel. The toolbox also includes revetments (sloping structures on banks to absorb a river's energy), dredging (to remove silt that gathers in river channels and reduces the amount of water they can contain), and weirs (small dams or barriers, typically below the water's surface, to alter its flow characteristics).[6]

Nevertheless, the Mississippi has delivered some of the largest floods in the nation's history, including in 1927, 1973, 1993, and 2019. There were significant but less historic floods in 2002, 2008, 2011, 2014, 2016, and 2017. In the 2019 event, rain falling in the river's drainage basin was as much as 250 percent of normal and the wettest in 124 years. The flood began in December 2018 and remained above flood stage for 235 days, the longest on record, finally ending in August 2019. At least twelve people died, and damages exceeded $20 billion. In the Mississippi Delta alone, 231,000 acres and 686 homes were swallowed by the flood and remained underwater for 150 days, preventing farmers from planting any crops. At its peak, the water covered an area twice the size of New York City.

Today's floods are less predictable, faster, bigger, longer lasting, and more destructive. Alexis Madrigal, who writes for the *Atlantic*, described the river this way:

> The Mississippi no longer fits the definition of a river as "a natural watercourse flowing towards an ocean, a lake, a sea, or another river." Rather, the waterway has been shaped in many ways, big and small, to suit human needs. While it may not be tamed, it's far from wild—and understanding the floods that are expected to crest in Louisiana soon means understanding dams, levees, and control structures as much as rain, climate, and geography. From almost the moment in the early 18th century, when

the French started to build New Orleans, settlers built levees, and
in so doing, entered into a complex geoclimatic relationship with
about 41% of the United States.[7]

But although the Mississippi is an exceptional case in the effort to
tame rivers, it is far from the only one. There are 3.5 million miles of
rivers in the United States, and only a quarter of the most significant
flow free. A deeper look at the history of structural flood control in the
United States will reveal what a long, strange trip it's been.

8

HOW THE FEDERAL
ROLE BEGAN

When a man decides he can control nature, he's in deep
trouble.

—Laura Dern

THE FEDERAL GOVERNMENT'S INVOLVEMENT in flood control evolved over
two centuries of disasters, court rulings, and acts of Congress.[1] The US
Supreme Court ruled in 1824 that the government could finance and make
improvements to rivers. Congress quickly passed the first law authorizing
the USACE to remove navigation obstructions in the Ohio and Mississippi Rivers.

Levees first appeared in national policy in 1849 and 1850, when two
new laws transferred floodplain lands from federal control to states, on
the condition that states sold the property and used the proceeds to
build levees and drainage channels.

In the years that followed, a succession of "great" floods drove more
action by Congress as well as disagreements about what the national
response should be. The Great Flood of 1862 took place in Oregon,
Nevada, and California. Nineteen years later, another big flood caused
millions of dollars in damages in Nebraska and Iowa.

However, it was a flood in Johnstown, Pennsylvania, that woke up
the nation to how deadly floods could be even where dams were present.

Johnstown was devastated by the Great Flood of 1889 when the South Fork Dam, 14 miles up the Little Conemaugh River, failed after days of heavy rain. It released 14.5 million cubic meters of water, at one point equaling the volume of the Mississippi River.

By the time it reached Johnstown, it was a 30-foot wall of water carrying trees, rocks, dead people, dead animals, houses, and even railroad cars. At one spot, debris collected into a 40-foot pile and caught fire, killing 80 people huddled there for protection. In all, more than 2,200 people died, including nearly 400 children and 99 entire families. Another 100 children were orphaned. Approximately 780 bodies were never identified. With so many fatalities and almost $500 million in damages (2016 dollars), it was the worst flood of the century.

Two years later, in 1891, W. J. McGee, an inventor, geologist, anthropologist, and ethnologist from Iowa, became the first person we know of to publicly question the wisdom of people living in floodplains. "As population has increased," he wrote in an article, "men have not only failed to devise means for suppressing or for escaping this evil [floods], but have with singular shortsightedness, rushed into its chosen paths."

Another dam failed in Austin, Texas, in 1911, destroying much of the city and killing 178 people. Two years later, a flood in the Ohio River

Aftermath of the Johnstown flood of 1889. *NOAA Archives*

Valley killed 415 people and damaged $200 million worth of property. Four years after that, Congress passed legislation that turned the responsibility for flood control over to the federal government.

The floods kept coming. The 1927 flood in the lower Mississippi River Valley was exceptionally destructive, inundating 27,000 square miles of land across ten states. Water reportedly reached a depth of 30 feet. The flood killed 250 people and displaced thousands more. The Great Mississippi Flood remains one of the most destructive flood events in US history. Its damages totaled more than $400 million, equivalent to more than $5 billion today.[2]

Congress took a big step toward a more aggressive response to floods in the National Flood Control Act of 1936. In effect, the act ordered the USACE to subdue rivers with dams, levees, concrete channels, and other structures, and it directed the US Department of Agriculture to reduce runoff in watersheds. "We [thought] we could build our way out of almost any problem, with engineers revered in American society then as only rock stars and sports heroes are today," the late water-law expert Robert Adler recalled in 1995.[3]

The same year that Congress passed the National Flood Control Act, USACE hydrologist Francis C. Murphy recommended that floodplain

The Mississippi River flood of 1927 caused more than $40 billion in damages. *Wikimedia Commons*

development be regulated to reduce the cost of floods and flood protection. He reported that only forty-nine communities in the United States had floodplain ordinances.

But back in Johnstown, Pennsylvania, the USACE was dredging the Conemaugh River in the city to create a 20-foot-deep channel with concrete walls designed to handle a "standard flood." The people there almost certainly felt safe because there were six dams upriver. When the corps finished the channel, it declared the flood problem solved.

A few more experts raised red flags about allowing people and communities to locate in the path of floods. In 1938, Harlan H. Barrows, a geography professor at the University of Chicago, chaired a subcommittee of President Franklin Roosevelt's Water Resources Committee. The full committee's recommendations to President Roosevelt focused only on dams, floodwalls, and levees—with one exception. The Barrows group suggested that the president consider floodplain zoning and the relocation of at-risk properties. It warned that flood-control reservoirs simply promoted human occupation of previously flood-prone lands, and this inevitably produced new demands for protection. It apparently was the first time an official government document recommended something other than engineering rivers to protect life and property.[4]

A Barrows protégé, Gilbert White, delivered the same message. As a young geographer, he wondered whether better land-use planning wasn't a sensible alternative to structures. While attending a national conference, he suggested that the federal government not build any dams in California until the state passed laws to control encroachment in floodplains.

"Floods are an act of God; flood damages result from the acts of man," White said. "Changing people's bad decisions about where to live would be more straightforward and effective than changing rivers."[5] He warned that the rising toll from extreme weather was "merely a foretaste of even greater disasters in the future if the nation continues to build and rebuild in its floodplains." In exchange for his advice, a congressional committee investigated White for his "un-American" ideas. White's career survived, but his suggestion did not.[6]

In 1942, White published his book, *Human Adjustment to Floods: A Geographic Approach to the Flood Problem in the United States*, which pointed out that the prevailing national policy was "essentially one of protecting the occupants of floodplains against floods, of aiding them when they suffer flood losses, and of encouraging more intensive use of floodplains." He advocated "adjusting human occupancy to the floodplain."

In 1958, White and his colleagues made the point again, summing up the previous two decades of flood-control policy: there were few incentives to stay out of floodplains, development in flood zones was increasing even where the population was declining, and the American people were learning that if a flood occurred, the federal government would come to the rescue. White went on to become America's most influential advocate for "accommodating nature instead of trying to master it" in the context of floods.

In 1959, the Tennessee Valley Authority told Congress "that local communities have the responsibility to guide their growth so that their future development will be kept out of the path of floodwaters." Its report introduced the idea of floodplain management.

At about the same time, yet another disaster was taking shape in Johnstown. In 1970, one of the dams above the city, a 42.5-foot-tall earthen structure on a creek called Laurel Run, was identified as a hazard risk. The USACE issued a warning of possible future flooding four years later, but people paid little attention. In 1977, 11 inches of rain fell in

Damage from Rapid City flood on June 10, 1972. *Rapid City Journal*

First responders remove one of the 238 fatalities in the disaster. *Rapid City Journal*

eight hours. The Laurel Run dam failed at 2:35 AM, releasing more than 100 million gallons of water. Forty-one people died in a village below the dam, most of them asleep at the time.

The five other dams above the city also failed and released an additional 27 million gallons of water, more than the concrete channel in Johnstown could contain. By the time the flood was over, it had killed 84 people in sixteen communities and left 50,000 others homeless. Damages totaled $200 million.

Congress finally confronted reality during the 1960s thanks to President Lyndon Johnson. His administration asked for a report on flood control. A task force that included the USACE, outside experts, state and local officials, and others delivered it in August 1966. It pointed out that the federal government had spent more than $7 billion on flood control since 1936.

Yet damages were still rising. For example, between 1900 and 1948 flood losses averaged $50 million or more about once every six years. Between 1940 and 1960, floods did not increase in magnitude or frequency, but the $50 million total was exceeded about every two years.

President Johnson wrote to the Speaker of the House and the President of the Senate, pointing out that "to hold the Nation's toll of flood losses in check and to promote wise use of its valley lands requires new and imaginative action."

"Nature will always extract some price for use of her flood plains," Johnson wrote. "However, this nation's annual flood damage bill of more than $1 billion per year is excessive, even in a growing economy."

With the passage of the National Environmental Policy Act in 1969, Congress finally recognized the ecological value of floodplains. In the Water Resources Development Act of 1974, Congress recognized the value of alternatives to flood-control structures. It instructed federal agencies to give them equal weight with dams and other engineered works when it planned flood protection projects.

Following the Great Flood of 1993 on the Mississippi and Missouri Rivers, Congress increased federal support for relocating flood-prone properties. It clarified acceptable conditions for federal "buyouts"—the practice of buying damaged homes, demolishing them, and using the land in perpetuity for open space, recreation, or wetland management.

Nevertheless, the risks of structural flood control are still evident today. In 2005, levee failures caused most of the 1,833 fatalities in New Orleans during Hurricane Katrina. At least 20 dams collapsed in 2015 during catastrophic flooding in South Carolina. Between 2015 and 2018, more than 80 state-regulated dams failed during hurricanes and floods in eastern and central South Carolina. They ranged from remote structures at farm ponds to flood-control projects upstream from hundreds of homes.

We have not accepted the third rule of water: it does not like and ultimately is not deterred by things we put in its way.

Today's Situation

With all due respect for states, it is time for the federal government to step in. It can't be a passive bystander, if for no other reason than the federal fiscal liabilities related to weather disasters. Over the years, several national task forces have looked at the status and performance of flood policy. It is time for another one. The next president should have all the federal, state, and private-sector Acronyms give us definitive knowledge of the condition of the nation's flood-control infrastructure, our options for protecting people and property from weather on steroids, the recommendations of past task forces that have not been implemented but should be, what infrastructure investments should be part of a national effort to modernize America, and what challenges we should prepare for, including the next mass migration (see chapter 13).

Among other things, the disaster-prevention community should have consistent data on crucial details such as the number of Americans in floodplains and the miles of levees in place to protect them. Estimates range from 30,000 to 40,000 miles of levees. FEMA says that 13 million Americans live in 100-year floodplains; Oliver Wing at the University of Bristol says more advanced technology tells us there are 41 million. There appear to be different estimates on the cost of repairing deficient dams, if that's what we should do. There should be better estimates of how much it would cost for a methodical nationwide "managed retreat," which on its face would seem the better plan.

Our risk-averse political leaders have two options. They can respond to flood disasters one by one as they occur, putting lives and federal spending at risk. Or they can act now to minimize, if not avoid, coming flood disasters. In other words, national flood policy can be reactive or proactive. There will be less suffering and cost if it's proactive.[7]

Educating People

To build political support for the proactive option, the Acronyms should collaborate on a national campaign to educate the American people about the spot we're in. The folks at the Association of State Dam Safety Officials (ASDSO) suggest what the messages should be. ASDSO literature warns, "The risks associated with dam failure and flooding in the US continue to increase dramatically. . . . A large majority of dams were not intended or designed to store enough floodwater to provide significant flood protection to areas downstream."

ASDSO's Mark Ogden says, "There are thousands of people in this country that are living downstream from dams that are probably considered deficient given current safety standards." ASDSO's executive director, Lori Spragens, adds that "regular citizens are unaware that dams around them may be risks, and there's not enough public awareness for people to be prepared, just like they would be for a tornado or an earthquake."

A case in point is how coastal residents underestimate hurricanes' destructive power, even if they've experienced them. Just before the 2019 hurricane season began, a polling firm asked more than 1,000 homeowners in the riskiest coastal states whether they felt prepared. About 43 percent said they thought weather forecasters exaggerate hurricane risks. Nearly 60 percent said they would only evacuate their homes if it became mandatory; 10 percent said they would stay no matter what.[8] Homeowners significantly underestimate the costs of repairs after a storm. Most thought $10,000 would do it, but average insurance claims ranged from $30,000 after Hurricane Irene to more than $100,000 after Harvey.

Urban Floods

Cities have unique problems with flood disasters. The federal government has programs to reduce riverine and coastal flood risks, but no single agency is responsible for overseeing urban mitigation support. In 2018, the University of Maryland at College Park and Texas A&M University at Galveston produced an urban flood vulnerability analysis.[9] They found that:

- There are unclear lines of responsibility among the federal, state, regional, local, and tribal governments that may be involved in disaster mitigation and response.
- Some cities don't have adequate human and financial resources to bring their stormwater and wastewater systems to the level they should be.
- Many local officials and residents do not understand the economic and social impacts of urban floods. Many homeowners and renters

do not know how to reduce their flood risks, and many don't have the resources to do so.

- City leaders don't have adequate tools to communicate flood risks. For example, many flood-prone areas in cities are not identified on FEMA's maps of hazard areas. About one in four claims submitted to the National Flood Insurance Program come from people outside FEMA's 100-year flood zone. A survey found that 85 percent of respondents said they had experienced floods outside designated hazard areas.

Other research has identified inequities in FEMA's buyout program. The people most affected by floods—low-income households and the elderly—are least able to cope. During Hurricane Katrina, many of the lowest and heaviest hit areas of the city were its poorest. Nearly half of the dead were seventy-five years old or older, and more than half were African Americans. More than 70 percent of the dead in Louisiana were over age sixty. At least sixty-eight died in nursing homes.

Researchers at Rice University concluded that federal buyout "disproportionately targets whiter counties and neighborhoods, especially in more urbanized areas where the program now concentrates."[10] The bias is not necessarily intentional; Rice researchers said it reflects racial inequities in neighborhoods that have long been segregated and served unequally by government programs. The researchers cited one case where residents and community leaders in a low-income housing area tried to suppress buyouts, believing they were a new type of urban renewal to remove Black residents from their neighborhoods.

A decade after Hurricane Katrina, Amnesty International found that many of the low-income residents who fled the storm have been unable to return because the public housing that was demolished during and after the storm was not entirely replaced. The organization cited a report by the Housing Authority of New Orleans that by 2015, the city had 3,000 fewer public housing apartments for low-income people than it had before Katrina.[11]

Talk Poverty, a website created by the Center for American Progress, reported in 2016 that eleven years after the storm, one in three

Black residents of New Orleans—96,000 in all—had not returned. "Most shocking is the Lower Ninth Ward, where the average resident was living on $16,000 a year before the hurricane," it reported. "You can still drive blocks there and not see a single home. The neighborhood is still missing more than half its pre-Katrina population."[12]

The low return rate was not for lack of effort on the part of the Ninth Ward's remaining residents. Within a year of Katrina, they created a nonprofit homeowner's association to "build the future of the Lower 9th Ward through affordable homeownership and resident-driven redevelopment." I served on its board for a time. Months after Katrina, two colleagues and I worked with a dedicated group of survivors as they developed detailed plans to rebuild the neighborhood. But thirteen years after the disaster, fewer than 40 percent of the residents had returned to the Lower Ninth. The association tells of multiple barriers in the way of the ward's recovery.[13]

The socioeconomic impacts of a substantial storm are often more devastating and long-lasting than the physical damages. A year after Hurricane Katrina, one in three residents of New Orleans was still unemployed. Research shows that 30 to 40 percent of the direct victims of natural disasters experience PTSD (post-traumatic stress disorder), compared to 5 to 19 percent in the general population.[14] Unfortunately, disaster victims frequently lose access to medical doctors and psychiatrists who could help them cope with post-traumatic stress and depression.

As we have seen, floods create victims in many different ways.

Coastal Floods

During the first half of the 1960s, Hurricanes Carla, Cindy, and Hilda invaded the Louisiana coast. The year 1965 began as one of the calmest storm seasons ever, but fall brought Hurricane Betsy, a Category 4 event that hit parts of Florida and the Gulf Coast.[15] Betsy reached wind speeds of more than 160 miles per hour, slammed into New Orleans with a 10-foot storm surge that lasted for days, and destroyed more than 164,000 homes. First responders found drowning victims huddled in their attics.

Elsewhere, hundreds of ships, barges, and oil rigs sank or were damaged. Eleven wrecked ships blocked the Mississippi River for 30 miles. At the time, it was one of the deadliest storms in the nation's history. The body count varies, but Betsy killed about 80 people and caused $1.43 billion in damages. It was the first event in the United States where losses topped $1 billion.

Then came Hurricanes Katrina and Rita in 2005. They attacked coastal Louisiana, Mississippi, Alabama, and parts of Florida, contributing to the most expensive hurricane season in history. Katrina killed more than 1,800 people and destroyed property worth $250 billion.

One after another, recent hurricanes have caused legendary devastation in the United States. Hurricane Sandy killed 147 people in 2012 after it made landfall in twenty-four states and all of the Eastern Seaboard. It drew particular attention because it threatened America's financial and government centers, New York City and Washington, DC. In 2017, Hurricane Maria left Puerto Rico looking like a nuclear bomb had detonated there. Two years later, Hurricane Dorian slammed into the Bahamas with wind speeds up to 185 miles an hour, the worst natural disaster in its history.

But Katrina had the most significant impact on our thinking about hurricanes. It made landfall as an intense Category 3 event with winds of 120 miles per hour. Before it was over, fatalities stretched across five states, 40 percent by drowning and 25 percent due to injuries. The storm forced more than 1 million people to flee the Gulf Coast.

These repeated blows were not a fluke. They are the beginning of the new normal on the nation's coasts. Coastal flooding will get worse as storms become more muscular and sea levels rise. Scientists at the Woods Hole Oceanographic Institution report that the Atlantic Ocean is 11 inches higher today than it was a century ago in New York City and Boston. It is 16 inches higher in Atlantic City. On the island city of Galveston, Texas, the Gulf of Mexico has gone up 25 inches over the same period. Scientists predict that the odds of extreme coastal flooding will double about every five years far into the future.[16]

People on shorelines already are feeling a variety of impacts from climate change. Coastal erosion is responsible for $500 million annually in land and building losses. The losses would be much worse if it were not for natural ecosystems. Marshes prevented $625 million in direct flood damages during Hurricane Sandy in 2012. Wetlands prevented $140 million in flood damages in New York and $425 million in New Jersey. Coral reefs reduce losses from wave energy by 97 percent.

Unfortunately, human activity, along with saltwater intrusion and changes in ocean chemistry, threaten these ecosystems. Louisiana lost about 2,000 square miles of wetlands in recent decades because of subsidence caused by oil and water extraction along with changes in sediment deposits from the much-manipulated Mississippi River. More than 80,000 acres of wetlands critical to species are lost every year, equal to seven football fields every hour around the clock. Urban development is blocking coastal wetlands from migrating inland as sea levels rise. And coral reefs are dying as oceans become more acidic from absorbing carbon dioxide (CO_2).

Coastal cities, including New York, Boston, San Francisco, New Orleans, Los Angeles, and Miami, are investing in adaptation measures, but federal scientists say their investments are too small to handle the challenges ahead.

Imagine living more than 10 miles from the Atlantic Ocean. You feel safe from the big waves that major storms generate as they approach the coast and make landfall. But one day during an exceptionally powerful storm, the force of the wind creates a bulge of water 40 feet high. It surges all the way to your home and beyond. You learn the hard way that you don't have to live on the coast to become a victim of its storms.

Storm surges like this are often a more dangerous threat to life and property than the storm itself. During Hurricane Katrina, many of the estimated 1,833 deaths were blamed directly or indirectly on the storm surge.[17] Between 1963 and 2012, an estimated 2,544 people died during floods along the Atlantic Coast, where flat and subsiding lands make people even more vulnerable. Storm surges drowned most of the victims, along with floods produced by heavy rain.

As the 2019 hurricane season began, nearly 3 million homes on the Atlantic Coast were vulnerable to storm surges. Louisiana took second place, followed by New York and Texas. The US Global Change Research Program's (USGCRP) Fourth National Climate Assessment reported in 2018 that 118 million people, or 37 percent of the population, live in counties adjacent to shorelines.[18] It said more than 49 million homes and more than $1 trillion worth of infrastructure are vulnerable to coastal flooding and sea-level rise.

The threat alone is causing coastal property values to plummet. Between 2005 and 2017, flooding caused coastal properties from Maine to Texas to depreciate by $16 billion.[19] Some of the highest losses relative to home values have taken place in small communities whose damages don't get much attention.

Military and Defense Risks

The Pentagon has warned in the past that the international effects of climate change will draw the US military into crises in other countries where there is a need for humanitarian assistance, a likelihood of border conflicts, or the destabilization of regions where tensions already are high. Military and intelligence leaders fell silent about this when President Donald Trump became commander in chief. By 2020, the military was considered unprepared for climate change.

Its installations are unprepared, too. Sea-level rise is invading US military facilities around the world.[20] In 2018, Hurricane Michael damaged every building at Florida's Tyndall Air Force Base, inflicting $4.7 billion in losses. Three Marine Corps installations in North Carolina experienced 36 inches of rain and suffered $3.6 billion in damages during Hurricane Florence in 2018. Severe storms affected operations in 2018 and 2019 at the Marine Corps base at Camp Lejeune, the Marine Air Station at Cherry Point, and the Offutt Air Force Base, where 60 of 130 structures were damaged beyond repair.

These incidents are only the beginning of what's to come. More than 1,700 installations worldwide, including two-thirds of the military's operationally critical facilities, are located in coastal areas at risk of flooding from storm surges and sea-level rise.[21] Flooding threatens an air force base in Virginia with a combination of land subsidence and sea levels that have gone up 14 inches since 1930. Fifty-three installations are already vulnerable to recurring floods from oceans and rivers. Coastal erosion is affecting military facilities in Alaska and on islands in the Indian Ocean and South Pacific. Former navy secretary Ray Mabus warns, "If we don't do something about sea-level rise caused by climate change within the lives of people alive today, Norfolk, Virginia, the biggest Navy base in the world, will disappear."[22]

The General Accountability Office (GAO) concluded in June 2019 that the military is not doing enough about this despite $9 billion in hurricane and flood damages at three of its bases in less than a year.[23] The reason, the GAO said, is that the Pentagon has not given the military branches any guidance on what to do. "The DoD is not adequately prepared for this," said retired Marine brigadier general Stephen Cheney, in large part because the White House has downplayed climate change. "It's been difficult to get them to even admit that climate change is causing destruction of major bases and interrupting training worldwide," he said.

President Biden fixed that on his first day in office by ordering the Pentagon and the Joint Chiefs of Staff to assess climate risks in the National Defense Strategy.

Shrinking and Sinking

If you have a current map of the United States, hold onto it. It will be a collector's item someday. While sea-level rise is shrinking the size of the continental United States, water withdrawals are sinking it. Subsidence is happening along the Atlantic Seaboard and the Gulf of Mexico, as well as locations inland. Eighty percent is due to water withdrawals, including the water consumed by oil and gas extraction. Lower land elevations and higher seas mean even more severe coastal floods.

Subsidence is one reason that Houston has claimed the dubious title of the most flooded city in the United States. Swamped by one record rainfall after another in recent years, it is a case study of urban vulnerability to bad weather. It is flat, only 50 miles from the Gulf of Mexico, barely above sea level, and covered with impermeable surfaces.

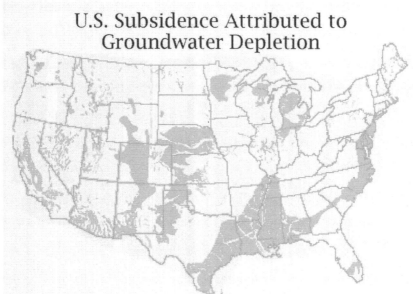

U.S. Subsidence Attributed to Groundwater Depletion

Areas where subsidence has been attributed to groundwater pumpage
(Land Subsidence of the United States, USGS Circular 1182)

Subsidence has taken place in 45 states over 17,000 square miles, roughly the size of New Hampshire and Vermont combined. Water withdrawals caused the subsidence shown here. USGS

The 35 Cities Most Vulnerable to Rising Seas

35. Secaucus, New Jersey
34. Hampton, Virginia
33. St. Simons, Georgia
32. Margate City, New Jersey
31. St. Helena Island, South Carolina
30. Long Beach, New York
29. Brigantine, New Jersey
28. West Ashley, South Carolina
27. Revere, Massachusetts
26. Little Ferry, New Jersey
25. Waccamaw Neck, South Carolina
24. Pennsville, New Jersey
23. Key Biscayne, Florida

22. James Island, South Carolina
21. La Marque-Hitchcock, Texas
20. Poquoson, Virginia
19. Tybee Island-Wilmington Island, Georgia
18. Middle Keys, Florida
17. Brazosport, Texas
16. Ventnor City, New Jersey
15. St. Pete Beach, Florida
14. Charleston Central, South Carolina
13. Ponte Vedra, Florida
12. Ocean City, New Jersey
11. Boca Ciega, Florida
10. Upper Keys, Florida
 9. Chesapeake, Virginia
 8. Pleasant, South Carolina
 7. Lower Keys, Florida
 6. Hilton Head Island, South Carolina
 5. Galveston, Texas
 4. Key West, Florida
 3. Atlantic City, New Jersey
 2. Hoboken, New Jersey
 1. Miami Beach, Florida

Development over the last quarter century has eliminated half of the city's wetlands, so the rain has no choice but to turn into destructive stormwater. At the same time, subsidence in the Houston-Galveston region is collapsing well casings, altering the flow of creeks, changing bayous, and damaging roads, bridges, and building foundations.

The suite of risks in Florida is even greater than Houston's. The state is vulnerable to tropical storms and hurricanes, coastal erosion, degraded protective ecosystems, rising seas, saltwater incursion, king tides, nuisance flooding on coasts, and inland floods. More than 440,000 square miles, home to 375 million Floridians, are destined to be swallowed by the sea. In Miami Beach, sea-level rise is combining with subsidence to make some properties even more vulnerable. Houses initially built on higher ground have sunk about 4.5 inches.

Agricultural operations in the San Joaquin Valley of California have relied on groundwater withdrawals since the 1920s. As a result, sections of the valley have sunk as much as 28 feet, risking damages to aqueducts, levees, bridges, wells, and roads. Since the 1960s, the state has spent about $100 million to repair water infrastructure destroyed by subsidence.

In other words, the United States is not the nation it used to be, geologically speaking. We are shrinking and sinking at the same time. We can't blame nature. We are taking too much water from the ground and putting too much carbon into the air.

We're Not Alone

Cities and coasts worldwide will be threatened by bigger floods in the not-so-distant future. In 2019 alone, nearly 4,500 deaths and $46 billion in economic loses were due to floods. By 2030, the number of people affected annually by coastal floods will double, and property damages will increase tenfold. That amounts to 15 million people and $177 billion in property. In cities, river flooding is expected to more than double, while property damages will triple by 2030. That's 132 million people and $535 billion in property.

These are the projections of a new tool the World Resources Institute (WRI) uses to measure flood risks around the world. The director of WRI's Global Water Programs points out that investments in natural and engineered infrastructure can make a big difference. India is an example. The tool calculates that every dollar India spends to improve flood protection from eleven-year to twenty-five-year events will avoid $248 in damages and reduce the likelihood of floods by half.

The tool, called Aqueduct Floods, uses the best available data to allow cost-benefit analyses for structural, nonstructural, and insurance investments in flood prevention.

9

PROBLEMS
WITH STRUCTURES

You can't argue with a river; it is going to flow. You can
dam it up, put it to useful purposes, deflect it, but you
can't argue with it.

—Dean Acheson

IN THE SPRING OF 2020, the National Oceanic and Atmospheric Administration (NOAA) issued its annual warnings about extreme weather. It
predicted lively flood and hurricane seasons and that there would be
widespread flooding, with twenty-three states likely to experience moderate to heavy events. As if on cue, central Michigan experienced rain
amounts 250 percent above usual in May. A few minutes after midnight
on May 19, an urgent evacuation order went out to residents in and near
Midland. There were two dams above the city, each holding back a lake.
The one farthest upriver, the Edenville dam, collapsed. Its liberated lake
rushed 7 miles downriver and overtopped the Sanford dam. The result
was a catastrophic flood that forced the evacuation of 10,000 people.
Michigan governor Gretchen Whitmer called it "unlike anything we've
ever seen before." Fortunately, no one was killed. However, there was
extensive downriver damage, and lakeside property owners above the
Edenville dam were suddenly living next to a mud field littered with
tree stumps.

More important, the incident was the latest example of some troubling, unresolved national issues. First, USACE data show more than 1,000 regulated dams in Michigan, 70 percent of them privately owned. Many were built for hydroelectric power between the late 1800s and the 1940s. Their average age is seventy-four.[1] The state has only two dam safety inspectors. Officials planned a forensic analysis of what caused the Edenville dam to fail, but the simple answer was that it was ninety-six years old, and its owner reportedly had not complied with repeated warnings to upgrade the structure so it could hold back the "probable maximum flood."

Second, state and federal regulations were insufficient to force the owner of the failed dam to fix deficiencies that were known for years. "The lesson to learn here," the *Detroit Free Press* noted, "is that Michigan must invest not just in its infrastructure—the Edenville dam is just one of the hundreds of aging dams across the state, and there are also bridges, roads, and god knows what else poised to fail—but in the kind of sensible regulations and enforcement authority that will give those we entrust to keep us safe the power to make that happen."[2]

Third, the disaster dramatized the danger of toxic chemicals and wastes in the nation's floodplains. Midland is home to Dow Chemical's world headquarters. Its property includes one of the nation's most extensive Superfund sites, and Dow announced that the floodwaters "comingled" with waste containment ponds at the facility. If ponds failed, people and farmland could be endangered for more than 20 miles downriver. The company said that no chemicals were released. However, environmental leaders pointed out that one of the environmental directives President Trump rescinded in 2017 would have required Superfund sites to update their infrastructure for protection against extreme floods.

Enormous Risks

Floods are still the most frequent type of weather-related disaster in the United States. The scope of flood risk is enormous. There are 250,000 rivers in the country, with enough combined length to circle the Earth 140 times. Three-quarters of them have been modified, often to protect communities and croplands from floods. But we might as well try to prevent thunderstorms. The creeks will always rise, and whatever gets in their way will get wet or much worse.

At last count, there were 91,468 dams across the country, not including the small ones.[3] About 17 percent were built for flood control, while others store water, guard crops, or provide recreation. There are cases where people live below dams built for other reasons than flood prevention and are not up to the standards necessary to protect lives.

Most dams are owned by states, utilities, farms, or local governments; only 5 percent are owned and managed by the federal government. We know less about levees. There are 30,000 miles of documented levees and up to 10,000 miles whose location and conditions are not known. They are supposed to protect 14 million people and $1.3 trillion in property.

The American Society of Civil Engineers (ASCE) issues a report card on the nation's infrastructure every four years. The most recent, in 2021, gave dams and levees grades of D. Nearly 15,600 dams, double the number twenty years ago, are classified as high-hazard structures, meaning their failures would kill people. More than 2,300 are deficient in

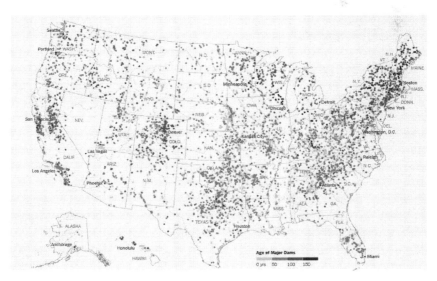

Major dams in the United States. *US Army Corps of Engineers*

some way. Another 12,000 are classified as "significant hazard potential" structures, meaning they might not kill people, but they definitely would cause economic and property damage. The cost would be $93 billion to rehabilitate all federal and non-federal dams, or $20 billion to fix only the "high hazard" structures.

News organizations, including the Associated Press and the *New York Times,* have done independent investigations into the risks of relying on dams for flood control or power production. During its two-year investigation, the AP evaluated dam conditions in forty-four states and Puerto Rico. It found that "some states declined to provide condition ratings for their dams, claiming exemptions to public record requests. Others simply haven't rated all their dams due to lack of funding, staffing or authority to do so."[4]

Five Reasons for Failing Grades

There are five principal reasons that dams and levees are so close to failing grades. I've mentioned several of them, but they deserve more explanation.

Inherent hazards

The ASDSO points out that while rivers and coasts are naturally hazardous places, dams are "innately hazardous structures." Nobody seems to know precisely how many dam failures there have been. "Engineers and organizations have documented dam failure in an ad hoc manner for decades," according to the Congressional Research Service.[5] But we do know that they've happened in every state. One estimate is that from 2005 to mid-2013, there were 173 failures and 587 cases where only quick action prevented disasters.

Even the biggest and most impressive dams can fail for the simplest of reasons. They might be poorly maintained or improperly designed, built, or operated. They can be overtopped by a storm that exceeds their design capacity. Earthen dams can fail because of erosion, burrowing animals, and tree roots. Unfortunately, the government has not fully assessed our national exposure to these risks.

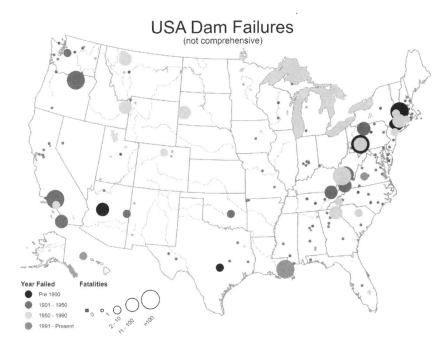

USA Dam Failures
(not comprehensive)

This map shows some dam failures in the United States since 1900, but federal officials caution that it is "not comprehensive." *NOAA*

Aging

Most flood-control dams were built to last about fifty years before problems would begin. Their average age today is approaching sixty. By 2025, three of every four dams will be at least fifty years old. Many levees were built in response to floods in the early half of the last century, so they also are more than fifty years old.

The federal government's research into climate change is centered in the USGCRP, which includes scientists from thirteen federal agencies. Its latest report says that aging and deteriorating flood-control structures are growing hazards, in some cases even during moderate rainfalls. In addition to the Midland disaster, recent structural failures include the Oroville emergency spillway in California in 2017, Missouri River levees in 2017, 25 dams in South Carolina in October 2016 and 50 more dams in that state in October 2015, and those 50 levee failures in New Orleans in 2005 during Hurricane Katrina.

Nearly 200,000 people were evacuated after the main spillway failed on the Oroville dam on February 7, 2017. The dam is located on California's Feather River. At 770 feet, it is the tallest in the United States. Between February 6 and 10, nearly 13 inches of rain fell in the Feather River Basin.
California Department of Water Resources

Changing dynamics

After those 50 levees failed in New Orleans during Hurricane Katrina, the USASCE developed principles for designing flood-control infrastructure. One is adaptability. It's a challenging requirement. Dams and levees are static structures, but rivers change over time. We designed dams and levees to meet needs when they were built, not conditions fifty, sixty, or more years later. How much rivers change and how long it takes depends on their speed, the amount of sediment loading, and the surrounding landscape.

Precipitation events are changing. Flood-control dams were designed to handle the probable maximum flood (PMF) event at their locations. In the past, engineers could get a sense of PMF by studying past floods, but that is no longer the case. Flood frequencies and intensities are now less predictable due to climate change.

In most places, the PMF was a 100-year event, but 500- and even 1,000-year events are becoming more common. Houston had three 1,000-year floods between 2015 and 2017. Thousand-year floods hit Texas, West Virginia, Maryland, Louisiana, and South Carolina in one five-month period in 2016. In the first nine months of 2018, there were five 1,000-year events east of the Rocky Mountains.

Over mid-Atlantic and northeastern states, the water volume of heavy rains has increased by more than 70 percent over the last six decades. FEMA predicts that river floodplains will be 40 to 45 percent larger by the end of the century than they are now.[6]

Inadequate inspections

The safety of 70 percent of the nation's dams is a state responsibility, but states are short of qualified dam inspectors. On average, each inspector is assigned to 200 dams today, an unreasonable workload that guarantees infrequent inspections. Staffing and funding have improved in recent years, but the ASDSO says that nearly every state needs more money and personnel in its dam-safety program.

Regular inspections are crucial because municipalities and private owners often defer maintenance in favor of more immediate expenses. FEMA has dam-safety guidelines for states, but they are not mandatory. States decide if and when to do safety inspections, and which dams are inspected.

Insufficient investment

The USACE, the nation's principal dam-building organization, estimates that levees will need $80 billion in maintenance and improvements over the next ten years.[7] The ASDSO, which represents state dam inspectors, says it would cost $70 billion to rehabilitate all of the nation's federal and nonfederal dams and more than $25 billion to fix dams owned by the government. The USACE says it would take fifty years to do the work at the current level of investment.

The Value of Mud

Flood-control structures have considerable ecological impacts that should be considered when communities consider how to mitigate flood damages.

Natural floodplains allow rivers to spread out, which reduces their speed and volume as the water is absorbed by soil and vegetation while replenishing the water table.

In their natural state, floodplains are excellent habitat. They make up only 2 percent of the planet's land surface, but they provide about 25 percent of all land-based ecosystem services.[8] When they are inundated from time to time, floodplains contain up to 1,000 times as many species as rivers.

The sediment that rivers carry has a great deal of value, too. The Mississippi River once collected sediment from all over North America and deposited it at the river's mouth on the Louisiana coast. The sediment hosted plant communities, which trapped more sediment, and eventually formed new land. Mississippi River levees have changed this process. As a result, Louisiana has lost more than 2,000 miles of land to the Gulf of Mexico since 1930.

Rivers deposit silt to make new land. This was the Mississippi River delta before much of it was destroyed by Hurricanes Katrina and Rita in 2005. *NASA*

The Colorado River developed a similar problem when the Glen Canyon dam and Lake Powell were built in the 1960s. When rivers meet lakes, they slow down, and their sediments sink. Inhibited by Lake Powell, the Colorado River's sediments no longer refreshed downriver sandbars to provide habitat for native fish as well as campsites for hikers and "river runners." Several years ago, federal water managers tried an experiment. They doubled or tripled the water volume released by the dam for a week at a time. Three years later, the US Geological Survey (USGS) found that sandbars increased in size on half of those it inspected.

Rivers also deposit sediment to create delta lobes. The rivers work around them for a time but eventually cut shorter paths and leave the lobes behind to provide fertile habitat for marsh plants and trees. Then, rivers start the process over in their new channels—unless we try to make them do otherwise.

Meanwhile, on the Coasts

Like rivers, shorelines are dynamic. The nonprofit Surfrider Foundation points out that "beaches are dynamic and natural [but] buildings, bridges, and roads are static. The problem occurs when there is a structure built on a dynamic, moving beach." That's why parables about foolish decisions use the metaphor of building on sand.

Most people living on coasts and riversides apparently reasoned that the benefits of living near the water were worth the risks. Global warming should be changing that calculation.

East Coast communities are experiencing a type of frequent flooding variously called sunny day, tidal, or nuisance floods. This is one of several problems created by rising sea levels. Seas are rising because oceans expand as their water warms, and new water is being added by melting land-based glaciers. Ocean levels are high enough now that seawater is pulled into coastal towns when the moon's influence is strong.

Then there are king tides, the highest each year. They take place in Florida for up to a week several times annually. The *South Florida Sun-Sentinel* describes them:

> Periodically throughout the year in South Florida, water from
> the sea invades our coast. It leaks out of bays, climbs over sea
> walls and docks, and floods out of sewer drains built to contain
> it. For hours, it sits like an unwelcome guest—swallowing up
> whole streets, parking lots, marinas, and driveways. It creeps
> under the doors of unsuspecting homes and businesses and seeps
> in through the cracks of futile sandbags. Then, like a thief in the
> night, it slips away.[9]

Sea levels will keep rising and even submerge entire cities. NOAA
reports that the frequency of annual high-tide flooding has doubled over
the last twenty years. Along the East and Gulf Coasts, 57 of 62 locations
experienced record high-tide flooding in 2019. By 2030, the frequency
of high-tide flooding nationwide is likely to increase two- to threefold,
NOAA says.[10]

Growing at-risk populations

The coastal population increased by nearly 40 percent from 1970 to 2010,
and it's expected to keep growing. Researchers anticipate that the population in 100-year floodplains will increase from 41 million to 60 million by
the end of this century. But in light of climate change, we should be paying
attention to the number of Americans living in 1,000-year floodplains.

Rising seas, storms, floods, and shoreline erosion currently threaten
about $1 trillion in national wealth held in coastal real estate, accord-
ing to the USGCRP. Along the Atlantic, Pacific, Gulf, and Great Lakes
coasts, governments and private property owners have installed seawalls,
bulkheads, and revetments, and poured 14,000 miles of concrete to prevent beach erosion. Nevertheless, erosion still causes $500 million in
property losses every year, and the federal government spends an average
of $150 million annually to replenish lost beaches.[11]

Federal scientists predict that if greenhouse gas emissions remain
high, "many coastal communities will be transformed by the latter part
of this century." In other words, all or parts of them will be underwater.

Who will pay for the damages is a contentious, unsettled question.
The Center for Climate Integrity (CCI), an organization created in 2017

to hold oil companies accountable for damages attributed to climate change, estimates that by 2040, the coasts will require 50,000 more miles of seawalls and other barriers to hold back rising seas. That would cost $416 billion. For nearly 180 small coastal communities, it amounts to $100,000 per person, making evacuation the only viable option.

Our Costly Legacy

So, here we are. The rising risks of extreme weather disasters are a consequence of national water policy over the last one hundred–plus years, combined with the government's failure to do anything about them. National leaders have known about these consequences since the 1960s when White House science advisors predicted with remarkable accuracy what the results of continuing greenhouse gas emissions would be. Yet today:

- Floods kill more of us than tornadoes, hurricanes, or lightning. They can happen anywhere at any time. Heavy downpours have grown 20 percent in the last fifty years, so while dams are getting older floodplains are getting larger, people keep moving into them, and flood recovery is straining the federal budget.
- Floods account for 90 percent of all our natural disasters and the costs are enormous.[12] There were fourteen weather disasters where damages exceeded $1 billion in 2019; the most widespread was flooding across fifteen states. Floods in Missouri, Arkansas, and the Mississippi River Basin caused $20 billion in damages, almost half of all US disaster damages that year.
- Analysts expect nearly 2.5 million properties worth more than $1 trillion to experience chronic flooding by 2100 and thirty cities to be underwater by then.[13] Trillions of dollars of infrastructure—from power plants to airports to military bases—are at risk.
- The number of billion-dollar disasters is rising. They averaged 15 yearly from 2016 to 2018, more than double the average (6.2) from 1980 to 2018. Weather and climate disasters in the United States have caused $1.6 trillion in damages since 1980, according to NOAA.

- Despite President Johnson's call in 1966 to "hold the nation's toll of flood losses in check," there were 32 billion-dollar floods in the United States between 1980 and 2019.[14]
- The Congressional Budget Office (CBO) expects that storm-related losses will average $54 billion annually over the long run, but the losses actually will be much higher.[15] CBO based its estimate on current policies and conditions, not the more destructive floods and vulnerable populations we will see.
- Homes and businesses are not the only structures at risk from floods and rising seas. At least 14 coal-fired power plants, 36 toxic coal-ash waste ponds, 2,500 toxic chemicals sites including 1,400 in areas of highest risk, 945 high-priority Superfund sites, 54 nuclear power plants, and 120 oil and gas facilities are located in places at risk of floods.
- The Weather Channel says that more than 100 people a year have died because of floods in the United States since 2015.[16] We will see the numbers rise as the weather gets more severe and rise dramatically when dams begin to fail.

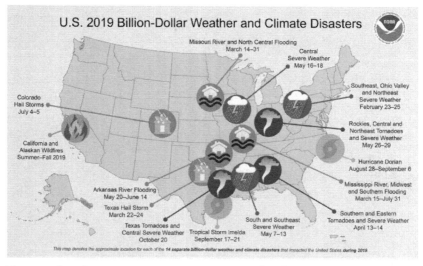

This graphic shows 2019 was an active year for disasters where damages exceeded $1 billion. *NOAA*

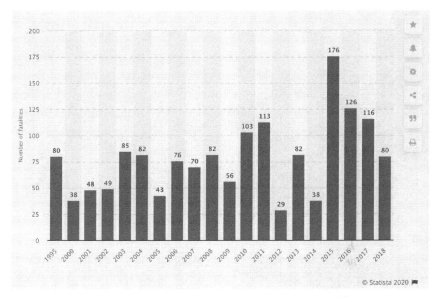

The data company Statista shows that deaths from floods vary a great deal from year to year, spiking sharply in years with mega-floods. *Statista*

The Human Cost

Facts and figures like these cannot convey the physical and psychological trauma that floods inflict on families.

Imagine that you and your family live in a river community. One day, without warning, a tsunami of muddy water slams into your neighborhood carrying toxins, snakes, sewage, animal carcasses, all kinds of debris including cars and dislodged buildings, and even coffins and corpses exhumed by the water.

Your family is safe because you fled the city. But now you'll have to wait until the flood subsides before you can get back to your home to assess the damage. If your house is still there, you find that toxic water has fouled everything—the floors, walls, and the framing behind them; every piece of furniture; every rug and mattress; *everything* below the high-water level. Mold is developing everywhere. There is no telling what foul substances the water left behind. Whatever it was, your house will have to be gutted to get rid of it. Your home will never feel the same.

Coffins exhumed by a severe flood in Calcasieu Parish, Louisiana. *Courtesy of the Calcasieu Parish Coroner's Office*

Next comes the post-disaster disaster. Many of your neighbors who fled the city have not come back. You have no friends or relatives to stay with, so you might try to ignore evacuation orders so that you and your family can squat in your damaged home. Or, you sleep on a gymnasium floor next to strangers, or crowd into a cheap motel room until FEMA provides one of its mini-trailers. When the trailers arrive, workers arrange them in Femavilles—neat rows in military-style formations. If you're unlucky, as thousands of Gulf Coast families were after Hurricane Katrina, you might end up in a trailer with fumes that threatens your health.[17]

Life after disaster: FEMA's trailers are lined up to provide temporary housing for victims of Hurricane Katrina. *National Archives*

If you evacuated the floodplain, it might be a long time before you're allowed to return to your house. Once you do, you and the neighbors who didn't leave town must pile your sodden unsalvageables on the curb for trucks to haul away—everything from sofas and mattresses to teddy bears, photo albums, and moldy clothes.

You wait weeks before the government finishes processing the paperwork for disaster-assistance payments. You learn that many of your neighbors who fled the city have decided never to return. Some homes are so disgusting and damaged that their owners simply walked away. Your kids finally go back to school, but they find a lot of empty desks there. It takes a long time for businesses to return, and many do not. On average, 40 percent of the small businesses in a flood do not reopen.

There is a moment—a small window of opportunity—when you resolve to never again let your family go through another flood. FEMA offers money to help your community buy your home and destroy it, and you consider selling. But as months pass with no word on when your house will sell, you get impatient, then angry, about getting your family's life back to normal. The fastest way to "normal" is to repair your house and move back into the floodplain so you can look forward to being home for Thanksgiving and Christmas.

As time passes, you learn that if you had agreed to a buyout, it would have taken various government agencies as long as five years to process and approve the paperwork. It is inhumane to keep people's lives in limbo that long.

There is another option. Several communities around the United States have done it. Neighbors are talking about selling their homes to the city and moving together to higher ground. The city will help because it wants to retain its property tax base. Your neighbors want to do it because it will keep their social networks mostly intact, and it presents an opportunity to build modern new homes that have not and never will be fouled by floods. This option is called a "managed retreat." It requires patience and compromise, like any effort to get a group of people to agree on anything. But there's something to be said about staying in a community where you and your kids have friends, and where you'll never be afraid of the rain again.

Unfortunately, managed retreats must compete with an array of less sensible government policies that encourage people to live in floodplains and help them move back in after disasters. Larry Larson, director emeritus of the Association of State Floodplain Managers, says federal policies should "create some incentives for states and locals to do the right thing. Right now, it's going in the other direction."

The inescapable reality is that the flood-control strategy of the twentieth century cannot work in the twenty-first. Our national water policy should be to avoid floods, not to control them.

10

SOUND THE RETREAT

Retreat, hell! We're not retreating, we're just advancing
in a different direction.

—General Oliver P. Smith, during the Korean War

IT IS TIME FOR US all to advance in a different direction in regard to
floods. There is no heroism or honor in standing our ground to defend
the flood-control philosophy of the last century, and it is folly to fight a
battle we cannot win. Think of the western wildfires and trains of hurricanes making landfall in the United States these days. Or the slow-moving
flood in 2019 that swamped 14 million people and halted farming in the
Midwest and South, causing $6.2 billion in damages. Then think of them
on powerful steroids. If we refuse to advance in a different direction,
what's coming will be much worse.

Of all the dissonances that signal climate change, weather is the
most obvious. By 2019, six of ten Americans told pollsters that heat
waves, floods, intense storms, and droughts were affecting their communities.[1] People want to know if we are experiencing a new normal.
The answer is a nuanced yes. In the old normal, nature's behavior was
fairly predictable. The new normal will be continuous abnormality as
the Earth warms and alters climates. Climate affects virtually everything, so virtually everything will change, from agriculture and public
health to energy consumption and pollution. I offer some details in
chapter 13.

Several retreats actually are necessary if we are to adapt to and survive climate change. We have to retreat from places that are uninhabitable. We must retreat from outdated attitudes about the relationship between human civilization and nature. I'll explore those topics later. Most immediately, we must retreat from the types of energy we used during the last two hundred years of industrialization.

The Carbon Cycle

Fossil fuels—coal, oil, and natural gas—powered the industrial era and made possible the quality of life that most Americans enjoy today. We owe the men and women who produced them a great deal of thanks. But they also filled the air, and still do, with dangerous pollutants. Nearly half of American people still live in places where it's dangerous to breathe due to pollution from vehicles and power plants. But the pollutant causing the longest-lasting threat is carbon dioxide, or CO_2, the principal cause of global warming. The lesson we must take from industrial era is that the biosphere has limits that we cannot ignore without consequences.

I explain the science of climate change in greater detail in appendix 1, but here it is in a nutshell: 80 percent of the energy the world uses comes from fossil fuels. Coal is 60 to 80 percent carbon, depending on type. As much as 85 percent of petroleum is carbon. Natural gas is mostly methane; when completely combusted, 16 grams of methane produce 44 grams of carbon dioxide. When these fuels burn, their carbon combines with oxygen to produce carbon dioxide. Carbon dioxide lingers in the atmosphere for hundreds and even thousands of years. It, and several other "greenhouse gases," allow the sun's energy to reach the Earth's surface but keep some from escaping back into space. The trapped solar energy warms the Earth's surface; the warming alters the planet's climate; and weather becomes more extreme. As oceans warm, they expand. Combined with the water from melting ice caps and glaciers, sea levels rise and invade land and property on the coasts.

Carbon dioxide itself is critical for all life on the planet. It ordinarily circulates through the environment (the carbon cycle), where it is absorbed by living plants, healthy soils, and the oceans. These are called carbon sinks. They release the carbon when they die or are disturbed. When the amount of carbon dioxide absorbed by sinks equals the amount released, the carbon cycle is in balance and all is well. But fossil fuels free enormous amounts of carbon dioxide that were safely sequestered deep underground for millions of years. Their use for energy has overloaded the carbon cycle and upset the balance. To stabilize the cycle, we must stop polluting the atmosphere with carbon dioxide and we must remove a significant amount that's already there. We have a very short time to do both.

The rush is not because we only recently discovered this greenhouse effect. A British physicist first noticed it 1859. In 1896, a Swedish chemist warned, "We are evaporating our coal mines in the air." The world's climate scientists began collaborating to monitor and study climate change in 1988, forming the Intergovernmental Panel on Climate Change, or IPCC. When the IPCC's findings became concerning, they convened an Earth Summit in 1992 and agreed on a document called the United National Framework Convention on Climate Change (UNFCCC). As its title indicated, the UNFCCC established a process for countries to meet every year with the goal of "preventing dangerous anthropogenic interference with the Earth's climate system" by reducing greenhouse gas pollution. The treaty recognized that although all countries shared the same goal, the responsibilities of developed countries would be different from those in developing nations.

After meeting annually for twenty-three years, the international community finally reached an agreement in Paris in 2015 in which all nations would voluntarily reduce their greenhouse gas pollution. But the plans that countries submitted to the UN fall far short of what's necessary to avoid catastrophic climate change. The scientists of the IPCC now have warned that unless nations work much more aggressively to stop carbon pollution, and unless they make substantial progress by 2030, climate change will become catastrophic.

Politics Gets in the Way

There are several reasons it took so long for nations to agree to limit their greenhouse gas pollution. Scientists at one of the world's largest oil companies warned their executives that the company's products were causing the climate to change. But the corporation hid those findings and instead launched an expensive public relations campaign to discredit climate science and scientists. Countries worried about the disruption and costs of transitioning to cleaner energy. Other countries worried about their sovereignty and were reluctant to commit to mandatory actions dictated by the UN. But in 2021, no credible leader can still deny that climate change is real because science's predictions are coming true with extreme, often unprecedented, weather disasters.

The issue today is not whether climate change is real; it's what to do about it. In the United States, fossil energy lobbies have worked hard to keep Congress from doing anything. It has taken no significant action on climate change since 1992. Energy politics has been an especially difficult barrier in the United States, where oil, gas, and coal companies have claimed that switching to cleaner energy would ruin the economy. They assert their influence on national policies by contributing money to election campaigns. During America's 2019–2020 election cycle, for example, oil and natural gas interests contributed nearly $140 million to presidential and congressional candidates, with 84 percent going to Republicans.[2] Oil and gas companies contributed $3.7 million to Donald Trump's campaign, more than twice their contributions to Joe Biden. The industry deployed 683 lobbyists to Congress during 2020 at a cost of nearly $111 million.[3]

Congress reciprocates by providing tens of billions of dollars in direct tax subsidies to fossil energy companies every year, with some subsidies going back more than a century. Estimates vary widely because there is no agreement on what qualifies as a subsidy, but the International Monetary Fund (IMF) estimates that in 2015, US government subsidies for fossil fuels totaled $649 billion, counting tax breaks and the social and environmental costs of producing and consuming the fuels. The US government also allows oil, coal, and gas companies to extract fuels from public lands at relatively cheap rates.[4]

Barack Obama and his team pushed hard for the Paris climate accord in 2015. But in 2017, President Donald Trump announced that the United States would withdraw. America was the only country to do so. In the first three days of his presidency, though, Joe Biden began reversing Trump's orders and directives. He declared a moratorium on oil and gas leases on public lands. Three days into his presidency, Biden signed an order to rejoin the Paris accord; America's reenrollment became official on February 19, 2021.

The United States is not the only country that still gives oil companies incentives to produce and consumers incentives to use fossil fuels. The IMF reports that worldwide subsidies for fossil fuels totaled a staggering $4.7 trillion in 2015. This is counterproductive, to put it mildly, because the world's efforts to reduce carbon emissions must include divestments as well as investments. We obviously cannot stop carbon dioxide emissions when our governments are paying oil, gas, and coal companies to produce them.

The Transition Has Begun

The world's transition to net-zero carbon economies must happen more rapidly than any major economic transition of the past, and it will not be easy. Fossil fuels are deeply embedded in the industrial world's infrastructure, economies, public policies, and lifestyles. Developing nations see only on prominent model of the path to prosperity, and it requires fossil fuels. To manage their transitions to net-zero carbon, nations must count and mitigate pollution from every link of the oil, coal, and gas value chains, or more accurately their "devalue chains," because fossil fuels emit greenhouse gas pollution not only when they burn, but also when they are taken from the ground, processed, and transported. Nations must begin now to retire and replace the old infrastructure that encourages or requires fossil energy consumption, build anew, retool the many policies they created for their old carbon economies, accelerate the market penetration of clean technologies, and help retrain their workforces. Procrastination is dangerous and costly. Energy Innovation, a policy group, estimates that delaying the transition to 2030 would make it twice as expensive. It would climb to $750 billion yearly by 2035 and more than $900 billion by the early 2040s.

The good news is that the energy transition already has begun in the United States and many other nations, sparked by technical improvements, economies of scale, and government subsidies that have allowed the costs of solar and wind power to drop rapidly. They now can compete with, and often are less expensive than, generating electricity with coal or natural gas. Over the ten years ending in 2019, the price of solar electricity declined 89 percent while onshore wind power dropped 70 percent. Carbon Tracker, a think tank, found in 2020 that it was cheaper to invest in renewables than in coal in every one of the world's energy markets.

Despite the four wasted years of the Trump administration and then the COVID-19 pandemic, renewable energy capacity in the United States nearly doubled in the first half of 2020 compared to the same period in 2019, driven in part by wind developers taking advantage of a federal tax incentive before it was due to expire. (The tax credit was later extended in one of America's COVID relief bills.) The stock prices of big wind and solar companies reached historic highs when the pandemic began easing.[5] By 2020, 60,000 wind turbines and nearly 1.5 million solar panels were producing electricity across the United States.[6] Yet, energy experts say clean energy markets still are not moving fast enough in the United States or worldwide. At present, the world is producing, consuming, and subsidizing fossil fuels at rates that will make it impossible to keep global warming in check. The International Energy Agency (IEA) reported in April 2021 that renewable energy was poised to provide more than half of the world's new electric supply that year. But the IEA also reported that global coal demand in 2021 would approach its 2014 peak due mostly to Asia, and the world's energy-related carbon dioxide pollution was heading toward its second yearly increase ever.[7]

Global banks are partly responsible for headwinds facing the world's transition to clean energy. From 2016, the year following the Paris Agreement, to 2020, the banks have invested more than $3.8 trillion in fossil energy.[8] They are doing so despite the risk that tens of trillions of dollars of fossil energy infrastructure and proved underground reserves will be stranded when climate change becomes so destructive that governments and markets force companies to leave their remaining fossil energy reserves in the ground.

Biden's Plan

The International Renewable Energy Agency (IRENA) says power production by renewable resources must grow eight times faster and nations will have to invest more than $130 trillion by mid-century to keep pace with the world's rising demand for electricity.[9]

In March 2021, President Biden proposed the first installment of the US share, his $2.2 trillion plan to modernize and improve the resilience of America's aging infrastructure. Biden's plan called for the nation's largest ever investment ever in the systems and workforce necessary to support a clean energy economy. Some of the money would come from reducing the government's fossil-fuel subsidies.

Unfortunately for energy investors and flood-prone communities, Biden's plan did not contain a few elements that would have made it even better. The first was a clear, comprehensive roadmap to 2050, complete with specific timelines, milestones, and how the pieces of the infrastructure puzzle fit together to create synergies. "America has to date offered no comprehensive outline of the goals and strategies it will use to tackle greenhouse gas emissions," the *Economist* noted correctly. A roadmap with bipartisan support would provide greater certainty in US energy policy, always a plus for investors. And it could identify the synergies between federal programs and those of states, localities, and businesses. Literally hundreds of companies, states, cities, and civil-society groups have pledged to achieve either carbon neutrality or 100 percent renewable energy in the decades ahead.

Second, Biden's plan doesn't even mention what is arguably the nation's largest climate adaptation challenge: what to do about the nation's rapidly aging flood control structures and the millions of people living in river and coastal flood zones. Should the government invest billions of dollars to fix old dams and levees, billions to build new ones designed to withstand climate change, or launch an aggressive program to help Americans move out of floodplains?

Congress isn't tackling this problem, either. It reportedly considers a retreat from floodplains to be one of those "third rail" issues that no one will touch. But it might help the president and Congress to know this: as politically difficult as it would be to push or pull people out of floodplains, it is far more cost effective for all concerned to do that rather than elevating or floodproofing homes. Over the long term, moving 1 million homes to safety would save $1 trillion compared to elevating or floodproofing them.[10]

Butterflies and Hurricanes

In chaos theory, the flap of a butterfly's wing in New Mexico can cause a hurricane in China. Similarly, we might say that the flip of a light switch in California eventually contributes to sunny-day floods in Florida. The human factors in climate change are the small decisions each of us makes every day about how much energy we use and where it comes from.

The adverse impacts of the wrong decisions will not be the same everywhere. Generally, dry places will get drier and wet places wetter. Some regions will welcome warmer temperatures to increase crop production. But over time, coastal and riverside communities will experience firsthand what happens when heat gets together with water. The Earth's warmer lands and oceans will cause surface waters to evaporate and build up in the atmosphere to produce more intense rains. Warm oceans also add energy to tropical storms and hurricanes as they cross over them.

As the temperature of oceans goes up, their water expands and rises, causing coastal floods and stronger storm surges. As icecaps and glaciers melt, they add water to oceans, and sea levels rise even more. Because of these effects, nearly 9 million are more vulnerable to coastal floods.

Inland, warm air holds more water, leading to more intense rainfalls and floods. More than 40 millions Americans live at risk of floods from rivers and streams.[11] In 2017, for example, Hurricane Harvey dumped 20 trillion gallons of rain on Texas, nearly 1 million gallons per person. That is enough water to raise the level of all the Great Lakes by a foot. In 2019, three major inland floods, eight severe storms, and two tropical cyclones contributed to what NOAA called a "landmark decade of billion-dollar weather and climate disasters."[12] Scientists in the

US Global Change Research Program (USGCRP) say the heaviest rainfall events in the United States have become heavier and more frequent, and significantly above average since 1991.[13]

These extreme weather events have compelled the USACE to look at floods differently. After monster floods inundated the Midwest in 2008, the USACE stopped using the term "flood control." Semantically at least, it has backed away from the notion that floods are controllable. It adopted the term "flood risk management."

Now, climate change has forced the USACE and FEMA to adopt yet another approach: managing people instead of floods. Thus, the term "managed retreats." Gilbert White has been vindicated eighty years after he was accused of being un-American for suggesting that we keep people out of floodplains.

Why Is Retreat Necessary?

FEMA allows new construction in floodplains and allows homeowners to repair their damaged buildings if the repairs include "floodproofing." The agency suggests several methods: elevating homes on pillars or earthen mounds above the 100-year-flood level, plus "freeboard"—a little extra height just in case; wet-proofing the building so that water can enter and exit the bottom floor without much damage; and dry-proofing, where the ground floor is sealed to keep water from entering. Each option has drawbacks.

The elevation option works best for people who are (a) not afraid of heights, (b) fond of climbing stairs, (c) partial to owning boats instead of cars, (d) confident that floating vehicles and other debris will not knock the stilts out from under them, and (e) comfortable with the possibility that their houses may become houseboats embarking on involuntary and unplanned river trips.

Wet-proofing can cause the deterioration of building materials when they are exposed to repeated flooding. Dry-proofing only works if the exterior walls are strong enough to withstand the water's hydrostatic pressure outside. As floods become more severe, or if a dam or levee failure sends a wall of water through town, hydrostatic pressure can increase enough to destroy a dry-proofed structure.

Unless a home is required to have an escape route to dry land, each of these options cuts families off from first responders, food, and evacuation until the water recedes. That can take days or even weeks.

All things considered, it is easier to move people out of the way of rivers and coastal storms than it is to move rivers and coastal storms out of the way of people. Retreat is the only option that completely eliminates flood risks. And in places that experience repetitive flooding, retreat is inevitable as home values decline because of damage and risks, and hazard insurance gets more expensive. The USGCRP says that retreat from parts of US coasts will be unavoidable in "all but the very lowest sea-level rise projections."[14] The same is true for Americans subject to repetitive record inland floods.

The Forecast: Cloudy with a 100 Percent Chance of Climate Change

As the Earth's surface temperature continues warming, weather disasters will get worse. Researchers at Princeton University say Category 3 and even stronger hurricanes will increase.[15] Sea levels on US coasts have gone up eight inches since 1900, including three inches just since 1993. Along the Atlantic Ocean and Gulf, rising seas are causing billions of dollars in property damage.

The Union of Concerned Scientists estimates that $1.07 trillion worth of property is currently at risk from encroaching shorelines in the United States. It estimates that 300,000 residential and commercial properties will suffer chronic flooding by 2045, causing $135 billion in property damages and forcing 280,000 Americans to adapt or relocate.[16]

Relocation is preferable. If climate change progresses as scientists say it will, the decision for tens of millions of Americans at risk of flooding will not be whether to move, but when and where. From the financial and safety standpoints, sooner and farther are better than later and closer. The value of floodplain property is declining from Maine to Texas and the cost of inland properties will rise because of greater demand from climate migrants.

Sooner is better for the nation as a whole, too. The $800 billion the federal government has spent after 119 billion-dollar disasters over the last decade could have been better used on pressing needs like modernizing the nation's deteriorating infrastructure. We already have seen the first indication that there are limits to the government's ability to pay for climate disasters. The National Flood Insurance Program (NFIP), in which FEMA provides below-market insurance premiums for many floodplain homeowners, has gone $50 billion in the red in recent years. Congress allowed the US Treasury to pay some of it, but the NFIP remains more than $20 billion in debt. As one result, FEMA is expected to begin basing all premiums on actual risk. The GAO warns that costs like these could create a trillion-dollar fiscal crisis in the future. The government is "ill prepared" for that, the agency says.[17]

Climate-related weather disasters make other federal programs vulnerable beyond those at FEMA and the USACE. The Federal National Mortgage Association (Fannie Mae) and the Federal Home Loan Mortgage Corporation (Freddie Mac) are publicly traded enterprises that purchase and guarantee mortgages held by low- and moderate-income borrowers. Fannie Mae and Freddie Mac hold about half of the country's $11 trillion in residential mortgages. Federal flood insurance subsidies are supposed to reduce some of the risks of flood losses for the two enterprises, but the NFIP's insolvency makes government-backed mortgage programs more susceptible to climate-related risks.[18]

"US taxpayers could be on the hook for billions of dollars in climate-related property losses as the government backs a growing number of mortgages on homes in the path of floods, fires, and extreme weather," Politico reports. "In short, the government's biggest housing subsidies—mortgage guarantees and flood insurance—are on course to hit taxpayers and the housing market as the effects of climate change worsen. A series of disasters in a single region could trigger a full-blown housing crash."

"Where catastrophe happens and physical climate really manifests itself, the public tab will end up carrying this. Everyone is exposed in this," adds Ivan Frishberg of Amalgamated Bank.

Federal expenditures only scratch the surface. We know little about how state and local government spending is affected. State and local governments qualify for federal disaster relief only after their resources are exhausted. Pew Charitable Trusts found in 2019 that a wide variety of state and local agencies become involved in weather disasters, including those in charge of policing, fire-fighting, agriculture, housing,

criminal justice, revenue, education, public health, environmental protection, public works, business and economic development, social services,
conservation, forestry, transportation, and emergency management.[19]
Most states do not thoroughly track their spending on natural disasters
across all of these agencies, Pew found, and spending varies widely.

However, we know that state and local expenditures on flood disasters also take money away from other important priorities, including
investments that help localities adapt and become more resilient to the
impacts of climate change. "The unaddressed financial costs of adaptation loom large and are unavoidable," CCI warns correctly. "The failure
of the American public and its elected representatives to come to grips
with the massive costs of climate adaptation is perhaps the most delu-
sional form of climate denial we currently face."

Why "Relocation" Rather than "Retreat"?

Another evolutionary change must take place in our response to floods.
We will focus not only on the places that disaster victims must leave but
also the places they will go. Climate change is expected to cause one of the
largest American migrations since the Dust Bowl. In fact, the movement of
"climate migrants" has already begun. Significant numbers of Californians
are moving out of state to avoid deadly wildfires, unbreathable air, and
power outages as it becomes apparent that dry conditions and strong winds
are not going away. In 2018 alone, tens of thousands of Californians left for
Texas, Washington, and Arizona.[20] "Managed retreat" addresses only half of
the problem that climate change is causing. The focus should be on relocation. The difference between retreat and relocation is more than semantic.

Managed retreat will result in lost tax base and declining public
services in flood-prone municipalities unless they can persuade homeowners to relocate within the same jurisdictions. Crops, wildlife, and
isotherms will shift too, forcing the people and industries that depend
on them to move. Some families are already moving away from frequent
fires, drought, heat, and water shortages, as well as flood. On the other
hand, demographers expect climate change to result in massive numbers
of displaced Americans moving to "climate havens" that are safer and
better prepared for changing weather. If migrants arrive in significant

numbers, havens will have to contends with additional demands on space, housing, transportation, and public services. Rural areas and cities with declining populations and tax bases might want to invite migrants to locate there.

Who Should Relocate?

It may not be easy for climate migrants to decide where to go. Few places will be completely safe from climate change, given the diversity of its impacts. For example, FEMA points out that "anywhere it can rain, it can flood." Even people living thousands of feet above sea level can experience flash floods during extreme rain events.

Many families may want to stay where they have longstanding social networks and other ties to their towns. There is no standard checklist for deciding whether to relocate locally or to move away. Every community is different. The variables range from topography (some places don't have higher ground) and demographics (the elderly are often less inclined to move) to the financial help that is available (especially for low-income households). Cultural and psychological factors come into play. In every relocation project I know of, some people refused to move because they loved their homes and riverside locations. Floods were the price they were willing to pay for staying where they were.

My guess is that a growing number of flood-prone communities will make floodplain evacuations mandatory. Municipalities will not want to continue providing infrastructure and services to the few homeowners who want to stay in the floodplain. Done correctly, relocation can create construction jobs, increase the tax base, and provide an opportunity for co-benefits like moving municipal wells out of flood-hazard areas and reducing demands on first responders.

How Buyouts Work

"Buyout" is the term that FEMA uses to describe a local government's purchase of a floodplain home. A buyout may be the only opportunity a homeowner will ever have to recover some of the equity in his or her home. That will be the case especially if the local government pays the greater of the fair-market value and the assessed value of flood-prone homes.

The buyout process currently goes like this: A community applies to FEMA for federal funds to help purchase homes in the floodplain. FEMA ordinarily provides 75 percent of home purchase prices, with state, local, or private funds covering the rest. FEMA has been known, however, to cover 100 percent. To qualify for FEMA's funds, the community must demolish the homes it buys (except where a home can be physically moved out of the floodplain) and conserve the property in perpetuity as floodplain. However, communities are allowed to retain some of the floodplain's economic value by developing trails, parks, and recreation facilities that are not badly damaged by floods and do not obstruct water flows.

FEMA does not require it, but communities are wise to couple flood-plain evacuation with other "nonstructural" measures that reduce flooding. Examples include restoring wetlands to filter pollution, recharge groundwater, and provide habitat for a variety of species; reforesting and revegetating the upriver watershed so it will stop raindrops where they fall; and reducing stormwater volumes with more green spaces and permeable surfaces so that soils absorb water. In cases I'll describe later, USACE helps communities by demolishing flood control structures it built in the past and restoring the natural features of rivers, including the snakelike meander that slows a river's flow.

FEMA's regulations require that all home purchases must be voluntary, but the agency has been criticized for funding buyouts for a few homes at a time rather than entire neighborhoods. The USACE's approach is different. It reportedly will begin requiring local governments to use eminent domain to purchase homes whose owners don't want to sell. That will be controversial because of property-rights issues, but it is constitutional so long as the purchase is for a public purpose. The purposes here are to reduce public expenditures on flood prevention and recovery and to leave floodplains unimpeded so rivers will slow down and spread out during flood events.

All three of the federal agencies typically involved in relocation projects—FEMA, the USACE, and the Department of Housing and Urban Development (HUD)—plan to encourage large-scale buyouts rather than one or two homes at a time, as in the past.[21]

How Far from the Floodplain Is Safe?

Technologies are getting better for predicting the types and severity of climate impacts at large and small scales. Still, a community can't be sure how large an area will be at risk of flooding. FEMA provides maps that identify the areas it determines will be affected by 100-year floods. It sometimes maps 500-year floodplains. But it has not mapped the 1,000-year floods that are happening with greater frequency, or the areas at risk if a levee or dam fails.

Insurance companies and federal agencies have relied on past flood data to anticipate future events, but climate change has made floods less predictable. In other words, the past is no longer prologue in the flood mitigation business. Although data are improving to help anticipate future events, scientists have been less able to predict at local scale. They have given most of their attention to studying climate at the global, national, and regional levels. But their confidence in projecting future floods is increasing as data and computer modeling capabilities improve.

One example is a recent study by the First Street Foundation, a nonprofit research group specializing in flood risk. It analyzed decades of peer-reviewed studies, gathered the experience of more than seventy experts, and used its model to assess the risk of future floods for millions of properties. The results differed dramatically from FEMA's flood maps. It showed that 14.6 million properties are at risk for 100-year floods, compared to 8.7 million identified by FEMA. The foundation now allows the public to obtain property-specific data through a web application called Flood Factor.[22]

Because federal data are still evolving to anticipate floods at small scale, New York City created its own Panel on Climate Change, an advisory board of climate experts appointed by the mayor. Using the panel's projections, the city's Department of City Planning developed a tool that allows people to map likely coastal flood hazards in the 2050s, 2080s, and 2100. The city also uses the panel's findings to build its $20 billion climate-resilience budget.

Common sense should be thrown into the mix, too. Farther and higher are better, of course. The closer a building is to a river or shoreline, the greater the risk. The closer a community's elevation is to sea level or historic high-water marks, the greater its risk.

Second, the fact that an area has not been flooded in the past does not mean it will not be flooded in the future. In 2018, researchers surveyed more than 700 stormwater and floodplain management officials in the United States. Eighty-five percent reported that their cities had experienced floods outside their mapped 100-year floodplains.[23] When Hurricane Harvey hit Houston in 2018, nearly 60 percent of the more than 200,000 affected homes were outside the 500-year floodplain and were not required to have flood insurance.

Changes in upriver and downriver land uses can make FEMA's maps obsolete. When a floodplain is evacuated and returns to its natural state, it can alter river characteristics upstream and down. Upstream real estate development usually adds to runoff, affecting water volumes downriver. Some communities—Charlotte in Mecklenburg County, North Carolina, is one—have created their own maps to supplement FEMA's, based on more up-to-date information about recent and projected upriver land-use changes.

Equity Issues

Difficult equity issues have surfaced in buyouts. A research team representing several universities found that FEMA buyouts are used more often in wealthy and populous counties than in rural counties, even though the latter are more likely to experience floods.[24] Similarly, if only middle- to upper-income families can afford to take buyouts, low-income families and elderly residents may be left behind in the floodplain. The assessed value of a house often is lower than its market value. If a community buys houses at their assessed values, homeowners may be left with too little money to obtain mortgages for new residences. For that reason, homeowners have more incentive to take a buyout when the community pays the higher of the two valuations.

Virtually every flood-prone city and village has low-income citizens who (a) are the most heavily affected by floods because they are least able to recover, (b) can't afford flood insurance, (c) may not receive a buyout price sufficient to build or buy a home outside the floodplain, and (d) live in floodplains not because they choose to, but because that is where land and housing is most available and affordable, especially in rapidly expanding cities. "Climate gentrification" has become a term to describe the disparities in how people are treated because of income, race, or age.[25]

Texas Southern University has produced a very good analysis of the social impacts of relocation projects.[26] It addresses how lower-income residents in Houston were affected by Hurricane Harvey. Its principal conclusion is that current buyout program is not well designed to serve low-income flood victims. Some of the most salient findings, quoted verbatim here, are:

- Many low-income residents perceive buyouts as "takings." Most of the wealth of low-income and poor people is often in their homes. A buyout is a wealth transfer. Once it is gone, they may never be able to attain it again.
- Relocation often means losing proximity to family, school, church, job, and transportation. These are irreplaceable resources for vulnerable residents. So, when possible, a relocation project should include more than homes. It should include features essential to the social, educational and spiritual needs of its residents.
- Low-cost housing is more likely to be deemed substantially damaged immediately after a flood, leaving [low-income residents] unable to afford to rebuild and therefore subject to an unwanted buyout, otherwise known as displacement. In a relocation project where one or more neighborhoods are being moved and reconstructed, the projects should provide a variety of housing options for families at all income levels, including rental and multifamily units.
- Current buyout policy is not need-based. Any programmatic decision based on economic valuation will value the properties of the wealthy more than those of the poor, which will produce subsequent demographic implications by race, ethnicity, age, gender, etc.[27]

Many well-regarded organizations specialize in equity issues.[28] Congress should consult them to identify and address systemic discrimination in FEMA's buyout program and other federal disaster policies. For their part, local organizations concerned about equity should participate in and become watchdogs during relocation planning. The concerns of low-income, elderly, handicapped, and minority people can get lost quickly in a project's complexities. In some cases, failing to plan for and meet the needs of these populations may be intentional. When many New Orleans residents fled to other cities after Hurricane Katrina, for example, the city was slow to rebuild low-income housing. It was accused of wanting to discourage poor families from coming back.

Streamlining the Buyout Process

In 2019, the Natural Resources Defense Council (NRDC) published an analysis based on thirty years of FEMA data.[29] It found that federally funded buyouts are far from adequate to keep up with the growing number of at-risk properties in the United States. "By the end of this century, as many as 13 million people in the United States will see their homes affected by sea-level rise," the NRDC warned. "Millions more who live, work, or travel through coastal or riverine areas will be subjected to repeated flooding as severe weather events become more frequent and cause greater damage. . . . Among the millions who could be displaced, many will need assistance to move to higher ground."

FEMA says it completed 46,734 home purchases from 1989 to 2017, but usually only one or two homes at a time.[30] Over thirty years, buyouts reached only a tiny fraction of the many millions of people living in river and coastal floodplains. The program's objective should be to buy out as many homes as possible in each floodplain and to do it as seamlessly and efficiently as governments can.

Judging by how rapidly the effects of climate change are accelerating in the United States, neither homeowners nor policymakers should be under the illusion that they have until the end of the century to evacuate the nation's floodplains and to help people move inland. The federal government will need adequate resources for a much more ambitious national relocation program.

Speed also is an issue for individual homeowners. The current process is untenable. With all three government levels involved—federal, state, and local—a three- to five-year wait before a home purchase is completed is common today. The long delays put homeowners in a bind after a disaster, forcing them to spend money to repair their damaged homes, a wasted investment when they move.

"Long wait times make buyouts less accessible, less equitable and less effective for disaster mitigation and climate adaptation," the NRDC study concluded. "Most important, many of the homeowners suffering through these long waits are those who can least afford it."[31] Rather than going through the buyout process, many homeowners rebuild and "hope the next flood misses them."

Pearlington, Mississippi, provides an example of the current buyout process. It is a small community that had never flooded before it was hit by Hurricane Katrina and a 30-foot storm surge in 2005. The city experienced flooding again in 2008 and 2012 from Hurricanes Gustav and Isaac. After Katrina, the state said it would spend $10 million to

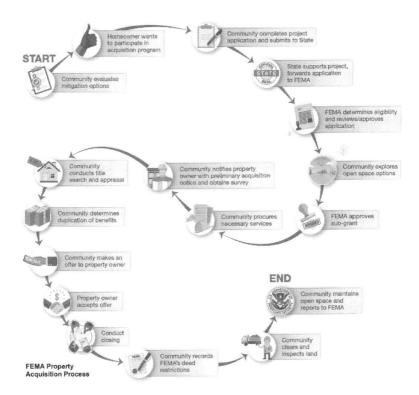

The buyout process: These are the steps necessary for a homeowner to obtain a buyout. The process typically takes five years or more to be completed. *FEMA*

buy homes in Pearlington's newly defined floodplain. But residents said the process dragged on for years because of government red tape and funding the government withdrew and restored again.

Nearly 120 homeowners signed up for buyouts. About half were found to be eligible, but a decade later, residents reported that purchases had been completed for fewer than ten homes. "I'll say it bluntly, and I want Washington, I want Jackson [the state capital], I want everybody to hear it: The buyout going on in Pearlington right now? The whole situation's been a joke," one homeowner said.[32]

Bloomberg Businessweek tells another story of how buyouts worked, or didn't work, in Sidney, New York, a town of 4,000 along the Susquehanna River.[33] More than 400 homes and businesses were flooded by Tropical Storm Lee in the fall of 2011. Some 2,000 people were impacted. Just as people finished rebuilding, the town was hit by a second flood. The result is that more people became interested in moving out of the floodplain.

The floods left a mix of damaged and abandoned homes in the floodplain. Sydney hoped to become a model of relocation rather than raising homes on stilts or using other floodproofing measures. The town bought the option on a nearby farm, intending to make it the site of a new neighborhood for flood victims. Then it learned it would cost $4 million to extend water and sewer to the site.

The buyout process became another disincentive, involving contracts, land surveys, lien checks, appraisals, and approvals from agencies all the way to Washington, DC. It showed "how unprepared the US is politically, financially, and emotionally to re-create even a single community away from rising waters in an organized way, preserving some semblance of its character and history," *Bloomberg* reported.

Only 32 families applied for buyouts. To pay the local 25 percent share, Sidney applied for grants from HUD. That encouraged another 127 families to sign up, but mixing two pots of federal money slowed the government approval process even more. Rather than go through it, some people left town.

FEMA should consider providing block grants to states and allowing them to take care of due diligence and approvals. It should consider giving the highest priority to communities applying for the largest numbers of buyouts.

Also, FEMA and USACE should encourage repetitively flooded communities to relocate before another flood rather than waiting for one to occur. The weeks and even years following a significant flood are preoccupied with finding food and shelter, salvaging belongs, getting insurance estimates, filling out paperwork, and so on. Pre-disaster relocations allow time for community involvement and thoughtful planning. If FEMA's approvals are already in hand, recovery funds arrive much sooner. Cities can also prepare ordinances and master plans in advance to organize and govern the post-disaster move. And some cities have had more luck than Sidney in purchasing and extending infrastructure to relocation sites in advance. East Grand Forks, Minnesota, arranged for FEMA to set up its trailers on the city's permanent relocation site and leave its infrastructure behind, a clever way to make infrastructure less expensive.

Communities will need technical assistance to manage the human, economic, and physical challenges of relocations, as well as the zoning and building codes they may want to put in place to guide construction. As Soldiers Grove demonstrated, buyouts at scale are opportunities to develop community-scale solar energy systems, energy-efficient buildings, other renewable energy systems such as geothermal heating and cooling, and so on.

If buyouts are the best way to avoid flood disasters—and they are—and if the law requires agencies to give them full consideration—which it does—then FEMA, USACE, HUD, and Congress must make them as equitable, user-friendly, and free of red tape as possible.

Tough Love

We may assume that we have the right to live almost anywhere we want in a free society. But if we choose to live at risk, we should not expect others to be responsible for the consequences. That should be the principle for a new national disaster policy: people can live where they want if they take responsibility for their decisions, respect the rights of others, and do not rely on taxpayers to bail them out if their decisions are bad.

On shorelines and along rivers, respecting other people's rights may be complicated because, as I pointed out earlier, the unintended consequences of a seawall, a levee, or a dam might shift damages to people living elsewhere. One option would be floodplain or coastal compacts in which every resident and town along a river or shoreline pledges to do no harm to others and if possible, take steps that reduce damages elsewhere.

If we wanted to implement the "take responsibility" principle, then a radical retooling of government disaster programs would be necessary. They might look like this:

- We would acknowledge the inevitability of floods in this age of climate change and deal with them before, rather than after, they occur.
- FEMA, USACE, and HUD would undertake a ten-year program to evacuate the nation's coastal and riverine floodplains using data and tools like the First Street Foundation's Flood Factor. To accomplish this, FEMA would reform its buyout program to eliminate long delays, promote pre-disaster buyouts, and encourage large-scale buyouts. During the first five years of the transition period, FEMA would provide communities with 100 percent of the fair market value of floodplain homes whose owners agree to relocate. In years six through ten, FEMA's share would decline annually from 50 percent to 10 percent of fair market value.
- In addition, FEMA, USACE, and HUD would eliminate inequities for disadvantaged, underserved, elderly, disabled, low-income, and minority residents in the buyout program.
- FEMA and HUD would help relocating communities identify development sites, plan the movement of floodplain residents to those sites, and learn about best available urban designs, clean energy systems, mobility options, ecosystem management techniques, and overall sustainable development of the new settlements.
- During the same ten years, Congress would phase out the perverse incentives that encourage and indemnify floodplain occupation, including the National Flood Insurance Program (NFIP). During the phase-out, the NFIP would shift entirely to risk-based premiums. This would cause steep increases in insurance costs. The First Street Foundation has found that the 4.3 million properties with substantial flood risks were expected to experience flood losses of

$20 billion in 2021. Estimated losses would grow 61 percent to more than $32 billion annually in thirty years because of climate change. Insurance for nearly 3 million homes would be more than five times higher, or about $2,484 annually; the cost for 1.5 million properties would go up four-fold to $7,895 annually, creating a substantial incentive for homeowners to move out of disaster zones.[34]

- Any property owner who experienced more than two floods during the transition would be immediately ineligible for further federal disaster assistance.
- The long-range goal of coastal relocations would be to establish continuous National Seashores along the Atlantic and Pacific Oceans and the Gulf of Mexico, and National Lakeshores along the Great Lakes.

The Numbers

When most of today's flood-control dams were authorized and built, there was little attention to their environmental impacts and long-term costs. Congress did not require federal agencies to conduct environmental assessments and write impact statements until 1969.

Contemporary impact analysis should assess the consequences of federal policies and programs much more holistically, looking at the full life-cycle impacts, good or bad, to society and the economy as well as the environment.[35] Structural flood-control projects would require an evaluation of whether nonstructural alternatives, including ecosystem services, would be safer and more cost-effective on a full-cost life-cycle basis.[36] Here are some data that should be considered.

Scope of the challenge

Different organizations have issued a variety of estimates of how many Americans live in floodplains. The First Street Foundation calculated that 14.6 million properties are in danger from 100-year floods.[37] The University of Bristol used upgraded technology and data to identify flood risks across the United States, including small streams. It estimated that 41 million Americans live in 100-year floodplains.[38] The New York University Furman Center indicates that an average of

15 million Americans lived in 100-year floodplains from 2011 to 2015, and 30 million lived in combined 100- and 500-year floodplains during the same period.[39]

Future cost of weather-related damages

Weather disasters attributed to climate change are costing the United States $58 billion annually, on average.[40] Flood damages average about $5 billion a year. But this estimate is conservative; it does not include inland floods caused by hurricanes or the many floods that result in less than $1 billion in damages. These costs will increase as the weather gets more severe. Costs also will rise if people keep moving into floodplains and assuming that structures will protect them.

The CBO estimates that based on current conditions (climate, sea levels, and property development), the annual cost of hurricane winds and storm-related flooding will be $54 billion over the long run.[41] The yearly cost to taxpayers is expected to be $17 billion. But these estimates are based on current climate change, sea-level rise, and government policies even though we know that climate-related costs are rising and will continue to do so.

Cost of fixing dams and levees

USACE estimates that the nation's existing levees will need $80 billion in maintenance and improvements over the next ten years. The ASDSO says it would cost $70 billion to rehabilitate all of the nation's federal and nonfederal dams. That means an upfront investment of $150 billion. It is not a static number: it grows continuously as these structures age and undergo wear and tear. Seventy percent of the nation's dams exceeded fifty years old in 2020.

In most cases, $150 billion would bring existing dams only to the condition necessary to protect people and property from 100-year floods. We don't know what the cost would be to upgrade or build new dams and levees for increasingly severe precipitation events. Moreover, investing more money in these structures commits their owners to years of more spending on maintenance and repairs.

Cost of new structures

As noted earlier, the Center for Climate Integrity estimates that by 2040 the coasts would need 50,000 more miles of seawalls and other barriers to hold back rising seas. That would cost $416 billion. For nearly 180 small coastal communities, it amounts to $100,000 per person, making evacuation the only viable option.

Cost of natural protection

A study published in 2020 found that in an area roughly the size of Colorado, leaving 100-year floodplains in woodland, wetlands, and/or grassland would be the most economical way to avoid future flood damages. The authors reported that in about 21,000-square miles of this area, a dollar invested in flood protection would save at least $5 in future flood damages. In other words, communities can avoid significant future costs by prohibiting development in floodplains, focusing real estate development on low-risk land, and buying existing buildings to evacuate flood-prone areas.[42]

Cost of relocations

The National Bureau of Economic Research estimates that there are at least 3.8 million homes in America's floodplains.[43] The National Institute of Building Sciences has concluded that it would cost $180 billion to remove one million of them. The investment would save $1.16 trillion over the next one hundred years or $6.50 for every $1 spent.[44] That puts the cost of relocating all floodplain homes at less than $700 billion with a savings of about $4.5 trillion over the next one hundred years.

Lost property values

As risk awareness increases on coasts and along rivers, the market value of homes slips, meaning less return on the owners' capital investments and lower property tax revenues to support local government services. Several studies show that coastal real-estate values are already dropping because of more frequent tidal floods. For example, the First Street Foundation evaluated housing market data in eighteen coastal states from Maine to Texas and found that floods eroded property values by nearly $16 billion between 2005 and 2017.[45] The National Bureau of Economic Research calculated that Americans are paying $34 billion too much today for floodplain homes.[46]

We can draw two conclusions from all of these numbers. First, there are many different and contradictory data about the number of people and amount of property at risk of flooding in the United States today, and what those risks are likely to be in the future. It would be useful for FEMA to convene a committee of public and private experts who have evaluated flood risks to develop a common set or range of numbers and a consensus on the scope of the challenge.

Second, no matter which data we accept, they tell us that governments at all levels, as well as the many millions of Americans living in harm's way today, have an enormous amount of work to do without a lot of time to do it. The nature of that work is not flood control, or flood loss management, or even managed retreats. It is the relocation of people out of floodplains and deliberate efforts see them resettled in places most advantageous to the environment, to them, and to the communities from which they come.

Third and most important, we must pick up the pace. Now.

11

NATURAL SOLUTIONS

This emergence of ecological restoration is, in my mind, the most important environmental development since the first Earth Day.

—Gary Paul Nabhan

WITH SUNNY-DAY FLOODS AND RISING SEAS, it may be obvious that Florida has a lot of problems, ecologically speaking. It gets worse. More than 3,600 miles of the state are in the 100-year floodplain. Parts are subsiding and making sea-level rise more dangerous. "Miami as we know it today—there's virtually no scenario under which you can imagine it existing at the end of the century," says environmental author Jeff Goodell.[1]

Fortunately, state officials recognize that ecosystem restoration must be part of their work to reduce adverse climate change. Florida has a deputy secretary for ecosystems restoration as well as offices in charge of ecosystem projects, coastal protection, and water restoration.[2] The state has created more than forty aquatic preserves that protect more than 2 million mostly underwater acres of coastal lands for wildlife and recreation. It monitors the condition of beaches along 825 miles of erosion-prone areas on the Atlantic Ocean, Gulf of Mexico, and Straits of Florida coasts and restores beaches and dunes to buffer wildlife habitat and human settlements from the ocean.

Many other states are getting busy, too. This sometimes involves projects in which the USACE reverses the work it did during the dam-building era. For example, the USACE has been helping restore ecosystems in urban and rural river corridors. Among them are the Trinity River in Dallas; Spring Brook in Naperville, Illinois; the Elwha River in Washington's Olympic National Park; the Penobscot River in Maine; the Muddy River in Boston; and the Upper Mississippi River in Illinois, Wisconsin, Iowa, Minnesota, and Missouri. Some projects are underway, and others have been completed. They involve activities ranging from dam removals to ecosystem restorations and combinations of both. Two of the most impressive are on Kissimmee River in central Florida and the Napa River in California.

Kissimmee River

In central Florida, the USACE is undoing a flood control project it did twenty years ago. The Kissimmee River once twisted and turned for more than 100 miles between two lakes. During heavy seasonal rains, its floodplain was as much as 3 miles wide, providing a rich habitat for waterfowl, largemouth bass, alligators, eagles, aquatic invertebrates, and a variety of plants.

In the 1960s, the USACE collaborated with the area's water management district to convert the river into the C-38 canal, a ditch 56 miles long, 300-feet wide, and 30-feet deep. Over nine years, the corps removed 26.5 million cubic yards of material and built seven locks. By eliminating the river's meander, the canal halved the time it took to get from one lake to another. C-38 succeeded in reducing flooding, but more than 90 percent of the waterfowl in the watershed disappeared. As oxygen levels dropped, largemouth bass were replaced by less popular species.

So, in 1999, the USACE began returning the river to some of its original character. It backfilled 8 miles of the canal and re-created 24 miles of the river's meandering course. The project is restoring 40 square miles of floodplain. By 2020, much of the flora and fauna had returned.

Wetlands came back, oxygen levels rose, and aquatic plants cleaned the river water again. The USACE increased the lakes' storage capacities to maintain the flood-control benefits the canal had provided.

The restored Kissimmee River alongside the backfilled C-38 canal. *USACE*

Napa River Restoration

The Kissimmee River restoration project is said to be the largest of its kind in the world, but similar work is underway in the Napa River Valley of California, where erosion threatened property, habitat, and scenic landscapes. The river runs 55 miles from Mount St. Helena (not to be confused with Mount St. Helens in Washington State) to San Pablo Bay. It originally meandered along a valley floor, supporting up to 8,000 migrating steelhead trout and chinook salmon. But after levees and berms were built for agriculture, erosion became a problem.

Today, the Napa River is three times deeper in some places than it once was. The restoration includes removing levees, reestablishing wetlands, and widening the floodplain. More than forty landowners agreed to dedicate portions of their vineyards to expand the floodplain and protect the rest of their vineyards from erosion and flooding. Federal and state grants are funding similar work on longer stretches of the river.

Restoring Floodplains

In other places, rivers are being reunited with their natural floodplains. This is happening in California's Central Valley and in several parts of the flood-prone Midwest.

Freshwater supplies have always been a problem in the arid West. The more intense droughts attributed to climate change have triggered debates about whether the region needs more dams. But with more attention on environmental impacts than there was a century ago, states are looking at nonstructural solutions. Floodplain expansions and wetland restorations are among the options.

In the Sierra Nevada Mountains, American Rivers restores meadows that collect spring rains and filter water pollutants. One project is the Hope Valley Meadow in a watershed shared by California and Nevada. In collaboration with several other organizations, American Rivers is repairing 400 acres damaged by a long history of heavy grazing. Once it is healthy, the meadow will provide fish and wildlife habitat as well as water storage and groundwater recharge.

Integrated Floodplain Management

Nonprofit groups in California have created the Multi-Benefit Flood Protection Project to encourage integrated flood management in the Central Valley. The goal is to protect more than 1 million people and $70 billion in homes, businesses, agriculture, and infrastructure. At last report, the organization was involved in twenty-three projects ranging from buying flooded farmlands to expanding the floodplain, using weirs (low barriers across the width of rivers that change flow characteristics), and restoring wildlife habitat.

Another initiative is Floodplains by Design, through which the Nature Conservancy works with the Washington State Department of Ecology and the Puget Sound Partnership. Communities compete for grants to improve water quality, recreation, and agriculture, and restore habitat along Washington's major rivers by integrating hazard reduction measures with ecological preservation and restoration. The initiative's sponsors point out that "floodplain management needs a rethink" because "practices have not kept pace with scientific advances or evolving public priorities."

Restoring Coasts

A virtual army of federal agencies, state governments, legislatively created councils, coalitions, and environmental organizations is involved in projects to restore the Atlantic, Gulf, and Great Lakes coasts and its river corridors. Complete information is scarce about how much money these organizations have invested or what all of their efforts are, but they include wetlands restoration, beach nourishment, natural methods to harden shorelines, marshland grass planting, and much more.

Great Lakes

The Great Lakes have been called inland oceans. They contain 21 percent of the world's surface water—the most massive collective freshwater expanse in the world. The Great Lakes system includes 5,000 tributaries and a drainage area of nearly 290,000 square miles. Many of the challenges in and around the lakes' 9,000 miles of coastline are similar to those on the ocean and Gulf coasts: beaches, dunes, and wetlands threatened by the freshwater version of sea-level rise. Wetlands have been destroyed by agricultural and residential development. In a collaboration called the Great Lakes Coastal Assembly, more than twenty organizations are working to conserve and restore critically important ecosystems in Great Lakes coastal zones. In addition, forty-three field stations of the US Fish and Wildlife Service (FWS) have collaborated on a Great Lakes Basin Ecosystem team that conserves islands and restores lake sturgeon populations.

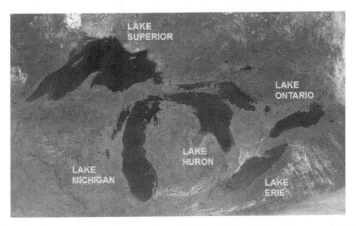

The Great Lakes. *SeaWiFS Project, NASA/Goddard Space Flight Center, and ORBIMAGE*

Gulf Coast

Congress created a coastal restoration trust fund in 2012 with penalties assessed against companies involved in the 2010 Deepwater Horizon oil spill. The overall effort is managed by the Gulf Coast Ecosystem Restoration Council, consisting of the governors of five states, the secretaries of five federal cabinet departments, and the EPA.

The funds are being used to stabilize banks, create marshes, restore barrier islands, control erosion, and monitor species. The USACE is involved, and so are young adults participating in a program called Gulf Corps, a three-year collaboration between the Nature Conservancy, NOAA, and the Student Conservation Association.[3] A nonprofit group, the Coalition to Restore Coastal Louisiana, works with volunteers on projects such as planting marsh grasses and trees.

Living Shorelines

Fourteen percent of the nation's continental coastline has been "armored" with hard structures such as seawalls and bulkheads. These structures block the power of waves, but they shift that power to adjacent areas. Hard structures take a toll on ecosystems. They often were built to replace natural systems that protected the coasts, such as oyster reefs, coral reefs, marshes, and wetlands. However, "living systems" offer multiple benefits over hard systems. For example, 15 feet of marsh can absorb 50 percent of incoming wave energy while also providing habitat for sea life. Salt marshes and mangroves grow higher by trapping sediment and organic matter.

Environmental scientist Dr. Rachel Gittman at East Carolina University points out that soft measures are not suitable in all situations, but they can supplement hard protections to cope with more extreme climate impacts. An example is the Big U project in New York City, where landfills will elevate a 60-acre waterfront park by 10 feet. Combined with retractable flood gates in neighborhoods, the park is expected to protect as many as 100,000 people from up to 16 feet of sea-level rise.

Elsewhere in the city, the New York Harbor School coordinates the Billion Oyster Project. Oyster beds are natural reefs that block the full power of waves. The project engages hundreds of thousands of children to grow 1 billion oysters in New York Harbor by 2035. Restaurants like it; they are donating their oyster shells rather than paying to have them carted away. Crews pick them up, clean them, and take them to the project's hatchery at the Urban Assembly New York Harbor School, a public high school that teaches marine sciences. Students grow oyster larvae and combine them with the shells. The larvae attach themselves and develop their own shells. Bags and cages full of the live shells are then put into the harbor to grow into reefs that reduce damage from wave erosion.

The living oysters also are natural filters that each clean 30 to 50 gallons of water a day and provide food and shelter for other marine life. By the spring of 2021, the project had put 1.6 million pounds of oyster shells into New York waters, created 15 reefs, planted 47 million live oysters, and filtered nearly 20 trillion gallons of water.

Rewilding

Again, climate change presents us with two principal challenges: ending the pollution responsible for global warming (mitigation) and adjusting to the climate changes that are already underway or in the pipeline (adaptation). Every community should engage in both. Flood avoidance is a form of adaptation not only for the community engaged in it, but also for other people, species, and ecosystems affected by the community's actions. Preserving biodiversity is one such opportunity. When we pay attention, we can see that biodiversity loss is happening. The FWS lists nearly 1,500 species that are already threatened or endangered in the United States.[4] The most threatened range from the gray wolf and polar bear to the Texas ocelot, Florida panther, and wood-land caribou. The government protects critical habitat for fewer than half of them.[5] Closer to home, elderly Americans might notice that the monarch butterflies they saw as kids seem to have disappeared. Farming and urbanization have destroyed milkweeds, which are food for Monarch larva.

The World Economic Forum, the organization that hosts thousands of elite leaders each year in Davos, Switzerland, issues an annual *Global*

Risks Report. Its 2020 report ranks biodiversity loss as the second most impactful and third most likely risk for the next decade. "The current rate of extinction is tens to hundreds of times higher than the average over the past 10 million years—and it is accelerating," the report notes. "Biodiversity loss has critical implications for humanity, from the collapse of food and health systems to the disruption of entire supply chains."

If the world does nothing about climate change, up to half of the planet's plants, mammals, birds, reptiles, and amphibians will be lost in the thirty-five most wildlife-rich regions. The greenhouse-gas reduction goals of the Paris climate agreement could cut the losses in half, according to the Tyndall Centre for Climate Change Research, but millions of species would still go extinct.

Biologist E. O. Wilson's goal is to set aside half of the planet for wildlife in an initiative he calls Half Earth. He believes that "rewilding" on this scale could save 80 to 90 percent of all species. After a three-year study by nearly five hundred scientists, a United Nations (UN) working group came to a slightly less ambitious conclusion: a third of the world's land and oceans should be protected, and 10 percent should be strictly protected to reverse species loss.[6] On either scale, the call is for a massive effort to restore and protect habitat.

The human species is not exempt from the impacts of climate change. In one generation, the climate of many cities is expected to change to resemble temperatures of places that are now hundreds of miles away. Some cities will experience environments "with no modern equivalent in North America."[7]

In rivers, lakes, and streams, droughts and shifting rain patterns will cause lower water levels that won't dilute pollution, American Rivers warns. High temperatures will cause more algae blooms that starve fish of oxygen. Trout anglers in the South will find that the fish have disappeared and been replaced by warm-water species. Trout and salmon that migrate upstream each season may notice that low water levels make them more vulnerable to predators.

Some species will attempt to move north or climb to higher elevations to escape warming temperatures. But there are complications. Suitable habitat is often fragmented. Writers at *Bloomberg* describe the lower forty-eight states as "a 1.9-billion-acre jigsaw puzzle of cities, farms, forests, and pastures." Many likely migratory paths are interrupted by cities and other human developments. Codependent species may be separated from one another as they move. For example, pollinators may be separated from their preferred plants.

Some cities and electric utilities are creating more habitat and wildlife corridors that give species paths to migrate or find new habitats that fit their climate needs. The Electric Power Research Institute (EPRI) promotes the development of wildlife corridors and habitat in the millions of acres of transmission rights of way in the United States, including areas suitable for conservation and wetland banking. EPRI says "vegetation management" to create these corridors has been evolving over the last fifty years. Research shows that biodiversity can be improved in corridors as narrow as 25 yards.

Chicago's Burnham Park includes a 100-acre wildlife corridor that runs through the heart of the city. Montana has created one of the nation's largest collections of safe crossings for wildlife along a 56-mile section of US Highway 93. There are forty-one crossings much appreciated by grizzly bears, cougars, elk, and deer. The Federal Highway Administration has joined the effort, too, with guidance on changing roadsides and medians from grasses to wildflowers for pollinators.

One of the more ambitious corridors is 2,000 miles long and connects 500,000 miles of protected habitat. It is the Yellowstone-to-Yukon Conservation Initiative (Y2Y). As its name implies, it connects the Greater Yellowstone Ecosystem to the Yukon Territory in Canada. It spans five US states, two Canadian provinces, and the traditional lands of seventy-five indigenous groups. To its credit, Y2Y conducts, commissions, and shares scientific research and indigenous knowledge, including how to adapt landscapes to climate and land-use changes.

More Net Zeros

"Net-zero energy" and "net-zero carbon" are becoming more familiar terms as goals for the economy in the era of climate change. What if our objectives included net-zero species loss due to human activity, net-zero loss of habitat, and net-zero loss of carbon sinks?

One model is called "compensatory mitigation." If a developer wants to build a housing project that will damage a wetland, stream, or river today, it must obtain a permit from the USACE. The permit requires the developer to avoid damage to the wetland, stream, or river. If the damage is unavoidable, the developer must invest in creating or restoring a comparable natural resource elsewhere. This requirement has resulted in a market for "wetland credits." Private investors can put their money into wetlands restoration, earn credits, and sell them to developers.

A study in 2016 found that compensatory mitigation had resulted in the creation of nearly 1,050 "mitigation banks" whose credits protected about 1 million acres of wetlands and 220,000 jobs in engineering, construction, and scientific professions. Among other things, compensatory mitigation would help states carry out Wildlife Action Plans, an item all states must have.

Conserving and Creating CO_2 Sinks

In the last months of its tenure, the Obama administration issued a Mid-Century Strategy for Deep Decarbonization that described what the United States could do to achieve net-zero carbon by 2050. The plan noted that the proper conservation and administration of natural carbon sinks could sequester as much as half the nation's carbon emissions by 2050 (see sidebar).[8]

Forests are major sinks. Although America underwent intense deforestation from 1600 to 1900, the total forested area has remained relatively stable since then. To maintain that stability—or better yet, to increase forested lands—forests must be preserved, tree planting must follow timber harvests, and trees should be planted on urban sites and reclaimed farmland.

Ten years ago, there were more than 751 million acres of forests, about a third of the country. A quarter of it was old-growth forest, 67 percent was secondary forest, and 8 percent was on farms and plantations. Now there seems to be a tree-planting competition underway. Several cities have programs to plant 1 million trees. In 2018, the National Forest Foundation launched a campaign to plant 50 million trees. The Arbor Day Foundation plans to plant 100 million trees by 2022, while the Nature Conservancy has a billion-tree program.

President Trump announced during his 2020 State of the Union address that the United States would join a Trillion Tree Initiative of the World Economic Forum.[9] Republicans in Congress have lined up behind the idea as a noncontroversial, nature-based way to do something about climate change. But reforestation and afforestation enthusiasts must do their work holistically, because trees affect the ecosystems in which they live. Forests can compete with other important land uses, divert groundwater needed elsewhere, and prevent other vegetation from growing if canopies provide too much shade. Like all other endeavors, environmental and otherwise, holistic analysis is necessary to avoid unintended consequences.

Carbon Sinks

The ability of forests, grasslands, soils, and wetlands to be "carbon sinks" will be one of the most critical ecosystem services in this century. They take carbon from the atmosphere and store it. In 2014, these systems offset 11 percent of the nation's carbon emissions. With conservation and proper management, they could sequester 30 to 50 percent of all the nation's carbon pollution by mid-century. Following are some carbon sink options.

Forests: Creating another 60 million acres of forests would be economical if CO_2 were priced at only $20 per ton. Sooner is better if the United States wants to achieve a net-zero economy by 2050. One danger is that 57 million acres of rural forestlands will be destroyed for housing in the coming decades—one of the reasons that smart urban planning is important.

Urban Forests: Urban trees could provide 10 percent of the nation's carbon sink, but urban tree cover is declining. The co-benefits range from lower inner-city temperatures and cooling costs to higher real estate values. Species with longer life spans, higher wood density, and good stress tolerance are best.

Grasslands: As many as 40 million acres of pasture and idle croplands could be planted in perennial grasses that serve as energy feedstocks. Rotational grazing will prevent overgrazing. "Carbon-beneficial biomass" varieties optimize the use of grasslands as carbon sinks.

Soils: Soils make an excellent carbon sink if they are not disturbed. The requirements include no-till farming, cover crops, residue management, and other practices that increase organic soil carbon. It can take years of proper management to improve soil structure and sequestration performance, but just one conventional plowing will reverse soil-carbon gains.

Wetlands: Wet organic soils can hold carbon in place for hundreds to thousands of years. There are nearly 100 million acres of wetlands in the coterminous United States and 144 million acres in Alaska. The best sinks are saline marshes, seagrasses, and mangroves. Wetlands are some of the most productive ecosystems, supporting water quality, fish and wildlife habitat, and flood protection. In addition to sequestering carbon, a single acre of wetland saturated to a depth of 1 foot retains equivalent water to cause thigh-deep flooding in thirteen average-size homes, according to American Rivers. Wetlands in the United States save more than $30 billion annually in flood damages.

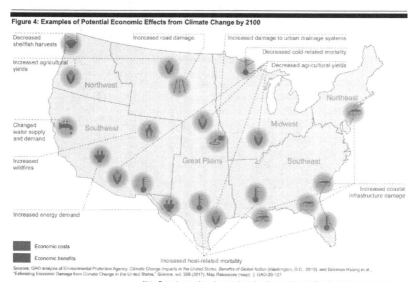

Figure 4: Examples of Potential Economic Effects from Climate Change by 2100

Sources: GAO analysis of Environmental Protection Agency, *Climate Change Impacts in the United States, Benefits of Global Action* (Washington, D.C., 2015), and Solomon Hsiang et al., "Estimating Economic Damage from Climate Change in the United States," *Science*, vol. 356 (2017); Map Resources (map). | GAO-20-127

Note: Examples are shown in approximate locations and do not reflect the relative magnitudes of potential economic effects. In addition, this figure does not depict Alaska, the U.S. Caribbean, Hawaii, and the U.S.-affiliated Pacific Islands, which are where some of the largest observed and projected risks are concentrated, according to USGCRP officials.

A few areas of the United States will benefit from global warming, but most will experience its adverse effects. *GAO*

Funding

Where would the money come from for these net-zero initiatives? The Federal Disaster Relief Fund is the usual source; state and local cost-sharing would be another.[10] Private mortgages for new construction would contribute. Congress should ensure that local banks that help finance relocations, including the energy efficiency and renewable energy systems they use, get credit under the Community Reinvestment Act.[11]

State policies like the tax incremental financing (TIF) that Soldiers Grove used would help. TIF allows local governments to retain the revenues they would ordinarily send to schools and other places when the money is used for redevelopment, infrastructure, and community improvement. Municipal bonds could contribute, as well as increased tax revenues when new construction replaces floodplain buildings. Soldiers Grove found federal funds when it divided its relocation into parts that fit into government "stovepipes"—economic development, sewer infrastructure, and roads, for example.

Congress and the Biden administration could contribute in several ways. Congress should ensure that Exxon and other fossil energy companies are not exempt from liability lawsuits by cities that have incurred costs and losses related to climate change. The Justice Department and state attorneys general should apply the model used to sue tobacco companies, which resulted in billions of dollars for states.

Congress should eliminate the tens of billions of dollars that fossil energy companies receive in federal tax breaks every year and redirect the recovered revenues to floodplain buyouts and relocations. If Congress taxes carbon, some of the revenues could go to states and localities for adaptation and mitigation.

Finally, Congress should create a program in FEMA that integrates the government's many related funds into a single pool of money for communities to not only buy floodplain properties, but also to relocate homeowners locally by providing sewer, water, streets, low-income housing, and other public amenities. Eligibility could be contingent on communities using sustainable development, resilience, and net-zero carbon principles. In other words, federal policy should not stop with retreat. As President Biden would say, it should help communities and families "build back better."

12

EARLY ADOPTERS

Never give up on a dream because of the time it will take
to accomplish it.

—Attributed to Earl Nightingale

NOW THAT THE ERA OF ROUTINE DAM BUILDING appears to have ended
and climate-related weather extremes are upon us, reducing the number
of families in floodplains is gaining more currency. But some communities have conducted voluntary buyouts and relocations for decades. They
recognized that moving out of floodplains was their best chance for secure
futures. Here are a few examples:

Harris County, Texas

Harris County is home to 4.5 million people and the city of Houston,
the self-declared flood capital of the United States. The Texas legislature
created the Harris County Flood Control District (HCFCD) in 1937 after
devastating floods in 1929 and 1935. It covers an area of flat terrain, clay
soils, twenty-two primary watersheds draining into twenty-two major
waterways, and several hundred thousand homes and businesses in the
identified floodplain.

The HCFCD has responded with a large buyout program combined with stormwater detention basins, bypass channels, wider waterways, and bridge replacements where water flows were previously
obstructed.

Buyouts began in 1985. Since then, the program has purchased more than 2,075 structures with FEMA funds, 960 properties with funds from its Flood Control District, and 30 more with USACE funds. Hundreds more are in the pipeline. By January 2020, the HCFCD had acquired more than 3,100 properties with county and local funds along with grants from the HUD as well as FEMA and the USACE. Between 1985 and 2017, the program returned more than 1,060 acres of land to the floodplain. The cost was $342 million.

In January 2020, the journal *Nature Sustainability* published a study that confirmed the wisdom of the HCFCD's buyouts. It found that purchasing floodplain properties and forbidding real estate development on at-risk land would cost the HCFCD $400 million, but the program would prevent $3 billion in damages by mid-century. The study's authors concluded that the same approach would be cost-effective in most of the nation's mapped 100-year river floodplains.[1]

Unfortunately, the HCFCD's program also became an example of the long delays involved in FEMA's buyouts. When Hurricane Harvey hit in the fall of 2017, more than 1,000 people volunteered for buyouts. It took the district more than a year to secure federal funds. The stress from these long waits caused some homeowners to drop out of the program and sell their homes to developers or investors, who flipped the buildings and kept them in the floodplain.

"It is clear that a different buyout model is needed if places like Harris County are going to efficiently and equitably help move the growing number of flood-prone residents to higher ground," says Anna Weber of the Natural Resources Defense Council, who authored a report on the program.

Blue Acres

In 2007, the New Jersey Department of Environmental Protection created an ongoing flood mitigation program called Blue Acres. Like Harris County, New Jersey used funds from FEMA's Hazard Mitigation Program as well as HUD's Community Development Block Grants, supplemented by state and local money.

After Hurricane Sandy, the New Jersey department planned to allocate $300 million in federal disaster recovery funds to buy 1,300 homes vulnerable to repetitive flooding. Within two years of the program's launch, 719 residents volunteered and received approval for buyouts. The state made offers on 690 homes and sellers accepted 519. More than 240 homes were demolished.

Charlotte-Mecklenburg Storm Water Services

Buyouts in Mecklenburg County, North Carolina, have been underway since 1999. The county's population of 1.1 million includes more than 900,000 residents in its largest city, Charlotte. The floodplain covers nearly 20,000 acres of land in the county. About 2,900 habitable and accessory buildings are vulnerable to floods.

Surface waters make up about 4 percent of the county's area. They include the Catawba River and a series of human-made reservoirs managed by Duke Energy to generate hydroelectric power. Between the river's origin in the Appalachian Mountains and its termination 220 miles away in South Carolina, the Catawba feeds and passes through eleven dams and reservoirs, six of them in North Carolina.

The Cowans Ford dam is one. It created Lake Norman, the largest freshwater body in the state, nearly sixty years ago. In addition to powering generators, the lake provides cooling water for a coal-fired power plant as well as a nuclear power plant. Lake Norman drains into Mountain Island Lake, which provides drinking water for the city and county as well as electric generation for the surrounding area.

Another reservoir, Lake Wylie, spans the border of North and South Carolina and a portion of the western border of Mecklenburg County. It was built in 1904 for electric generation. Its dam was upgraded in 1924 to raise the level of the lake.

Fortunately, Mecklenburg County has never experienced a presidentially declared flood disaster, but it has gone through medium-size events, the most recent in June 2019, when the Catawba River left its banks and caused more than $3 million in damages to homes. Because it is located 165 miles from the Atlantic Ocean, the county also is vulnerable to floods from slow-moving tropical storms and the remnants of hurricanes.

In 1994, the county, the city of Charlotte, and several surrounding communities formed the Charlotte-Mecklenburg Storm Water Services utility to comply with the federal Clean Water Act. But after floods in 1995 and 1997, the utility added stormwater management, flood reduction, and floodplain restoration to its mission. Between 1999 and the spring of 2020, the program spent $789 million to purchase and demolish 438 properties so the land could be returned to the floodplain and put to compatible uses with economic and social value, such as gardens, a forest, wetlands, and recreational facilities. This program is exemplary for several reasons:

- While FEMA typically provides 75 to 100 percent of the money to purchase floodplain buildings, the Charlotte-Mecklenburg program has raised much of its own money by charging residents $1.25 on their monthly water bills. Overall, its money has provided about 60 percent of the purchase costs compared to 40 percent from federal and state governments.
- Homeowners must floodproof their homes if they choose to remain in the floodplain.[2] New and substantially improved or repaired homes must have access to dry land so families can evacuate or get medical help without relying on first responders and boats.
- The utility uses aerial photography to identify and measure impervious surfaces such as rooftops and driveways. It assigns each single-family home to one of four classes based on the amount of impervious surface on its property. The utility bills homes in each class at the same rate; it bills multifamily and commercial buildings based on their actual amount of hard surfaces.
- FEMA maps the county's floodplain based on 100-year and 500-year rain events, as it typically does. However, the Charlotte-Mecklenburg program was one of the first in the nation to supplement FEMA's maps by identifying how its floodplain would be affected by actual and anticipated land uses upstream. Risk-mapping technology allows the utility to update floodplain maps to reflect where land is likely to be flooded, how deep the water is expected to be, and which areas are vulnerable to repetitive flooding.
- The utility prioritizes its buyouts based on a home's likelihood of flooding, the damages that are likely to occur, and whether the long-term benefits exceed the purchase costs.

- The utility keeps a "rainy-day" fund to avoid the delays involved in FEMA buyouts. The fund allows the utility to purchase damaged or distressed buildings before their owners invest in repairs.
- The utility offers technical and financial assistance for selected flood mitigation measures for residents who choose to remain in the flood zone.
- About 85 percent of the homeowners who go through the early stages of the buyout process complete it.

Valmeyer, Illinois

Many relocations have taken place in small rural towns, possibly because smaller projects are easier to manage. Stronger social bonds in small towns help make relocations more successful. Valmeyer, Illinois, is an example located 30 miles south of St. Louis. The original village was located in the "American bottom" along the Mississippi River, an area whose trees were cut down to fuel steamboats in the nineteenth century. Floods occurred in 1910, 1943, and 1944, leading to levy construction by the USACE.

The levees protected Valmeyer for fifty years, but the Great Mississippi River Flood of 1993 breached them and put the village under as much as 18 feet of water for more than a month. Over the following two years, the community rebuilt on top of a bluff 400 feet above and about 1.5 miles east of the old town.

One of the assets that made Valmeyer's move successful was a tireless champion, then-mayor Dennis Knobloch. Knobloch recalls that abandoning the floodplain was difficult for people who had just seen 95 percent of their town destroyed. Many moved away at least temporarily, while others lived in FEMA trailers and with relatives while the old town was evacuated and the new one constructed. Knobloch credits the villagers with "commitment, dedication, perseverance, and blind faith" that the relocation would succeed. Like many other leaders who facilitate relocation, Knobloch praises the people who took part and is reluctant to acknowledge his role. But the perseverance and faith that are necessary in a relocation are sustained by the spirit, optimism, and personalities of community leaders like him.

It's common for people who relocate to miss some of what they left behind. Relocation projects can minimize this by reflecting the old town in the new. Buildings can re-create familiar architectural styles. People can establish museums in public buildings to exhibit photos and memorabilia that show the original town's history. They can name streets after historic events and prominent citizens.

Still, "When we decided that we were going to move the town, we knew we were not going to re-create Mayberry on the hill," Knobloch told an interviewer. "We knew that physically, it's not going to be the same. All you can do is hope that the heart of the community is there. People need to be proud of what they've done."

With nearly 400 modern homes, a post office, school, senior apartments, and a couple banks, the community looks like a modern, well-planned suburb of St. Louis. One indication of success is that Valmeyer's population grew from about 600 people in the old town to 1,263 a decade later.

Kingston, North Carolina

Hurricanes Fran, Dennis, and Floyd damaged more than 75 percent of the homes in the county, so the city of Kingston, population 20,000, began relocating entire neighborhoods. It bought nearly 1,600 homes in the Neuse River floodplain and left more than 70 percent of the vacated floodplain in forest. Kingston did several other things right. It avoided the long delays in FEMA's buyout process by developing its funding application before and submitting it to FEMA immediately after Hurricane Floyd.

The first 100 homes the city purchased avoided $6 million in property damages from the next big storm, according to Adam Short of the city's planning department.

Kingston prevented sprawl and the loss of property tax revenue by making sure that neighborhoods remained within its tax district. It encouraged evacuees to stick together to sustain the parents' and kids' social networks. Nevertheless, people experienced some feeling of loss about their old neighborhoods, especially the residents of a historically Black neighborhood.

East Grand Forks, Minnesota

In 1997, the Red River crested 26 feet above flood stage in East Grand Forks due to the thaw of the previous winter's heavy snow accumulation. A 54-foot crest overwhelmed levees and destroyed nearly $57 million worth, or 38 percent, of the city's residences. The total damages were $400 million, 100 times the community's annual budget of $4 million.

The city planned buyouts at neighborhood scale rather than home by home. With funding from FEMA and other sources, it bought 507 of its repetitively flooded homes during the three years following the flood. Local officials reported that 97 percent of eligible homeowners decided to take the buyouts. The city paid preflood fair market value and offered forgivable loans and tax abatements that encouraged people to move to properties within the town.

East Grand Forks was the city that struck a deal with FEMA to install permanent rather than temporary utilities and electric service at the site of a Femaville, then offered the land for subdivision development.

Some vacated homes were sold at auction and moved to other parts of the city or nearby lakes to become vacation homes. The city hired a private company to develop a greenway plan in the floodplain with the involvement of citizens and experts on wildlife, wetlands, and recreation.

At the time, FEMA's coordinating officer Ron Sherman called the city's recovery one of the largest post-disaster relocations in the United States. "This event showed an amazing level of involvement from local residents, not just elected officials, in the recovery planning process. . . . That deployment is one of the most memorable of my long career. Events like this are 'life markers' and they don't go away."[3]

In the end, East Grand Forks' disaster prevention program included ring dikes and a water diversion system constructed by the USACE to make sure that all properties had flood protection. That made the city an example of integrating structural and nonstructural measures.

Any community considering a floodplain relocation should send a delegation (including a skeptic or two) to one or more of these towns. As we found when the mayor of Soldiers Grove saw a home rolling down the street in Niobrara, Nebraska, seeing is believing.

Happy in the Floodplain

No matter how much sense it makes to leave a floodplain, some individuals and communities are not interested. They are happy where they are. Chelsea, Iowa, is an example. It was another casualty of the Great Mississippi River Flood of 1993. About 85 percent of the homes in the community experienced repeated flooding. The 1993 flood was so bad that meals had to be delivered by boat for more than a month. In 1994, the city council voted to relocate as many floodplain homes as possible, but only 40 of the city's 250 residents participated. As their congressman explained, "People have been living in this low-lying area for over 150 years and they are a hearty people."

When Chelsea flooded next in 2008, Susan Saulny of the *New York Times* reported: "Now here is Chelsea again, under about six feet of water at the lowest point, second-guessing everything but also staunchly defending its right to exist exactly where it wants to." People pointed out that nobody had died in a flood since 1944. Because the terrain is hilly, some homes weren't damaged. Many residents felt they couldn't bear to trade the rich history of their community for a "generic" dry place. There also was evidence that Chelseans were very independent and didn't feel they needed help. When the Red Cross opened a shelter after the 2008 flood, no one showed up.

When Chelsea flooded again in 2013, *USA Today* reported that the victims took it in stride.[4] "Floodwater doesn't keep us down," said one. "We just keep on working."

"It's survival, and why not be happy every day," another said. "We've been here a long time, and we plan to be here a lot longer. . . . This is home." That is a common sentiment among people who live along rivers and coasts. They may not have reached the point of "I can't take it anymore." These are the cases in which the USACE required communities to use eminent domain, but a better approach would be to provide stronger positive incentives for people to move.

13

THE NEXT MASS MIGRATION

Impacts from storms can disperse refugees from coastal areas to all 50 states, with economic and social costs felt across the country. Sea level rise might reshape the US population distribution.

—Fourth National Climate Assessment

IN THE COLD-WATER TRIBUTARIES OF THE PACIFIC OCEAN, river temperatures rose above 65 degrees Fahrenheit in 2015, beyond the tolerance of the sockeye salmon and steelhead trout in the Northwest's Columbia, Snake, and Salmon Rivers. A headline in *USA Today* said bluntly that the fish had been cooked alive. The kill-off left the 3,500 enrolled members of the Nez Perce tribe without much of their food supply for the year. It was not a one-time event. Water temperatures will get even higher as climate change alters the ecology of cold-water fisheries.

Researchers at the University of Exeter in the United Kingdom tell a similar story about the Athabaskan people of Alaska and northwestern Canada.[1] They share a subsistence culture in which natural resources provide their needs, from food and shelter to religious rituals. Vital salmon stocks are threatened there, too.

Pacific salmon require the higher oxygen levels found in cold water. The gravel beds in which they lay and fertilize their eggs must have water flows sufficient to supply oxygen to the young when they are born. But now, melting permafrost erodes riverbanks and creates silt that smothers eggs. Floods and faster river flows disturb the gravel beds that hold the eggs. Warmer waters bring parasites and invasive species. When salmon are lost, so are the birds and animals that depend on them for food.

Farther north in Alaska, thirty-five villages face imminent threats from flooding, coastal erosion, and melting permafrost. Warmer waters are literally poisoning members of the Alaskan Alutiiq tribe. Like nearly all of Alaska's rural people, they depend on foraging and hunting for subsistence. Shellfish are a critical food source, but rising water temperatures are ideal habitat for a type of algae that produces a toxin responsible for paralytic shellfish poisoning.

Clams are one of the ocean's most efficient water filters, but when they filter water containing the toxin, the poison can become a thousand times more deadly than sarin gas. Eating just one infected oyster can be fatal. The Nez Perce are responding by hiring a "climate change coordinator" to identify all the ways that climate change is likely to affect their lives.

Down south on the Isle de Jean Charles, a small island off the coast of Louisiana, the Biloxi-Chitimacha-Choctaw and the United Houma Nation tribes have watched all but a sliver of their land disappear because of rising seas, erosion, and saltwater intrusion blamed on canals dredged by oil and gas companies. Levees contributed by cutting the island off from the Mississippi River and the sediment that once replenished the land.

The tribes settled the island to escape the forced marches of Native Americans to the West, but the original 15,000 acres are now a strip of land a quarter-mile wide and a half-mile long. Congress has appropriated some money to help the residents relocate.

On the East Coast, the Tuscarora Nation, one of six nations more commonly known as the Iroquois, is preparing for the biocultural impacts of climate change, including the tribe's ability to adapt its traditional foods to warmer temperatures. The tribe has a seed-banking program to preserve heirloom varieties of beans and squash. Tribal members are teaching food preservation with canning workshops and using GIS technology to map the natural resources—soils, timber, water, and so forth—needed to sustain the tribe's self-sufficiency. To make sure they can grow enough food, the Tuscarora restored 80 acres of grassland on their 6,250-acre reservation, using warm-season grasses to capture carbon and adding organic matter to the soil.

We're told that if we want to experience what our cities will feel like in 2080, we should drive about 600 miles south. Cities in the Northeast will feel like today's cities in the Southeast and Midwest. New York will feel more like Arkansas; San Francisco will feel like Los Angeles. To better understand the plants and animals they will see in the future, Tuscarora tribal members hiked along the 80-mile path their ancestors took 300 years ago when they migrated from the Carolinas to New York.[2]

At least fifty Native American tribes in the United States are studying their risks and developing adaptation strategies. For some, the most apparent changes are shoreline erosion; for others, it's wildfires; and for others, it's the effect global warming is having on important species and habitat.[3]

Of all the cultures and subcultures in the United States, Native Americans are likely to be the most affected by climate change. They are the people who depend most on natural resources for their livelihoods, traditions, and religious practices. "Climate change is affecting the quantity and quality of resources—such as water, minerals, and various plants, animals, and fungi—that tribes depend upon to perpetuate their culture and livelihoods," according to researchers who studied the interface between climate change and tribal cultures.[4] The loss of these resources threatens the cultures, economies, and even the sovereignty of tribes.

Human Impacts

What might the human-on-human impacts be? Scientists and other researchers warn that climate change could displace 1.2 billion people worldwide by mid-century.[5] It has already begun. The International Organization for Migration (IOM) reports that "millions of men, women, and children around the world move in anticipation or as a response to environmental stress every year. . . . Disruptions ranging from extreme weather events to large-scale changes in ecosystems are occurring at a pace and intensity unlike any other known period on Earth. Anthropogenic climate change is expected to increasingly affect [human] migration and other forms of people moving to manage these changing risks."[6]

We have to be ready for much larger relocations than those in flood-prone communities. We are not nearly prepared to manage them. The adverse impacts of climate change will force millions of Americans to evacuate entire areas along the Atlantic, Gulf, and Pacific coasts because of sea-level rise, coastal erosion, and extreme precipitation associated with tropical storms and hurricanes. People living in 500- and 1,000-year floodplains may have to evacuate, too. Other extreme changes in weather and resources, including fires, droughts, water scarcity, and intolerable heat, will also cause population shifts. Populations will move in human trickles and waves, forcing the cities that lose them and the cities that receive them—so-called climate havens—to adapt. The planning for these mass human migrations should start now.

Creating Climate Havens

Some cities have already become climate havens at small scale. When people evacuate their hometowns during and after major disasters, they often settle in other cities and remain there. More than a million Gulf Coast residents left during and after Hurricane Katrina, ending up in Baton Rouge, Dallas, Atlanta, and San Antonio, for example. Some 250,000 people went to Houston; a decade later, as many as 100,000 were still living there. "Tens of thousands swapped one of the nation's most distinctive and historic cities [New Orleans] for the car-centric urban sprawl and homogenous modern suburbs of a metro areas of six million that is today about five times larger than greater New Orleans," the *Guardian* reported.[7] After Puerto Rico was devastated by Hurricane Maria in 2017, thousands fled to New York City, Philadelphia, and Florida. Many remain there.

Buffalo, New York, has been a popular choice for hurricane refugees. The city has thousands of vacant or little-used lots.[8] *Quartz* news reports that Mayor Byron Brown has designated Buffalo as a "Climate Refuge City" and he promotes the use of solar panels on public buildings.

Victims of repeated fires in California and other hurricanes on the Gulf Coast have said on national news that they've had enough; they are leaving, too. Demographers have identified several major cities that they think will become climate havens. However, they anticipate that most climate migrants in the United States will go to the nearby counties and cities where there are plentiful job opportunities and higher salaries.

Climate havens will have to invest in new housing and infrastructure to accommodate large numbers of migrants, but many American cities are now economically strapped because of the COVID-19 pandemic. The Urban Institute anticipates that the pandemic could cost states $200 billion by mid-2021.[9] Several cities that were preparing to become "climate havens" before the pandemic are now facing financial concerns. For example, Duluth, Minnesota, expected a budget shortfall of about $12 million despite austerity measures. Buffalo reportedly lost $32.5 million in state aid and more than $18 million in revenue in its 2020 fiscal year.[10]

One idea in circulation would have Congress create a national carbon tax and use the revenues to help communities relocate at-risk families and help "climate haven" cities build affordable housing and infill development for climate migrants.

Another challenge is that experts predict gentrification as property safe from floods grows in value while property values in floodplains decline. Low-income populations could find that relocation is unaffordable without government intervention. Researchers at Harvard University have labeled this widening gap between the value of floodplain property versus safe property the "elevation hypothesis" and the "nuisance hypothesis."[11]

How Massive Will Massive Be?

Experts anticipate that 13 million coastal residents in the United States will be displaced by sea-level rise.[12] More than 160 million Americans, nearly half of us, are expected to move because of excessive heat and the lack of fresh water. At least 4 million could find that they live "in places decidedly outside the ideal niche for human life." One study predicts that 12 million Americans in the South will move toward the Northwest, the Mountain West, and California over the next forty-five years to escape adverse climate impacts.[13] Others call what's coming the Third Great Migration, comparable in size to mass migrations during the Dust Bowl in the 1930s or the movement of African Americans from the South to the industrial North during the last century.

"The potential need for millions of people and billions of dollars of coastal infrastructure to be relocated in the future creates challenging legal, financial, and equity issues that have not yet been addressed," federal scientists warned in their Fourth National Climate Assessment in 2018.[14]

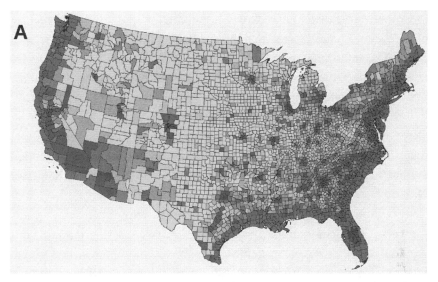

Researchers from the Georgia Institute of Technology, University of Southern California, Los Angeles, and the University of Waterloo in Canada developed this map showing where climate migrants are most likely to relocate if sea levels rise 6 feet by 2100. The darkest areas on the coasts indicate flooding. Inland, the darker the location, the more climate migrants it would receive. *Creative Commons*

The National Climate Assessment specifically mentioned future outmigration from Massachusetts, New Jersey, and New York. Other analysts point to Florida. One analysis predicts that 60 percent of Miami could experience chronic flooding by 2060, and more than 90 percent of the city could be under water at least twenty-six times a year by 2100.

Much will depend on the degree of global warming. Computer models show that if global temperatures increase more than 4 degrees Celsius above preindustrial levels, sea levels will rise 6 feet. Mathew E. Hauer, a geographer at the University of Georgia at Athens, calculates that a 6-foot rise would displace the 13 million coastal residents by the end of this century. If we continue business as usual, 4°C of additional warming is not unlikely. A paper published in the *Proceedings of National Academies of Sciences* in June 2019 projects that the Earth's average temperature will rise 5°C if the growth in greenhouse gas emissions goes unchecked.[15]

America's climate migrants will seek out cities less affected by adverse climate changes and those with adequate land, housing, infrastructure, and jobs. "The infrastructure challenges of accommodating millions of sea-level rise migrants in largely unprepared inland municipalities is virtually unexplored," Hauer emphasizes. "There's not a state unaffected by this."[16]

Population shifts will disrupt local revenues, businesses, and even states' representation in Congress. Social, economic, and environmental justice issues will loom large as poor and low-income families are left behind because they don't have the resources to relocate, or if urban climate havens do not have adequate affordable housing.

On the other hand, there could be opportunities if the nation plans for them. The populations of cities like Detroit, Cleveland, and Flint are among the dozens of American cities whose numbers have declined more than 3 percent in recent years.[17] Rural areas may offer opportunities for climate migrants; rural populations are already growing slightly in more densely settled areas near cities or natural beauty.[18] Government programs could target those places for economic development, infrastructure improvement, and affordable housing and offer incentives for clean energy industries to locate there.[19] Wind and solar jobs have increased about 60 percent in recent years, for example, and the United States' inevitable shift from carbon fuels to clean energy will continue. Economic research shows that every $1 million shifted from electricity generated by fossil fuels to clean energy produces a net increase of five jobs.[20]

At-Risk Industries

We should prepare for coastal businesses and industries to "migrate." Global warming will adversely affect commercial fishing, marine farming, tourism, recreation, shipping, and power plants. Some industries will follow the migration of the natural resource on which they depend, leaving the regions that depended on them for jobs and resettling in others. Sap harvests vital to the maple sugar industry in New England and the iconic populations of Maine lobsters are already affected. California's winemaking is vulnerable. And what might New Orleans be like without crawfish, oysters, and shrimp if Louisiana's wetlands succumb to subsidence and saltwater intrusion? The economic disruption could be substantial.

In 2016, the coastal economy included 154,000 businesses that employed 3.3 million people with collective earnings of nearly $130 billion. Oceans added more than $300 billion to the national economy that year.

The shift in industries, jobs, and populations, along with the growth in demand for "havens," may occur much sooner than we think because climate change is advancing more rapidly than scientists expected. There will be cultural as well as economic disruptions. "Governments have not yet addressed the cultural losses we are all facing as a result of global climate change, and this could have catastrophic consequences," warns William Neil Adger, a professor of human geography at the University of Exeter. "It is vital that the cultural impact of climate change is considered, alongside plans to adapt our physical spaces to the changing environment."[21]

Climate Refugees

The people who study international and global population shifts distinguish between "climate migrants" and "climate refugees." For our purposes here, I define climate refugees as people whose lives and livelihoods are threatened by climate change and who seek refuge in countries other than their own. The residents of island nations inundated by rising seas are in this category. So are people fleeing violence due to state failures, resource conflicts, and other geopolitical global warming impacts.

International officials estimate there may be as many as 1 billion environmental migrants worldwide by 2050. Disasters displaced nearly 3 million people in 2017 alone. As of 2018, however, there were no international conventions to deal with climate migrants and refugees.[22]

The Pentagon has long predicted that global warming will be a "threat multiplier" that leads to state failures and violence, possibly resulting in US military involvement. A frequently cited example is the major drought that was a factor in the Syrian civil war, which forced millions of Syrians to flee that country. The US military attributes the reignition of civil war in Iraq to that refugee crisis, resulting in the involvement of American forces. Yet the Army War College, among others, warns that "the Department of Defense is precariously underprepared for the national security implications of climate change-induced global security challenges."[23]

Millions of climate refugees are likely to seek sanctuary in the United States due to adverse and even deadly climate-related impacts. It has already begun. Drought has been underway in El Salvador, Guatemala, and Honduras since 2014, leaving farmers unable to grow food. People from those countries have been among the large groups of refugees at the United States' southern border.

Experts at the World Bank predict that about 2 million people will be displaced from Central America alone by 2050 by climate change. A study published in the *Proceedings of the National Academy of Sciences* in 2010 estimated that poor crop yields may force as many as 7 million Mexicans to emigrate to the United States during the next seventy years.[24] Other scholars estimate that the number of climate refugees from these places could be twice as high if their farmers don't adapt to global warming.[25] The US government's international programs, the Peace Corps, and private organizations all would be wise to help them begin adapting now.

Yet, the United States has no coherent plan to cope with the multiple stresses of climate change, and it has no consistent immigration policy.

A scene in Nicaragua. Central America is suffering a food crisis because of drought, water shortages, and crop disease. Experts say these kinds of conditions may force climate migrants from the region to go north. Some have been among the recent migrants seeking refuge in the United States.
Center for Climate and Security

The State Department has not been preparing for climate refugees. The GAO criticized the Trump administration for removing any mention of climate change from foreign policy.[26] The US government was inactive internationally and domestically on climate issues from 2017 to early 2020 and Congress has not acted since 1992.

Whether the challenge is domestic climate migrants or foreign climate refugees, a human tide is coming, and the first signs are here. If the American people do not force the federal government to do something about it, more frequent and deadly weather events will. Although many states and cities have tried to take up the federal government's slack, climate change requires cooperative action by all government levels including a proactive, well-resourced, timely, and well-coordinated federal response.

The Mass Migration of Species

The impact of climate change on millions of other species will be profound, too. Experts say that half of all species in the world are on the move, and it is happening more rapidly than scientists thought. "We're talking about a redistribution of the entire planet's species," according to Gretta Pecl, a specialist in climate change ecology.[27] Shifting plant and animal populations create new ecosystems, ecological communities, and even new species as they find themselves among unfamiliar mates. Some species will adapt to warmer temperatures. Others will not be able to. They'll move north or move higher until they run out of space and disappear.

The McKinsey Global Institute says about 25 percent of the world has already experienced a shift of flora and fauna compared to the early twentieth century. The institute projects that by 2050, 45 percent of the Earth's land area will experience a biome shift. Land-based plants and animals are said to be moving an average of 10 miles per decade. Ocean species are migrating four times faster. Plants bloom earlier in the spring; changes in trees and shrubs are altering the ecologies of entire forests.

Millions of acres of trees in North America have been lost to insects no larger than grains of rice. Although the trees have natural defenses against bark beetles, drought weakens them, and warmer winters give the insects two chances to hatch larvae each year. There is uncertainty about

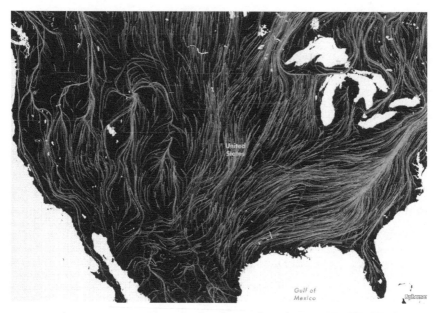

Dan Majka, a geospatial web developer for The Nature Conservancy, created "Migrations in Motion: Visualizing Species Movement Due to Climate Change," a series of animated maps that shows how mammals, amphibians, and other animals will migrate to new habitats because of climate change. This snapshot is static and converted to black and white but Majka's maps, color-coded and in motion, are available at maps.tnc.org/migrations-in -motion. *Dan Majka/The Nature Conservancy*

whether bark beetles perform a service for forests by attacking weaker and older trees, but there is no question that they exact a high price in regard to global warming. As they rot or burn, trees release the carbon they stored. They no longer help control runoff to modulate stream flows or filter the sediment that reduces the capacity of river channels.

In thousands of different ways, "human-caused climate change is altering life for plants and animals and in the process having direct and sometimes profound impacts on humans," *National Geographic* explains. How people make a living, what they eat, diseases that affect them, the traditions that define them, and entire cultures are changing.[28] In other words, climate change is resulting in large and sometimes reciprocal impacts: species on other species, humans on other humans, and humans and species on each other.

14

REVISITING
SOLDIERS GROVE

LET'S RETURN TO WHERE WE BEGAN. What has happened to Soldiers Grove?

It took nearly thirty years for the Kickapoo River to prove the wisdom of relocation. Sadly, many of the men and women who helped make the move possible did not live long enough to see the next big flood. Cecil Turk, the amiable village president and grocer, died in 2001 at the age of eighty-six. Ron Swiggum, who also served as village president and went up and down Main Street collecting contributions to repay me for printing the relocation proposal, moved from Soldiers Grove to a Madison suburb before dying at home at age fifty-six. Jerry and Eileen Schoville, who were dedicated to the Soldiers Grove community, both passed away years after selling me the *Kickapoo Scout*.

"Bullet Bob" Peterson published a haunting book about his experiences as an infantryman in Vietnam. He married a wonderful woman, Joni Peterson, from Soldiers Grove after he came home paralyzed from a bullet in his spine. Joni wrote the opening of his book and revealed that Bob never recovered psychologically or physically from the war. He died in her arms of a heart attack in 1994. A few weeks before, he told her something he told no one else: he had been paralyzed by friendly fire.

The first severe test of relocation didn't come until 2007: an unprecedented 500-year flood that devastated all the other river towns. It was followed a year later by another 500-year flood. Gays Mills, whose apple orchards made it the most prosperous of the villages, was virtually wiped

The Kickapoo River spills over Soldiers Grove's old levee during the 2008 flood. *Courtesy of Kate Walter*

out. Back in the 1970s, Gays Mills decided not to follow Soldiers Grove's example, and it was still trying to recover from the 2007 flood when the 2008 event happened. Residents gathered in a town meeting and finally supported relocation. "Almost everyone in the downtown area is affected in one way or another," a member of the city council said. "It's time we look toward relocating the village to higher and drier ground."

Reporter Chris Hubbuch of the *La Crosse Tribune* visited Soldiers Grove to see if it had escaped damage after the 2008 disaster. He inspected the floodplain park where the old downtown had been:

> The water tore playground equipment and benches from the ground, chewed up blacktop, ate swaths of land and dumped tons of rock and mud onto the land that was once downtown Soldiers Grove. . . . Last August, when the river flooded, the park was cleaned up in three weeks, but Soldiers Grove's [old temporary] levee held during that flood. This time it didn't. When the surging Kickapoo River breached the dike, the churning water ripped through the park. Benches and playground equipment once anchored in concrete footings lay in piles where the currents left them. A parking lot resembled a hastily cut chocolate cake.

Floodwaters gouged ravines in what once was a good spot for a picnic and cut a six-foot trench through Highway 131.[1]

The relocated business district and homes were untouched. The village had the park back in shape within three months, in time to host a previously scheduled art fair.

The flood was instructive. Thirty homes in the original village chose to floodproof in place rather than relocate. They all were damaged when the 2008 flood overwhelmed the old levee. One of them belonged to the granddaughter of the original owner. The flood put 29 inches of water onto her first floor. "I think it's time to move out of here," she said. It was evidence that elevating buildings would not be enough to protect them from the big floods on the horizon.

Today, most buyouts and retreats in the United States have been voluntary. Several communities have completed successful relocations larger than Soldiers Grove's, but they are still pioneering the process. Many more communities in the United States will follow in the years ahead, whether they want to or not, but the federal government is not prepared for it. Neither FEMA, the USACE, nor Congress has yet developed a national plan for relocating flood-prone properties. President Biden's massive infrastructure plan does not address how infrastructure investments should factor in the potential for significant climate migrations.

A. R. Siders, an assistant professor at the University of Delaware's Disaster Research Center, estimates that 49 million housing units are at risk of flood damage, and more than $1 trillion worth of infrastructure is within 700 feet of the coast. The government isn't prepared to relocate even one-tenth of that development, she says.[2] "If we're going to build a road, is this for today's population or is this for tomorrow's population?" one expert asks.[3]

Biden's plan also does not address what the government's flood avoidance strategy should be now that so many dams and levees are past retirement age.

Meanwhile, back in the Kickapoo Valley, what became of the La Farge dam and lake? After Congress finally deauthorized the project, bitterness and relief settled into an uneasy coexistence in the Kickapoo Valley. Trees and wildlife have reclaimed the land the USACE acquired.

In 1996, Congress ordered the corps to transfer 1,200 acres to the Ho-Chunk Nation, whose ancestors lived in the valley. The rest of the land was transferred to the state of Wisconsin. The nearly 9,000 total acres are now known as the Kickapoo Valley Reserve, managed to "promote, preserve and enhance its unique natural scenic and cultural features."

Today, the Kickapoo Valley has two monuments that symbolize the nation's still unfinished shift from flood control to flood avoidance. At the site of the proposed La Farge dam, a concrete tower rises five stories against deep green foliage. It was built to control the outflow of water from the lake, and it is the only evidence of what almost happened there.

The second monument is in Soldiers Grove, a plaque that commemorates the completion of relocation. It reads:

> Respectfully dedicated to all the minds who had the courage to dream,
> to all the hands who helped make the dream a reality, and
> to all the souls, some yet to come, who will nourish this idea:
> That people working together can make a better life.

The control tower is all that remains of the plan to dam the Kickapoo River.
Courtesy of Wisconsin 101

PART II

THE BIOCENE

15

INTRODUCING THE BIOCENE

Reconnecting the human species with the rest of the world is the great work of the twenty-first century.

—Thomas Berry

LEMMINGS, THE ADORABLE NORTHERN COUSINS OF MICE, hamsters, and gerbils, have been the topic of false facts for hundreds of years. The Norwegian lemming in particular is an interesting species. It reproduces rapidly, goes through population explosions every few years, and migrates in hordes of thousands to find new food supplies.

When the lemming population explodes, there might be as many as 3,000 in an area the size of seventeen football fields. Their large numbers inspired the myth that they periodically fall from the sky. They are grumpy. If you were to walk on the Arctic tundra, they would pop up, jump around, and shriek. This led to the myth that lemmings explode when they get angry.

But the most persistent myth has been what lemmings do to control their populations. They are said to stampede by the thousands and commit suicide by jumping off cliffs into the sea. In the 1958 nature film *White Wilderness,* Disney showed film of this behavior: lemmings leaping off a cliff-edge, falling hundreds of feet through the air, and splashing into the ocean.

"A kind of compulsion seizes each tiny rodent and, carried along by an unreasoning hysteria, each falls into step for a march that will take them to a strange destiny," the narrator explains. "That destiny is to jump into the ocean. They've become victims of an obsession—a one-track thought: 'Move on! Move on!' This is the last chance to turn back, yet over they go, casting themselves out bodily into space."

There were a few things wrong with this scene, however. It was filmed in a landlocked province of Canada rather than on the Arctic coast. The rodents in Disney's film were a different breed than the Norwegian lemmings known for mass suicides. They jumped into a river in the film, rather than into the ocean. And they didn't actually jump. One account is that the Disney crew, hidden by the camera angle, pushed them over the edge of a cliff; another is that they were dumped out of a truck.

A few lemmings do fall over cliffs during their mass migrations, but their deaths are accidental. So why has the myth of their compulsive rush to death been so enduring? The editors of Encyclopedia Britannica theorize that the myth "provides an irresistible metaphor for human behavior."

"Someone who blindly follows a crowd—maybe even toward catastrophe—is called a lemming," the editors explain. "Over the past century, the myth has been invoked to express modern anxieties about how individuality could be submerged and destroyed by mass phenomena, such as political movements or consumer culture."[1]

In other words, it's a myth for our times, when individual thought is subverted by conspiracy theories and falsehoods from national leaders, and when climate change is our compulsive rush toward catastrophe.

I'll leave our vulnerability to falsehoods for others to explain. Instead, I'll offer a theory about what's behind our rush to the edge of the planet's limits and our plunge into climate catastrophe. Unsurprisingly, it has to do with our dysfunctional relationship with nature.

In the 1960s and 1970s, several catastrophes in the United States triggered a heightened awareness of the natural environment. In response, Congress passed, and President Richard Nixon signed, a series of landmark laws to protect the country's natural resources. This period was the golden age of environmentalism in America.

One new law in particular created an aspirational foundation for the others. The National Environmental Policy Act (NEPA) of 1969 required federal agencies to analyze possible environmental impacts and consider alternatives to avoid them before building dams, highways, pipelines, and other projects.[2] NEPA created the Environmental Protection Agency (EPA) and the Council on Environmental Quality (CEQ), an office in the White House that is supposed to oversee the government's compliance with the law.

A new bureaucracy dedicated to the environment was not the most interesting part of the new law. More interesting was what Congress intended the new bureaucracy to do. It was to help the nation achieve a new vision for the relationship between society and the natural world. It instructed the federal government to use "all practicable means and measures" to "maintain the conditions under which man and nature can exist in productive harmony." Congress explained that productive harmony was necessary to accomplish the following:

- Fulfill the responsibilities of each generation as trustee of the environment for succeeding generations;
- Assure for all Americans safe, healthful, productive, and aesthetically and culturally pleasing surroundings;
- Attain the widest range of beneficial uses of the environment without degradation, a risk to health or safety, or other undesirable and unintended consequences;
- Preserve important historical, cultural, and natural aspects of our national heritage, and maintain, wherever possible, an environment which supports diversity and variety of individual choice; and
- Achieve a balance between population and resource use to allow high living standards and a wide sharing of life's amenities.

Regrettably, we are farther away from that vision today than when Congress wrote it. Atonalities rather than productive harmonies characterize our relationship with nature. In attempting to explain why I'll offer information that isn't new to those involved in environmental science and public policy. But I will present it in a different context than usual and hope it will be helpful to the generations who were not yet born when the golden age took place.

As far as we know, we humans are the only animals capable of "mental time travel"—the ability to go back in time to learn from experience and forward to use what we learned to shape the future. We might call it the opposable thumb of our intellect. We waste that unique ability when we know that what we're doing is self-destructive but we keep doing it anyway. The danger is the ignominious end to the great human experiment with a nuclear bang or a climate whimper. Between those extremes are the degradations of life's quality, threats to our security, assaults on our health, environmental injustices, species extinctions, and a lot else.

We've been amply warned. We have the intellectual tools and the advanced technologies to change course in the United States and internationally. We've expressed the desire to change in documents like the Paris climate agreement and our environmental laws. But we lack the will. I will suggest that there are forces in society that want to keep our political will suppressed.

The atonalities are all around us. The United States has had the world's largest economy since 1871; we account for a quarter of the global economy today. Yet we ranked only thirty-fifth among nations in 2019 on ending poverty, recognizing gender equality, transitioning to clean energy, saving the oceans, and building sustainable cities.[3] We placed only nineteenth among nations in the 2019 *World Happiness Report*, where a prestigious groups of corporations, academic institutions, and philanthropies rank countries annually on factors such as environmental quality, social environments, and life satisfaction in cities and rural areas.[4]

The 2020 *Environmental Performance Index* ranked the United States twenty-fourth among 180 nations on various environmental factors, from air quality and water resources to climate change.[5] Of the countries that are consistently at the top of the list—the Netherlands, Denmark, Sweden, Finland, Norway, and Iceland—only the Netherlands was among the world's twenty wealthiest countries, indicating that wealth and health have been decoupled.[6]

We have the resources to do much better, so why don't we?

16

THE DEVALUE CHAIN

> Build a dam to take water AWAY from 40 million people.
> Build a dam to pretend to BRING water to 40 million
> people. Who are these gods that govern us? Is there no
> limit to their powers?
>
> —Arundhati Roy, *The Cost of Living*

THE PROCESS IN WHICH CORPORATIONS take raw materials and turn them into products, then market, sell, and service them, is called the value chain. For example, fossil fuels' value chains begin when they are extracted from the earth. The chain continues as they are refined, distributed, and combusted to produce energy.

Unfortunately, industries also have the "devalue chains" I mentioned in Chapter 10. In the oil, coal, and natural gas sectors, adverse environmental, economic, and social impacts show up in each link of the chain: extraction, transportation, processing, combustion, and waste handling. Along the devalue chain, coal, oil, and natural gas result in land disturbance and toxic wastewater; methane leaks that add a potent greenhouse gas to the atmosphere; spills that foul lands, oceans, and wildlife; toxic wastewater from refining and processing; air pollution when they are transported from one link of the chain to the next; mercury, methane, carbon dioxide, particulates, nitrogen dioxide, and other pollutants linked with cancer; the risk of economic disruptions from oil supply and price shocks; the expense of maintaining the strategic petroleum reserve and guarding foreign shipping lanes; and the many costly and deadly consequences of climate change. The Centre for Research on Energy and Clean Air estimates that in 2018, the worldwide economic and health costs of burning fossil fuels were about $8 billion per day.[1] The American Lung Association says that more than 140 million Americans still live in counties with unhealthy particle and ozone levels, mostly from power plants and vehicles.[2]

These are unacceptable costs, especially when safer, cleaner, and cheaper alternatives are available. The coal industry in Appalachia is one of the most unfortunate examples in the United States.

Coal Country

The Appalachian region runs parallel to the Atlantic coast through thirteen inland states, from southern New York to northern Mississippi and Alabama. President Lyndon Johnson announced his War on Poverty there in 1964 and President Barack Obama launched a program to make the region a special economic development zone. But the region's persistent poverty rate remains higher than the nation as a whole, and eighty counties are economically distressed.[3] Most of them are in Central Appalachia, particularly Kentucky and West Virginia. The region is one of the most biologically diverse places in the United States, all thick forests and rolling hills, freshwater streams, and wildlife. But most people who don't live there know Appalachia less for its biome than for its coal production and persistent poverty.

The United States has the world's largest coal reserves, and three of the five states where most US coal is produced—Kentucky, West Virginia, and Pennsylvania—are in Appalachia.

Coal was king in this area for generations. The people who live there have been universally stereotyped, going back to a newspaper article in 1900. It called them "hillbillies" and described the typical person as "a free and untrammeled white citizen of Alabama, who lives in the hills, has no means to speak of, dresses as he can, talks as he pleases, drinks whiskey when he gets it, and fires off his revolver as the fancy takes him."

But the Appalachians are far more diverse and sophisticated than this stereotype suggests. The rest of the nation underappreciates the

The Appalachian region. *Appalachian Regional Commission*

President Lyndon Johnson visits with Appalachian coal miner Tom Fletcher in 1964 to announce his "all-out war on human poverty and unemployment."
Courtesy of LBJ Presidential Library

region's cultural heritage and rich history, from its role in the American Revolution and the Civil War to its music and its impressive list of writers and artists.[4] The Appalachian people are justifiably proud of risking their lungs and lives for generations to power America's industrialization. Many of them have known for a long time that the region's economy must diversify and that generations of coal-mining families must develop new skills, but it isn't easy. Coal mining goes back a very long time in many families, and although the industry is in decline, it is not going gently into the good night. There is conflict, some of it physical, between people who still depend on coal jobs and people, many of them young, who want the region to take its place in a twenty-first-century America.

Central Appalachia is a victim of the same curse found in undeveloped countries rich with natural resources. Outside interests rather than the indigenous people own the rights to most of the resources. By 1810, absentee owners controlled more than 90 percent of the area that is West Virginia today. In the 1800s, many landowners did not understand the value of the mineral deposits underneath their feet. Outside investors offered them ridiculously small amounts of money to buy rights to coal and natural gas as well as timber. In 1981, a task force that looked at land ownership reported that corporations or outside individuals owned 40 percent of the property and 70 percent of the mineral rights in the eighty counties it sampled across six states.[5]

In the 1960s, coal companies changed their operations from underground mines to mountaintop removal. Bulldozers removed trees and topsoil to expose coal seams so that demolitions experts could blow 600 feet or more off the hill tops. A federal law, the Surface Mining Control and Reclamation Act, required coal companies to return the land to its original contours after mining, unless it could be put to a "higher and better use." Mining companies obtained waivers by claiming that factories or stores could be built on the flattened hills. The result has been a permanent degradation of the land and its forests, all done with less labor than traditional underground mining required.

In 2002, the George W. Bush administration classified mining rubble as "fill material" under the Clean Water Act, allowing companies to

Mountaintop removal in Central Appalachia. *Courtesy of Jack Spadaro*

do the opposite of the law's intent. They dumped the overburden, as they call it, into valleys below mine sites, burying thousands of miles of headwater streams or polluting them with toxins such as arsenic, lead, and manganese leached from the rubble. The enormous amounts of dust created by the blasts contain the same poisons. It covers the surfaces of nearby communities as well as the lungs of those who breathe it.

In December 2016, after years of reviews and public comments, the federal agency in charge of mine reclamation issued a Stream Protection Rule intended to end the dumping of mine wastes into streams. Three months later, recently inaugurated President Donald Trump signed a bill to repeal it—another act the Biden administration should reverse.

In short, Central Appalachia has been, and remains, a "deeply cynical capitalist experiment" in which the people who own and profit from the minerals do not live in the region and do not suffer the consequences of destructive mining practices. And like the fossil fuels industry in general, companies make their profits by passing on the environmental, health, and climate costs to the public and future generations.[6]

Mountaintop removal has destroyed more than 500 mountains, cleared more than 1 million acres of forest, altered the hydrological cycle, ruined wildlife habitat, buried those miles of streams, changed others' chemistry, and exposed fish, bird species, and people to toxic contamination. A study in 2012 found that human mortality rates for lung, colon, and bladder cancer and leukemia in affected counties were significantly greater than those in non-mining areas from 2003 to 2007.[7] Miners have paid a heavy price with black lung diseases and accidents. One of the worst in recent history took place in April 2010. A coal-dust explosion at Massey Energy's Upper Big Branch Mine in West Virginia killed twenty-nine. The court sentenced the mining company's chief executive to a year in federal prison on a misdemeanor charge of violating mine health and safety standards. When he got out, he ran for the US Senate. He lost.

Market Forces and Lost Jobs

In recent years, hydraulic fracturing has created a boom in natural gas production in the United States. Oil companies inject pressurized mixtures of water, sand, and chemicals into the ground to crack rock formations and release trapped gas deposits.

This practice, often called fracking, has produced a bonanza of cheap natural gas. Many coal-fired power plants have converted to gas, and many others have been permanently retired. The growth in

Hydraulic fracturing or "fracking" has led to a boom in natural gas production, lowering its price below that of coal. *Bruce Gordon at EcoFlight*

cost-competitive solar and wind power has contributed to the decline of coal, too. From 2011 to the end of 2019, jobs in coal production declined by half. Appalachia is the hardest-hit region. More than half its coal mines have closed. Market forces combined with mining mechanization, not government regulations, are mostly responsible.

The coal industry is not dead, however. In 2019, it still provided 23.5 percent of the nation's utility-scale electric generation and exports to at least fifty other countries. The industry's dangerous contribution to global warming continues in the United States and elsewhere in the world.

Coal byproducts have caused problems, too. Coal is washed after it is mined to separate it from soil and rock. The process creates large amounts of liquid waste called slurry. Coal companies usually store slurry in impoundments they build by damming valleys with solid waste generated during mining. The waste contains carcinogens and heavy metals. In addition, the coal is mixed with water and dumped into "ash ponds" that are often unlined. One writer compared these impoundments to "a pool of gravy in a mound of mashed potatoes."

In 1972, a slurry pond collapsed and sent 130 million gallons of lava-like sludge into sixteen communities in Logan County, West Virginia. The sludge killed 125 people, injured more than 1,100, destroyed 550 residences, and left 4,000 people homeless. The mining company blamed heavy rains and called the disaster an "Act of God."

Appalachian communities have lived with another hazard of coal mining known as flyrock—rock fragments launched into the air when miners blast mountaintops. Flyrock deaths include a bulldozer operator in West Virginia in 1989, a sixteen-year-old riding in a car in Tennessee in 1993, a fifty-five-year-old man after he parked his ATV too close to a blast in Kentucky, and a thirty-two-year-old equipment operator in Pennsylvania in 1999. Flyrock penetrated his pickup truck's windshield. In 2005, a sleeping three-year-old boy in Virginia was killed after a bulldozer operator dislodged a boulder at a strip mine. The half-ton boulder crashed through the wall of the child's bedroom and crushed him to death.

A larger-than-usual example of flyrock. *Courtesy of aggregateresearch.com*

Floods Follow Deforestation

Floods compound the insult of mountaintop removal. The people who live at the bottom of treeless mined hills can expect them. The online news site *Inside Climate News* commissioned Duke University scientists to evaluate the flood risk in some Appalachian areas.[8] They identified 1,400 square miles in the Ohio River Basin where coal companies had blasted mountains and filled valleys with rubble. The scientists produced digital maps showing that 2,400 communities, urban and rural, from New York to Tennessee will experience heavier rains and floods in the nearly 1,000-mile Ohio River watershed.

This is how it goes in regions that suffer from the resource curse. Coal mining changed the Appalachian culture when it began, changed it again as the industry declined, and now is changing it as global warming takes effect. Central Appalachia, in particular, will never be the same as it once was, but it can be a lot better than it is today. There are a remarkable number of activists in the region working to bring in new types of jobs and enterprises.

For example, a program called the Appalachian Regional Reforestation Initiative restores the region's hardwood forests and accelerates
the natural succession of species that takes place after deforestation. It
will be generations before the new forests hold back runoff, but it's an
investment in the future and the kind of legacy that many people there
want to leave.

The coal industry's legacy includes about 48,500 abandoned mines
around the United States. Pennsylvania, West Virginia, and Kentucky
have 60 percent of them. People representing Kentucky have lobbied
Congress to pass a bill that would earmark $1 billion to reclaim the
abandoned mines along with the watersheds and waterways affected by
them. They also want to fund community projects intended to revitalize
mined areas for economic development.

They say the money would not come from taxpayers; it already
exists in a coal mine reclamation fund. And the reclamation project
would go well beyond Central Appalachia. It would fund states and
Native American tribes to reclaim mines in Virginia, Illinois, Colorado,
Tennessee, and Ohio. Unfortunately, one of the services that compute
the odds that Congress will pass a specific bill gives this one only a
3 percent chance.

The Devaluation of Fossil Fuels

There have been many notable incidents over the years in the fossil fuel
chain. Here are just some representative examples of the consequences
of fossil fuel energy.

There are 1,400 dumps where coal-fired power plants store ash in the
United States. In 2008, a billion gallons of coal ash slurry escaped when
the dike in a storage pond erupted at the Tennessee Valley Authority's
(TVA) Kingston coal-fired power plant. The cleanup cost TVA $1 bil-
lion. Within ten years, workers at the engineering firm hired to remove
the slurry developed brain cancer, lung cancer, and leukemia. More than
forty died.

TVA shipped 4 million tons of ash from the Kingston disaster
300 miles to a landfill near Uniontown, Alabama. The dump was twice
the size of New York City's Central Park. Uniontown's population was

90 percent African American with a median income of about $14,000. When they objected to dumping the ash at the landfill, the company that operated it filed a $30 million lawsuit against them. Residents responded with a civil rights complaint, but the EPA rejected it, ruling that there was insufficient evidence that operating the landfill near the town violated the Civil Rights Act.[9]

In 2000, a slurry impoundment owned by the coal company Massey Energy broke into an underground mine in Martin County, Kentucky. More than 300 million gallons of slurry escaped through openings in the mine and entered two river tributaries. The spill, which contained arsenic and mercury, polluted hundreds of miles of the Big Sandy River, its tributaries, and the Ohio River, contaminating the water supply for 27,000 people. The spill was thirty times larger than the *Exxon Valdez* disaster in which a tanker ship spilled its oil into Alaska's Prince William Sound in 1989.

An oil rig off the coast of Louisiana has been leaking between 380 and 4,500 gallons of oil into the Gulf of Mexico each day for more than fifteen years. The oil platform, owned by the Taylor Energy Company, was damaged by a hurricane in 2004. By the summer of 2019, the unstoppable spill exceeded the Taylor Energy Company's initial estimate by as much as 1,000 times.

Elsewhere in the Gulf, the *Deepwater Horizon* rig caused the biggest marine oil spill in history when it exploded in April 2010. British Petroleum, which rented the platform, estimated that the leak amounted to about 1,000 barrels a day, but government officials determined it was actually 60,000 at its peak. The well was not sealed until the following September. The resulting oil slick covered thousands of square miles in the Gulf and polluted an estimated 1,100 miles of shoreline in Mississippi, Alabama, and Florida. Fishing was closed in more than a third of federal waters in the Gulf. The aftermath depressed tourism and put between 8,000 and 12,000 people out of work.

In 1962–1963, industrial accidents spilled 3.5 million gallons of oil into the Minnesota and Mississippi Rivers. The spill was caused by bursting pipes after workers neglected to open steam lines at the Richards Oil Plant in Savage, Minnesota. The oil was traced back to the Richards plant in January 1963. Nevertheless, the company continued

Oil from the *Deepwater Horizon* spill covers pelicans in 2010. The spill continued for five months before it was stopped, but there were reports that the well was still leaking early in 2012. *"Gulf-Oiled-Pelicans-June-3-2010" by International Bird Rescue Research Center is licensed under CC BY 2.0.*

draining oil into the rivers until March because state officials could only take action if it were a public health emergency.

In Greenpoint, a neighborhood in Brooklyn, New York, oil has been leaking from refineries since the 1870s, putting toxic chemicals into Newton Creek. Accumulated oil and gas exploded in 1950, but the leaks were not noticed until 1978 when a pump started spewing oil from creek-side. The ongoing spill reportedly contaminated an aquifer meant as a backup water supply for the city during droughts. In 2009, a federal jury ordered ExxonMobil to pay the city nearly $105 million, and the contaminated area became a Superfund site. The *New York Times* reports that there are hundreds of similar spills across the United States from old facilities that were not regulated.

The biggest oil spill on US land may have been the 2010 eruption of the Lakeview Gusher in Taft, California, about 100 miles north of Los Angeles. Hydrocarbons erupted from a pressurized oil well in the Midway-Sunset Oil field. The spill lasted for 544 days, released 9 billion barrels of crude oil, spewed oil more than 200 feet into the air, and became a tourist attraction. The gusher finally stopped when the well caved in on itself.

In the past, some Americans reacted to industrial assaults on the environment by gently encouraging companies to have a greater appreciation for unspoiled nature. Aldo Leopold watched changes in his Wisconsin farm's ecology, then wrote the *Sand County Almanac* in 1949 and introduced the idea of a land ethic. Sigurd Olson became a lifelong advocate for wilderness while living in northern Wisconsin and serving as a guide in northern Minnesota and northwestern Ontario. He helped draft the Wilderness Act of 1964 and helped create several national parks and wildlife refuges. But it was about that time that four incidents set off alarms loud enough to wake up the American people and Congress to the need for environmental protection.

17

THE FOUR ALARMS

Well, here's another nice mess you've gotten me into.

—Oliver Hardy to Stan Laurel

THE FIRST ALARM WAS RACHEL CARSON'S BOOK, *Silent Spring*, published in 1962. Carson was a marine biologist and a superb writer who presented evidence that chemical pesticides such as DDT were destroying ecological balances and had even entered the food chain to cause congenital disabilities, liver disease, and leukemia. She pointed out that pesticide production grew 500 percent between World War II and the 1960s. She described a dystopian future where pesticides had silenced the natural world.

Some additional context might help explain why Carson wrote the book. Scientists had harnessed the atom to make a weapon with such profound power that it could destroy civilization. World War II general Omar Bradley pointed out, "Ours is a world of nuclear giants and ethical infants. We know more about war than we know about peace, more about killing than we know about living. We have grasped the mystery of the atom and rejected the Sermon on the Mount." Carson cautioned that despite science's achievements, it was naive to think that we could dominate and control nature.

The *New York Times* serialized *Silent Spring*, so it was widely available. It eventually was translated into thirty languages and sold 6 million copies in the United States alone. It triggered fierce and predictable opposition from the chemical industry. One of Carson's biographers recalled, "Even a former US secretary of agriculture was known to wonder in public 'why a spinster with no children was so interested in genetics.' Her offense was that she had overstepped her place as a woman." But the woman produced the spark that ignited the environmental movement.

A Senator Sees a Spill

Alarm number two took place in 1969. An oil-well blowout spilled 3 million gallons of crude oil into the ocean near Santa Barbara, California. The oil slick grew to 35 miles long and devastated wildlife. The leading environmentalist in Congress, Senator Gaylord Nelson of Wisconsin, witnessed it from the air while flying to a conference in Seattle. The tragedy gave him the idea of dedicating a special day each year to environmental awareness. Nelson announced the idea at the Seattle conference. He recruited a young activist, Denis Hayes, to organize the event. Hayes turned out to be an organizational dynamo, putting together a staff of eighty-five and a diverse network of supporting groups.

The United States celebrated the first Earth Day the following year. "The wire services carried the story from coast to coast," Nelson recalled. "The response was electric. It took off like gangbusters. Telegrams, letters, and telephone inquiries poured in from all across the country. The American people finally had a forum to express its concern about what was happening to the land, rivers, lakes, and air—and they did so with spectacular exuberance."[1]

Twenty million people took part, one of every ten Americans at the time.

A Flaming River

Alarm number three also took place in 1969. On August 1, *Time* magazine published an article about the ecological crisis in the United States. *Time* illustrated the piece with a photo of a fire on the Cuyahoga River in Cleveland. The fire in the picture took place in 1952, but pollution had caught fire on the river at least thirteen times since 1886, including an incident three months before *Time*'s article. A spark from a passing train ignited the waste in the river.

Industrial pollution burns on the Cuyahoga River in 1952. *Cleveland Plain Dealer*

Like urban rivers in many other cities, the Cuyahoga passed several industrial sites that contributed to its pollution, including an oil refinery, a steel mill, a ship-building facility, and a paint factory. Rivers in those days provided convenient sewers for industrial wastes. Pollution was considered the price of progress. But *Time*'s photo was the first time most Americans saw the anti-intuitive image of burning water. It was as dramatic an image as most people would ever see of industrial pollution.

Back-to-Back Oil Crises

The fourth alarm was a pair of events in the 1970s. In 1973, the United States imported about 30 percent of the oil it consumed. In October of that year, US defense secretary James Schlesinger received a cable from the Saudi oil minister on behalf of King Faisal. "I am instructed to cut off all supplies to the Sixth Fleet in the Mediterranean and to your forces in Europe," it read. The embargo was a protest against US aid to Israel during the Yom Kippur War. Before long, it applied to all oil from the

Arab nations that belonged to the Organization of the Petroleum Exporting Countries, or OPEC.

President Nixon ordered gasoline rationing, which led to supply shortages and intolerably long lines at gas stations. Some of us will remember that year as the one when Americans turned off their Christmas lights to conserve energy. By the time OPEC lifted the embargo March 1974, the global oil price had gone up nearly 400 percent. The result was a recession that lasted until 1975.

The embargo was a rude reminder of America's vulnerability when it depends on oil imports.[2] Within a month after the embargo began, Nixon vowed the United States would "meet our own energy needs without depending on any foreign energy sources." Two years later, in 1975, Congress passed the nation's first fuel economy standards for vehicles.

The second oil shock took place in 1978–1979 when Iran's production slowed because of the Islamic Revolution. The price of crude oil shot up again, and long lines returned at gas stations. Governments at all levels reacted through the 1980s with policies that significantly improved their energy efficiency. The United States shattered the myth that economic growth required lockstep increases in energy

In January 1974, the Federal Energy Office printed gasoline ration coupons to help control fuel use during the Arab oil embargo. The embargo was lifted that year and the coupons were never used. *Wikipedia Commons*

consumption. Economic output more than tripled compared to 1970, but energy demand grew only 50 percent.

In 2006, the United States still imported 60 percent of the oil it consumed. President George W. Bush drew headlines by declaring during his State of the Union address that "America is addicted to oil" and proposing that we replace 75 percent of our Mideast imports with alternative fuels. Twelve years later, in 2018, with hydraulic fracturing opening up new oil and gas reserves, the United States became the world's top oil producer. For the first time in more than seventy years, we exported more oil than we imported. In his 2020 State of the Union Address, President Trump reported, "We are energy independent and we do not need Middle East oil."

But he was wrong on two counts. We are not energy independent. In 2019, we still imported more than 9 million barrels of oil per day from nearly ninety countries, including Saudi Arabia and Russia.[3] We still deploy US military forces to patrol foreign oil shipping lanes, and we are still vulnerable to oil price and supply shocks triggered by other nations. The dramatic proof came in March 2020 when the Saudis and Russia got into a price dispute that caused world oil prices to plummet so low that it was no longer profitable for American companies to produce. The standoff ended with a truce the following month, but oil prices turned negative, meaning producers were paying buyers to take it.

The oil-price crash coincided with the COVID-19 pandemic, when travel virtually stopped. But we learned once more that the United States does not command oil prices. An international market sets them, and other nations can still manipulate supply and demand. And in a global economy, any nation's oil crisis becomes a crisis for everyone.[4]

There should have been an even louder environmental alarm in the 1960s, but it failed to go off. In November 1965, President Lyndon Johnson's science advisors informed him about climate change and gave him a prescient warning:

> Man is unwittingly conducting a vast geophysical experiment. Within a few generations, he is burning the fossil fuels that slowly accumulated in the earth over the past 500 million years. The CO_2 produced by this combustion is being injected into the

atmosphere; about half of it remains there. . . . By the year 2000 the increase in atmospheric CO_2 will be close to 25%. This may be sufficient to produce measurable and perhaps marked changes in climate and almost certainly cause significant changes in the temperature and other properties of the stratosphere.[5]

However, Johnson made only passing reference to this in an environmental address to Congress, and it didn't make an impression. Neither Johnson nor Congress took action to prevent those predictions from coming true.

Lawmaking Booms, Then Stalls

The four alarms resulted in a wave of landmark lawmaking. Congress approved, and President Nixon signed, the Clean Air Act in 1970, the Clean Water Act in 1972, and the Endangered Species Act in 1973. Nixon signed NEPA in 1970 to create the US Environmental Protection Agency and to require federal agencies to assess environmental impacts before they embark on projects.

In more or less rapid succession, Congress also created NOAA and passed the Federal Water Pollution Control Act; Coastal Zone Management Act; Marine Mammal Protection Act (the first to call for an ecosystem approach to wildlife management); Maritime Protection, Research, and Sanctuaries Act; the Federal Insecticide, Fungicide, Rodenticide Act; Resource Conservation and Recovery Act; Federal Land Policy Management Act; Whale Conservation and Protective Study Act; Toxic Substances Control Act; Soil and Water Conservation Act; Surface Mining Control and Reclamation Act; National Energy Act; Endangered American Wilderness Act; Wild and Scenic Rivers Act; and the Antarctic Conservation Act.

Then came the long legislative drought that continues today despite the indisputable evidence of climate change and the direct experience of unprecedented weather disasters.[6] Presidents have the power to fight climate change without Congress, but in modern times they have had very different opinions about the environment. The result has been an on-again, off-again commitment to environmental protection and reductions of the pollution responsible for global warming. Presidents George H. W. Bush, Bill Clinton, and Barack Obama took a few steps forward, while Presidents George W. Bush and Donald Trump responded with several steps back. The result is that the United States is the world's second-biggest source of carbon dioxide pollution, yet we have no consistent federal government policies to reduce it.[7]

The rest of the world has acted against the climate crisis (see sidebar), but much too timidly. It took more than twenty years for nations to reach a consensus agreement on climate action. It finally achieved one in 2015, the Paris Agreement, but only with voluntary and unenforceable commitments for each nation to cut its greenhouse gas pollution.

Slow Progress on the World Stage

1972: Stockholm Declaration In 1972, the United Nations convened history's first international conference to address environmental problems. More than 100 nations and 400 nongovernmental organizations formally declared that a healthy environment is a fundamental human right. They issued more than 100 actions to preserve and protect the environment.

1987: Brundtland Commission "Sustainable development" entered the international lexicon in 1987, compliments of the Brundtland Commission. The UN created the commission in 1987 to study how to prevent the deterioration of natural resources. The commission defined sustainable development as "meeting the needs of the present without compromising the ability of future generations to meet their own needs."

1992: First Earth Summit 178 countries met in Rio de Janeiro and produced the UN Framework Convention on Climate Change (UNFCCC). It established the architecture for decades of negotiations on how nations would tackle global warming.

1997: Kyoto Protocol Negotiated under the UNFCCC, this agreement was the first in which industrialized countries set targets to limit greenhouse gas pollution. The US Senate responded that any agreement had to include commitments from developing nations, too, and President George W. Bush refused to sign it.

Harmony with Nature resolutions Between 2009 and 2018, the UN General Assembly adopted ten resolutions on Harmony with Nature. "Devising a new world will require a new relationship with the Earth and with humankind's own existence," the UN explained.

2015: Millennium Development Goals World leaders endorsed seventeen Millennium Development Goals, including access to clean water and an end to poverty. The goal is to accomplish the objectives by 2030.

2015: The Paris Agreement After twenty-three years of negotiations, nations agreed to make voluntary self-determined cuts in carbon pollution. The collective goal is to hold global warming to 1.5°C to 2°C above the preindustrial level.

2017: US withdrawal Newly elected President Donald Trump withdrew from the Paris Agreement, making the US the only nation to do so.

2018: New Warning The IPCC warned that the world would have to make "rapid, far-reaching and unprecedented changes in all aspects of society" by 2030.

2021: US reenrollment In one of his first actions as president, Joe Biden notified the United Nations that America would reenter the Paris accord. The reentry became official on February 19, 2021.

The United States not only ignored climate change during the Trump presidency; it also became the world's leading oil producer. To build on George W. Bush's metaphor, we were not only addicted to oil; we are now both an addict and a dealer. There is no law against producing and exporting oil, but it is a de facto crime against humanity. Only America's voters can stop it.

Earth Rise

While environmental alarms were signaling danger in the 1960s and 1970s, there was a much more positive consciousness-raiser. Apollo 8, the first manned mission to the moon, achieved lunar orbit on Christmas Eve 1968. When the three astronauts on board—Frank Borman, James Lovell Jr., and William Anders—were 25,000 miles from the Earth, Anders looked back at the planet, and it reminded him of "the classroom globe sitting on a teacher's desk." It was no big deal.

But when their capsule emerged into the light from the dark side of the moon, the crew performed a rolling maneuver, "and up came Earth," Anders said. "I don't know who said it; maybe all of us said, 'Oh my God. Look at that!'" They were trained to focus on lunar orbit, but no one prepared them for the sight of an exquisite oasis in the blackness of space.

That evening, the crew held a live broadcast and showed pictures of the Earth and moon as they had seen it. They ended the broadcast by taking turns reading from the book of Genesis. William Anders began:

> We are now approaching lunar sunrise, and for all the people back on Earth, the crew of Apollo 8 has a message that we would like to send to you.
>
> In the beginning, God created the heaven and the Earth.
>
> And the Earth was without form, and void, and darkness was upon the face of the deep. And the Spirit of God moved upon the face of the waters.
>
> And God said, Let there be light: and there was light.
>
> And God saw the light, that it was good: and God divided the light from the darkness.

James Lovell continued:

> And God called the light Day, and the darkness he called Night. And the evening and the morning were the first day.
>
> And God said, Let there be a firmament in the midst of the waters, and let it divide the waters from the waters.
>
> And God made the firmament, and divided the waters which were under the firmament from the waters which were above the firmament: and it was so.
>
> And God called the firmament Heaven. And the evening and the morning were the second day.

Frank Borman concluded:

> And God said, Let the waters under the heaven be gathered together unto one place, and let the dry land appear: and it was so.
>
> And God called the dry land Earth; and the gathering together of the waters called the Seas: and God saw that it was good.
>
> And from the crew of Apollo 8, we close with good night, good luck, a Merry Christmas—and God bless all of you, all of you on the good Earth.

On December 30, 1968, the National Air and Space Administration (NASA) released a stunner of a photograph with the moon's surface in the foreground and the blue Earth in the distance. Titled *Earthrise*, it was called the most influential environmental photograph ever taken and one of the "100 Photographs That Changed the World."[8] These many years later, it is still a reminder of Earth's abundance compared to the emptiness of space and the moon's barren surface.

Astronaut William Anders took this photo during the Apollo 8 moon mission. In color, the Earth looks like a blue jewel hanging in space. *NASA*

Yet the impact of that reminder has waned. We might have thought that *Earthrise* would inspire an earnest international effort to take care of life on the planet. It hasn't, not at scale. As we shall see, the Earth has limited tolerances for the pressures we put on it, and we are not yet doing what's necessary to respect them.

The Stroke of a Pen

Congress is in charge of passing bills; presidents and presidential administrations implement them. But presidents also have a range of powers they can use without Congress's permission. They can move the government in one direction or another with executive orders, memoranda, and directives. When presidents believe an issue is of paramount importance, but Congress won't act, they can use one of these tools to get the job done.

There is a problem, however. As the old saying goes, "What can be created with the stroke of a pen can be deleted with a stroke of the pen." In other words, a subsequent president can easily undo what his or her predecessor has done. Executive directives do not have the relative permanence of laws.

When Barack Obama became president in 2009, his political party ruled the House and Senate. He focused on two urgent priorities: preventing the global economy from collapsing, and getting Congress to pass health-care reform, an issue that lawmakers had failed to address for decades. Obama succeeded at both. But in 2011, Republicans took control of the Senate and began blocking anything Obama tried to accomplish. Senate Majority Leader Mitch McConnell said his top priority was to keep Obama from being reelected. It was a cynical statement that showed clearly how winning elections was more important than doing the people's business.

On a sweltering summer day at Georgetown University, Obama gave a speech to students and said, "I refuse to condemn your generation and future generations to a planet that's beyond fixing." He was willing to work with Congress, he said, but he would bypass the House and Senate if he had to. "We don't have time for a meeting of the flat earth society," he said. Obama carried through on that promise. He used his executive authorities to address climate change, especially during his last two years in office. In 2014, he went to China and signed a historic agreement with its president Xi Jinping, who committed his country for the first time to cap its carbon emissions. In 2015, Secretary of State John Kerry and his chief climate negotiator, Todd Stern, worked tirelessly on a first-ever international agreement on climate action, which nearly two hundred nations signed in Paris that December.

On September 3, 2016, the United States and China symbolized their seriousness about international collaboration by delivering their formal paperwork for entry into the Paris Agreement to UN Secretary-General Ban Ki-moon. The Obama Administration created a climate action plan that included the nation's first-ever limits on carbon pollution from power plants and established historic increases in car and truck efficiency. The goal was to reduce US carbon emissions 26 to 28 percent by 2025 compared to their level in 2005. Obama's team also created a detailed plan to decarbonize the economy by mid-century.

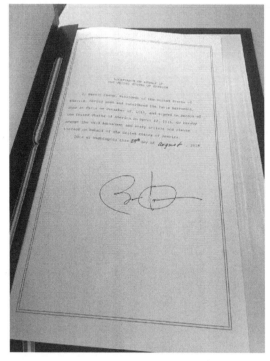

President Obama's signature on the Paris Climate Accord. *Courtesy of The White House*

But on June 1, just months into his presidency, Donald Trump announced he would withdraw the United States from the Paris deal, saying he would "cease all implementation of the non-binding Paris Accord and the draconian financial and economic burdens the agreement imposes on our country."[9]

Trump claimed the Paris pact would cost the economy close to $3 trillion in lost GDP. Fact-checkers reviewed Trump's statement and cited scientists who calculated that the United States would lose $8.2 trillion in GDP by not participating in the accord and would be about 5 percent poorer.[10] The losses would come from the additional increase in the atmosphere's temperature because of continuing US emissions. Nevertheless, Trump spent his term systematically cancelling environmental-protection regulations and the climate action plan that Obama and his team created.

Only hours after he took the oath of office in January 2021, President Biden began reversing Trump's actions, in some cases by restoring Obama's directives and in others by improving on what Obama did. Biden made US action on global warming second only to recovering from the pandemic. In addition to reenrolling the US in the Paris accord, Biden named former Secretary of State John Kerry to the new position of Climate Envoy, appointed former EPA Administrator Gina McCarthy as his White House Climate Advisor and the charismatic former governor of Michigan, Jennifer Granholm, as Secretary of Energy. Granholm worked with the Obama Administration to save the automobile industry during the Great Recession, then set about diversifying Michigan's economy with green industries.

Recognizing how pervasive a crisis climate change has become, Biden instructed the entire federal government to factor climate change into its work. This seemingly simple directive was an important precedent in a government where crosscutting issues like climate change were "stovepiped" in certain agencies—in this case, EPA and DOE—without sufficient coordination across the bureaucracy. Biden's directive reflected that global warming touches on virtually everything in society, and all parts of society must contribute to preventing it.

As DC's cherry blossoms bloomed in the spring of 2021, it appeared the pandemic's fever was finally breaking so that society could bloom again, too. But the most important development was that the long winter of climate denial, public indifference, and political resistance seemed finally to be ending. *Time* described it in its April–May issue: "For decades, the idea that climate change touches everything has grown behind the scenes," the magazine reported in its cover story. "Now, spurred by alarming science, growing public fury and a deadly pandemic, government officials, corporate bosses and civil society leaders are finally waking up to a simple idea whose time has come: climate is everything."

"The course of climatization—the process by which climate change will transform society—will play out in the coming years in every corner of society," *Time*'s article continued. "Whether it leads to a more resilient world or exacerbates the worst elements of our society depends on whether we adjust or just stumble through."[11]

"The world is crossing the long-awaited political tipping point on climate right now," Al Gore said. "We are seeing the beginning of a new era."

But the most surprising sign of thaw came when Cecil Roberts, president of the United Mine Workers of America, announced he would support Biden's clean energy plans if the government helped train mine workers for good-paying jobs and benefits in the post-carbon world. "Change is coming whether we seek it or not," Roberts said. "We can look away no longer. . . . We must act."[12]

Systemic Inconsistency

Still, the test of a democracy's ability to deal with long-term crises is far from over. Trump's trashing of Obama's climate policies proved how tenuous a president's initiatives can be and how important it is to codify climate action in law. Whether the government is finally ready to act on climate change and whether the United States can reestablish its credibility among other nations depends entirely on Congress now. Executive orders are not enough anymore.

The 2020 elections illustrated how important it is for both parties in Congress to stop treating climate change as partisan. The election produced a 50-50 split between Senate Republicans and Democrats, essentially putting the future of civilization in the hands of one centrist Democrat from the nation's second-biggest coal-producing state. Whatever the outcome of the next elections in the United States, the nation's long-term future will depend on some Republicans, preferably many, breaking from GOP doctrine to acknowledge the threat of global warming, its link with fossil fuels, the need to decarbonize the economy, and the importance of working with other nations on solutions. Members of Congress typically side with whoever is most able to help them keep their jobs. For years, it has been the fossil energy lobby. Now it must be voters in sufficient numbers to overwhelm whatever influence Donald Trump tries to assert. Because the world cannot tackle greenhouse gas emissions with America on the sidelines, it is not an exaggeration to say the quality of life on the planet is in the hands of America's voters.[13]

President Biden still has significant legal authorities to take his own actions on climate change, as he immediately showed. President Obama had them, too. Those authorities are likely to remain in place for future presidents. There are 112 provisions that give presidents the power to act on energy and environmental matters, including 96 that specifically address climate change, global warming, or greenhouse gas emissions. But whether a president can use those powers ultimately depends on the American people, too.

The two Roosevelt presidents are cases in point. Teddy Roosevelt subscribed to a stewardship theory of presidential power and explained it this way:

> My belief was that it was not only [the president's] right but his duty to do anything that the needs of the Nation demanded unless such action was forbidden by the Constitution or its laws. . . . In other words, I acted for the common well-being of all our people whenever and in whatever measure was necessary, unless prevented by a direct constitutional or legislative prohibition.

To deal with the Great Depression, President Franklin Delano Roosevelt put the legislative branch on notice that "in the event that Congress should fail to act, and act adequately, I shall accept the responsibility and

I shall act." Obama said the same thing to Congress during one of his State of the Union addresses, but Republicans in the Senate made sure that nothing Obama did would stand. The difference was that FDR's bold New Deal programs had strong popular support, and Congress knew it. Seven of the New Deal programs became so deeply rooted in the nation's life that they remain in force today.

On complicated issues, voters often take their lead from the people they elected to represent them. We should pray the leaders of both parties tell their voters that the days of partisanship are over in regard to global warming. From here on, the electorate must guarantee that every person chosen for public office continues the nation's commitment to a permanent net-zero-carbon economy.

Is There a Mandate?

Have environmental stewardship and climate action begun to take root in the US electorate? There is still a deep and senseless divide between conservative Republicans and everyone else. However, there are some positive signs. In January 2020, before the coronavirus pandemic hit, the Pew Research Center found that 64 percent of American adults considered the environment a top policy priority compared to 67 percent who considered strengthening the economy to be most important. The result was within the poll's margin of error. It was the first time in two decades that Pew found the two issues to be equally important to most Americans. More than half of Pew's respondents, 52 percent, said that climate change was a top priority for the nation, fourteen percentage points higher than three years before.[14]

But the poll was taken when the economy was booming and voters were not worried about it. Pew checked again in late April and early May when the COVID-19 pandemic was well under way, the economy was crashing, businesses were closing, the nation was in lockdown, and millions of Americans could not work. Pew found that 60 percent of adults still considered climate change a major threat to the well-being of the United States, as high a number as any Pew Research Center survey found going back to 2009. Sixty-five percent of adults said the federal government was doing too little about it.[15]

As the year progressed, climate change became a top issue in the presidential election. Twenty-nine Democrats ran for their party's nomination, and virtually all of them made climate change a major plank in their platforms. It was impossible to tell how many Republican voters or members in Congress considered global warming a top-ranked issue because the party marched lockstep with Donald Trump, who openly labeled climate change a "hoax."

Whatever action the US government does or does not take in the years ahead, we should ask how we became so careless about the Earth's ability to support life as our species has known it for ten thousand years. I believe two mindsets—one going back to the earliest days in the nation's history, and one that later institutionalized that mindset as a political philosophy—help explain America's cavalier attitude. The first is "frontierism"; the second is greed. Until we change them, we will continue degrading life on our planet.

18

FRONTIERISM

> The conservation of our natural resources and their
> proper use constitute the fundamental problem which
> underlies almost every other problem of our national life.
>
> —Theodore Roosevelt

IMAGINE WHAT IT MUST HAVE BEEN LIKE for the pilgrims when they landed on the North American shore, free at last from the harsh conditions in Europe and the much harsher conditions on the two-month voyage to the New World. They recorded some of their first impressions in letters describing good soil, abundant wildlife, and healthy forests that amazed people from England, where virtually all woodlands had been cut down for cropland, pasture, and fuel.[1]

Even so, the first settlements were decimated by starvation, mainly because the newcomers arrived insufficiently prepared. Many who didn't starve to death died of disease. Those who survived became farmers with the help of indentured servants and slaves or moved west into wildlands where there were even more abundant resources and no government constraints on using them.

Like starving people confronted by a feast, the settlers "rapidly consumed the natural resources of the land," according to professor Kamala Doršner at University of the People: "After they depleted one area, they moved westward to new frontiers. . . . A frontier ethic assumes that the earth has an unlimited supply of resources. . . . This attitude sees humans as masters who manage the planet. The frontier ethic is completely anthropocentric, for only the needs of humans are considered."[2]

Frederick Jackson Turner, the historian born in Wisconsin to pioneer parents in 1861, believed that the American people's unique attributes grew from the frontier experience. He wrote that the movement west was not motivated by government incentives but rather by the feeling of expansive power that sought to dominate nature. Turner believed "restless, nervous energy" and "dominant individualism" led frontiersmen to "squander seemingly inexhaustible natural resources . . . with an abandon unknown elsewhere."[3]

In other words, the Europeans were an invasive species. They invaded not only the North American environment but also its Indigenous cultures. After frontiersmen depleted the Midwest's beaver populations, they moved farther west to trade in buffalo robes and tongues. They slaughtered an average of 200,000 buffalo every year. Gilbert King, a writer at the Smithsonian Institute, describes it:

> Massive hunting parties began to arrive in the West by train, with thousands of men packing .50 caliber rifles, and leaving a trail of buffalo carnage in their wake. Unlike the Native Americans or Buffalo Bill, who killed for food, clothing and shelter, the hunters from the East killed mostly for sport. Native Americans looked on with horror as landscapes and prairies were littered with rotting buffalo carcasses. The railroads began to advertise excursions for "hunting by rail," where trains encountered massive herds alongside or crossing the tracks. Hundreds of men aboard the trains climbed to the roofs and took aim, or fired from their windows, leaving countless 1,500-pound animals where they died.[4]

Settlers who claimed western lands eked out a living with backbreaking labor. But there was plenty of greed, too. White settlers violated treaties and invaded Native American lands for access to gold and other resources. Official government policy forced Native Americans off their ancestral places so White farmers could grow more cotton. Estimates vary, but records suggest that White settlers forced 100,000 Indigenous people from their homelands during a "removal period." Tens

A mountain of American bison skulls in the mid-1870s. *Wikipedia Commons*

of thousands walked more than 5,000 miles to government-designated "Indian territory."[5] About 15,000 died on what became known as the Trail of Tears.

The early settlers were like a swarm of locusts devouring as they went. Turner believed that the frontier experience influenced everything in American history up to the 1800s. But frontierism, as I'll call it, didn't end there. The frontier has changed dramatically, but the frontier ethic is still alive.

The right to exploit natural resources as though they are unlimited, along with the resistance to government constraints on the freedom to do so, remains a strong influence in the economy and public policy today. Energy is an example. The US government has used tax dollars to subsidize oil production for more than a century. It became apparent in the second half of the twentieth century that fossil fuels were too much of a good thing, but we continue to subsidize them as they pollute the air, ground, and water. The oil and gas industry produces record amounts of fossil fuels while knowing they are the principal cause of worsening climate change. The United States is now the world's biggest oil producer, despite warnings that most underground oil, gas, and coal reserves must remain unused to avoid catastrophic impacts from global warming.[6]

The oil and gas industry has spared no expense to buy influence in Congress. It gave more than $87 million as of September 21, 2020, to congressional candidates in the 2020 elections.[7] It spent more than $116.5 million and deployed 635 lobbyists to oppose or stall congressional action on climate change and clean energy.[8] Renewable energy companies lobby too, but fossil energy interests outspent them thirteen to one in the 2017–2018 midterm elections, and so the exploitation of our resources continues unabated.[9]

Frontierism on a Finite Planet

Teddy Roosevelt is justifiably famous as the president who saved some of the nation's most precious landscapes. He created 150 national forests, 51 federal bird reserves, 4 national game preserves, 5 national parks, and 18 national monuments covering 230 million acres of public land. But President Roosevelt also believed, correctly of course, that natural resources should be put to work to benefit people. That has never been in question. The issue was and still is how we manage those resources.

In Teddy Roosevelt's time, resource management was the key to water availability in the West. He told Congress that "great [water] storage works" were necessary to irrigate the arid lands, with massive dams, reservoirs, canals, levees, and ditches to collect runoff from croplands. The government began building these structures regardless of the ecosystems they destroyed. Water projects flooded lands on Indian reservations, drained rivers, and destroyed salmon runs.

It was Franklin Delano Roosevelt who declared during his presidential campaign in 1932 that the party was over. "Our last frontier has long since been reached," he said. "The day of enlightened administration has come."[10]

"Our task now is not the discovery or exploitation of natural resources," but rather "the sober, less dramatic business" of administering the resources already in hand, FDR declared. He created the Civilian Conservation Corps to plant hundreds of millions of trees on the Great Plains. During his presidency, Congress formed the Soil Conservation Service and the Grazing Service (later the Bureau of Land Management) to manage grazing on public lands.[11]

A Vision of Prosperity

In the second half of the twentieth century, frontierism influenced aggressive industrialization and economic development. The deprivations of the Great Depression left Americans hungry for prosperity. As the Depression ended in 1939, New York hosted the World's Fair with the theme of "The World of Tomorrow." A writer for the *New York Daily News* recalled that "the fair featured all manner of weirdness and magnificence."[12] Exhibits gave glimpses of futuristic products, including television, color photographs, air conditioning, and nylon pantyhose. A seven-foot robot with a seventy-word vocabulary bragged, "My brain is bigger than yours" as people passed it.

One exhibit was especially popular, attracting more than thirty million visitors. It was called Futurama: 35,000 square feet of large models including more than 500,000 buildings, 1 million trees, and 50,000 vehicles. Fairgoers were so fascinated that they ignored an exhibit called the "Life of Wool" to stand in lines that sometimes stretched a mile.

When visitors all were seated, a moving track transported them through the panorama of a city twenty years in the future. General Motors sponsored the exhibit, so it focused heavily on the mobility that future transportation systems would provide. It showed freeways with cloverleaf exits so stoplights wouldn't inconvenience drivers. The freeways linked suburbs and rural areas conveniently to the city. There were dioramas of skyscrapers, parks, and elevated walkways. There was lots of glass and chrome. Futurama attracted more people than the other exciting features at the fair, including a burlesque dancer whose clothes were removed by trained birds.[13] Before people exited, they received badges that read "I have seen the future."

As it turned out, they had. A world much like Futurama materialized when World War II ended. Factories began producing consumer goods again. Science and engineering improved life, food supplies were plentiful, car sales took off, highways proliferated, suburbs mushroomed, and the modern car-centered society was born.[14] We had harnessed the atom, cured deadly diseases, and manufactured products that enhanced our quality of life. It seemed that science and technology gave us unlimited opportunities.

Moving seats transport visitors through General Motors' Futurama exhibit at the 1939 New York World's Fair. *New York Public Library*

"To a populace whose forebears had within living memory colonized the interior of a vast continent and whose country had never lost a war, arguments for limit and constraint seemed almost unpatriotic," wrote biologist E .O. Wilson.[15] The nation enjoyed "an ethic of limitless progress." It was frontierism, Great Generation style. But it wasn't long before we encountered some undesirable byproducts of the new prosperity.

FDR's critics complained that his conservation initiatives did not change the United States' fundamental attitude about natural resources. Alexis de Tocqueville described it in 1931: "As one digs deeper into the national character of Americans, one sees that they have sought the value of everything in this world only in the answer to this single question: How much money will it bring in?"[16]

It probably annoyed many Americans that a Frenchman passed judgment on their character, but there was plenty of evidence that he was correct. There still is.

19

AVARICE

The great tragedy of the climate crisis is that seven and a half billion people must pay the price—in the form of a degraded planet—so that a couple of dozen polluting interests can continue to make record profits. It is a great moral failing of our political system that we have allowed this to happen.

—Atmospheric scientist Michael E. Mann

IN THE 1987 FILM *WALL STREET*, businessman Gordon Gekko gives this short speech on the benefits of greed:

Greed, for the lack of a better word, is good. Greed is right, greed works. Greed clarifies, cuts through, and captures the essence of the evolutionary spirit. Greed, in all of its forms; greed for life, for money, for love, knowledge has marked the upward surge of mankind.

Greed for life? OK. Greed for knowledge? Sure. Greed for love? "Longing" is better. But greed for money? In a system so often rigged to favor the rich, that kind of greed works for the very few, usually at the expense of the very many.

The venerable Sunday evening news show *60 Minutes* told of an example. The trade sanctions that President Trump imposed on China, and China's retaliation, put family farms in danger. When COVID-19 took over in 2020 and people stopped going to restaurants, farm products jammed up in the food pipeline, and prices fell to the point that small operators were losing a great deal of money. The Department of Agriculture used a 1933 law to provide $28 billion in relief. Farm owners, or those who had a stake in a farm, were allowed to receive $250,000 each.

That arrangement allowed owners and shareholders in corporate farms to receive significant amounts of money. Leslie Stahl interviewed an attorney who specialized in helping farmers game the system. He acknowledged that he had once put together sixty-six people in a partnership involving one farm. Each qualified to receive bailout money. Some recipients of $250,000 were city relatives of a farmer. The report reminded me of a book from 1967 by sociology professor G. William Domhoff. Domhoff quoted an investment manager who worked with wealthy clients and described how the system works for them:

> A highly complex and largely discrete set of laws and exemptions from laws has been put in place by those in the uppermost reaches of the US financial system. It allows them to protect and increase their wealth and significantly affect the US political and legislative processes. They have real power and real wealth. Ordinary citizens in the bottom 99.9% are largely not aware of these systems, do not understand how they work, are unlikely to participate in them, and have little likelihood of entering the top 0.5%, much less the top 0.1%. Moreover, those at the very top have no incentive whatsoever for revealing or changing the rules.[1]

Data show that only upper-income families have been able to build on their wealth. As of 2016, upper-income families had 75 times the wealth of lower-income families and 7.4 times more wealth than middle-income families.[2] But the wealth of most American families is no higher today than it was two decades ago. Codified inequality paid off for the richest Americans even during the pandemic. Nearly 8 million people sank into poverty between June and November 2020, especially among Blacks, children, and people with a high school education or less. But between March 18, 2020, and April 12, 2021, the combined wealth of America's billionaires reportedly grew 55 percent to $4.56 trillion—a third of its growth over last 31 years.[3]

Why does this matter? It matters because lower-income families have less economic opportunity and mobility and less political influence to change the policies that lock in wealthier Americans' advantages. Gordon Gekko's "upward surge of mankind" is producing a downward surge in America's future, illustrated lately by the rollback of national environmental protections and ongoing carbon pollution that will continue causing climate change for many generations to come. Families with the fewest resources will be least able to cope.

Conspiracy theorists on the far right often refer to a "deep state," an alleged secret group of unelected government officials and military leaders who run things behind the scenes and foil the plans of duly elected leaders. This idea has been injected into public discourse so much that it has become part of our lexicon and many people believe this group is real. In early 2018, a Monmouth University poll found three of four Americans think the deep state exists.[4]

Conspiracy theories abound in culture today, particularly on the far right. But there is a grain of truth to the deep state. Its members are called neoliberals.

Neoliberalism

Liberalism in this context is defined as Europeans use the term; it's the opposite of what "liberal" means in the United States. An American liberal believes in an active federal government. A neoliberal believes that the government's only role besides national defense is to protect private property rights and the free-market economy. Neoliberals believe that the profit motive, not government, should provide what society needs. They believe in small government and free markets, and they don't like social programs and safety nets.

"The narrative is appealingly simple," explains Hunter Lovins, a prominent lecturer, educator, and author who believes we should be creating "an economy in service to life" rather than profit. Neoliberalism is based on the idea that "you, as an individual, are the only legitimate economic actor. Money is the measure of success, and your unfettered freedom to go get it is the paramount value." It is Darwinian economics, convinced that some people are rich and others poor because that is the natural order of things.

Neoliberalism liberates corporations and governments from any sense of obligation to society and any moral code, empathy, compassion, or ethical standards. The distinction between right and wrong is simple: profit is right; barriers to profit are wrong. It is a heartless and soulless view of the world, but it helps explain a few things. We've heard political commentators say President Trump's views on social programs, taxes, the environment, and other issues are not the problem but rather the symptom of a larger problem. They are correct. The larger problem is the neoliberal influence.

It is why President Trump killed ninety-five federal environmental protection rules during his first three years in office. He did nothing about global climate change because it would get in the way of a big industry's profits, in this case oil, gas, and coal.

It's why the president and members of Congress who voted for the 2017 tax-reform bill added $1.5 trillion to the national debt, ostensibly to create jobs and help middle-income Americans. Instead, corporations used $1 trillion of their substantial tax benefits to buy back their stocks, a practice that raises their stocks' prices. It's why the wealthiest fifth of Americans received nearly two-thirds of the benefits. By 2027, the richest 1 percent will receive 83 percent according to the Tax Policy Center.[5] And it's why President Trump promised that if he were reelected, he would cut safety net programs, possibly including Medicare and Social Security, to pay down the deficit that the Republican tax bill created.

A significant problem for the neoliberal view is that free markets do not exist and never will. Markets are distorted by tax subsidies and government services in the United States as well as by hidden costs. The price we pay for oil, for example, does not reflect its actual costs to the environment and society, among them the impacts of climate change. Most economists say that fossil fuels receive somewhere between $20 billion and $30 billion in taxpayer subsidies each year in the United States, but that does not include the subsidies that society at large provides, from childhood asthma to water pollution and climate change. The International Monetary Fund found that the value of social and environmental support for fossil fuels in the US was nearly $650 billion in 2017.[6] The fact that the fossil energy sector gets these "services" free is not what "free markets" is supposed to mean.

How Neoliberalism Began

After President Franklin Roosevelt's New Deal helped end the Great Depression, a group of influential men worried that FDR's aggressive federal programs and the public's confidence in government would lead the United States and Europe into socialism and even communism. They launched an initiative to persuade policymakers that national governments should be very limited and that free markets and the profit motive should rule the economy without interference. They called themselves the Mount Pelerin Society. Members of the group helped found and fund several conservative think tanks to promote their point of view.

One of them is the Heritage Foundation. It is not shy about its influence on Presidents Ronald Reagan and Donald Trump. "Heritage was President Reagan's favorite think tank, and Reagan was the embodiment of the ideas and principles Heritage holds dear," a Heritage member wrote in 2004.[7] Heritage provided Reagan's transition team with an eleven-hundred-page "Mandate for Leadership," including two thousand recommendations that shaped the incoming president's agenda. United Press International called it "a blueprint for grabbing the government by its frayed New Deal lapels and shaking out 48 years of liberal policy." Heritage bragged that the Reagan administration adopted nearly two-thirds of its ideas.

A year before Donald Trump announced that he would run for president, Heritage began assembling a database of three thousand "trusted movement conservatives." Heritage called it the "Project to Restore America." As the *New York Times* reported in 2018:

> Heritage has achieved a huge strategic victory. Those who worked on the project estimate that hundreds of the people the think tank put forward landed jobs in just about every government agency. Heritage's recommendations included some of the most prominent members of Trump's cabinet: Scott Pruitt, Betsy

DeVos (whose in-laws endowed Heritage's Richard and Helen DeVos Center for Religion and Civil Society), Mick Mulvaney, Rick Perry, Jeff Sessions and many more. Dozens of Heritage employees and alumni also joined the Trump administration—at last count 66 of them, according to Heritage, with two more still awaiting Senate confirmation. It is a kind of critical mass that Heritage had been working toward for nearly a half-century.[8]

Heritage also gave Trump a new Mandate for Leadership that contained more than 330 policy ideas. The foundation boasts that Trump and his administration embraced nearly two-thirds of them in his first year as president. Among them were Trump's decisions to leave the Paris climate agreement, open more federal lands and offshore areas to oil drilling, increase military spending, and reduce the size and scope of federal agencies.[9]

To be fair, many interest groups, lobbyists, nongovernment organizations, and left-leaning think tanks attempt to affect presidential policy. But few have had the influence of Heritage and its fellow conservative organizations.

DeSmog, a website launched to clear up "PR pollution" about climate science, says it obtained records showing that Koch foundations created or funded by the libertarian Koch brothers put more than $100 million into more than fifty groups connected to Mont Pelerin Society members.[10]

Others have looked into the society, too. Author David Harvey found there have been massive shifts of wealth to the top tenth of the top 1 percent where the neoliberal agenda has been adopted in the world. "The conditions that neoliberalism demands in order to free human beings from the slavery of the state—minimal taxes, the dismantling of public services and social security, deregulation, the breaking of the unions—just happen to be the conditions required to make the elite even richer, while leaving everyone else to sink or swim," Harvey wrote.[11]

What Happens Without Regulations?

Over time, neoliberals have proved that an unconstrained profit motive creates the human toll we've seen from tobacco, opioids, and climate change. To be protected, society needs governments to intervene. When conservatives and libertarians ask why the government thinks it should regulate industries, the answer is simple. The government must regulate bad behavior because many industries do not regulate themselves.

Instead, some of our biggest industries employ a common strategy when they produce harmful products. If their research shows that the product is dangerous, they bury it. If outside research shows their product is harmful, they discredit it. They launch well-funded disinformation campaigns, use their money and influence to discourage Congress from passing legislation and intimidate whistleblowers. The objective is to keep earning profits as long as possible and, if necessary, play dirty.

Chemicals

After Rachel Carson wrote her seminal book *Silent Spring* to disclose the danger of toxic chemicals in the environment, chemical companies issued an assortment of anonymous complaints about her. "If man were to follow the teachings of Miss Carson, we would return to the Dark Ages, and the insect and diseases and vermin would once again inherit the earth," one critic said. The writer called Carson a "fanatic defender of the cult of the balance of nature." Critics attacked her knowledge and character.[12]

They accused Carson of being responsible for large numbers of deaths because of restrictions on DDT use, a claim shown to be false. The neoliberal Competitive Enterprise Institute (CEI) established a website and posted, "Millions of people around the world suffer the painful and often deadly effects of malaria because one person sounded a false alarm. That person is Rachel Carson." Forty-five years after *Silent Spring* was published, CEI was still criticizing Carson on a website that included pictures of children who died from malaria.[13]

Even though it looked like a win when Carson's disclosures set the stage for Congress to pass the Toxic Substances Control Act in 1976, the chemical industry's clout was evident. The act grandfathered sixty-two thousand chemicals without testing, and required the EPA to prove that a chemical was dangerous rather than requiring chemical companies to show that their products were not. By 2016, the EPA had only banned nine of the more than eighty thousand chemicals on the market.[14]

Tobacco

More than 16 million Americans live with a disease caused by smoking—cancer, heart disease, stroke, lung disease, diabetes, chronic obstructive pulmonary disease, tuberculosis, eye diseases, or rheumatoid arthritis. More than 480,000 people die each year from cigarette smoking. That's 1,300 deaths every day. The economic cost exceeds $300 billion each year.[15]

After the US Surgeon General concluded in 1964 that cigarette smoking was linked to cancer, the CEOs of the largest tobacco companies swore before Congress that they did not believe their products caused the disease. But a study at the University of California Los Angeles found that tobacco companies knew from their own research as early as 1959 that radioactive particles in their products were connected to lung cancer.[16]

One controversial issue was the industry's practice of marketing cigarettes to kids. The American Lung Association says that strategy has not ended. "It was then and continues today to be their business plan" to hook kids on an addictive and harmful product.[17]

Pharmaceuticals

By the fall of 2019, the opioid epidemic addicted two million Americans and resulted in more than four hundred thousand deaths. Overdoses involving opioids killed nearly forty-seven thousand people in 2018, two of every three drug overdose deaths that year. A lawsuit named nearly 350 defendants ranging from pharmaceutical companies to medical associations and drugstores.[18]

The roots of the opioid epidemic go back decades. In 2001, the federal Drug Enforcement Administration (DEA) and twenty-one healthcare groups called for better safeguards against the diversion of opioids from medical uses. But in 2016, Congress passed a bill that made it difficult (some critics said "all but logically impossible") for the DEA to block a drug company from distributing opioids when there was an imminent danger to a community. The industry backed the bill with $21 million in contributions to members of Congress.[19]

The DEA's chief administrative judge coauthored an analysis of the bill and pointed out, "If it had been the intent of Congress to completely eliminate the DEA's ability to ever impose an immediate suspension on distributors or manufacturers, it would be difficult to conceive of a more effective vehicle." An analysis published by the *American Journal of Medicine* concluded that the bill "proves that money and power can subvert the best intentions of many."[20]

"The failure to control the scourge of America's present opioid epidemic has many similarities to America's long fight to limit tobacco use, another drug protected by the money and power of an industry," the authors wrote.

Oil and gas

This industry keeps producing petroleum even though it knows that its products cause global climate change, which makes many types of weather more extreme and deadly. Some of the carbon dioxide pollution from oil and gas will linger in the atmosphere for millennia.

Shell, Chevron, Exxon, and BP reportedly made $2 trillion in profits over the last thirty years while denying climate change and trying to discredit climate science. Exxon, which covered up warnings about climate change from its own scientists, led the four companies in profits, earning $775 billion.[21]

Inside Climate News and the *Los Angeles Times* uncovered the coverup.[22] They found in 2015 that Exxon's (now ExxonMobil) and Shell's own scientists warned them in the 1970s and 1980s that their products were responsible for climate change, but the companies collaborated to discredit climate scientists and to persuade the American people that climate science was unsettled.

Climate scientists calculated a few years before that about 80 percent of the world's underground reserves of oil, coal, and natural gas would have to remain unused if we are to avoid catastrophic climate change. Nevertheless, armed with technologies such as directional drilling and hydraulic fracturing the United States experienced a boom in gas and oil production and became the world's largest producer in 2018.[23] That production combined with President Trump's announcement that he would pull the nation out of the Paris Agreement made America both an outlier and an outlaw in the international effort to control global warming.[24]

The Benefits of Regulation

Let's settle the regulation issue once and for all. Can government overreach? Yes. Does it? Sometimes. Do regulations hurt the economy? Not when they are well designed. Do they kill jobs? Same answer. Do honest industries welcome reasonable regulations? It may surprise you, but they do.

I have talked about regulations at length with oil and gas executives. They said in private that they welcome reasonable rules because companies benefit from them. Regulations weed out the bad actors whose practices damage an industry's "social license to operate." Laws put competing companies on a level playing field so that polluters can't undercut the investments that good companies make to safeguard the environment. Good environmental regulation doesn't meddle with good practices.

What neoliberals in the United States do not accept is that the most important organizing force in the United States of America is not profit. It's life, liberty, and the opportunity for happiness.

It's Not Partisan

Finally, although climate change became a hot partisan issue, it is not inherently political. The oil industry and conservative politicians weaponized it. In 2008, the Republican Party platform supported market-based solutions to carbon pollution. Four years later, it opposed any action at all. It called coal "clean," declared that support for renewable energy was "the triumph of extremism over common sense," and demanded an immediate halt to US support for international efforts to curb global warming.[25]

The Pew Research Center poll that found two out of three Americans want the federal government to do something about climate change also found a big partisan split: 90 percent of Democrats agreed, compared to only 39 percent of Republicans.

It is a persistent and disappointing result. Floods and the other disasters linked to climate change don't distinguish between conservative and liberal households. But the oil and gas industry's strategy has been to politicize it. So long as the industry controls national energy policy, we can expect carbon emissions to continue, climate change to get worse, and its adverse impacts to grow.

20

SAFE OPERATING SPACES

The Earth will not continue to offer its harvest, except
with faithful stewardship. We cannot say we love the
land and then take steps to destroy it for use by future
generations.

—John Paul II

GREED IS NOTHING NEW AND USUALLY NOTHING to be admired, but it
is the core tenet of neoliberalism and a characteristic of frontierism.
It pays little attention to its impacts or to its logical conclusions: the
overconsumption of resources, a disregard for the biosphere's tolerances,
and damages that can be permanent and negatively transformative. The
planet has "safe operating spaces" beyond which we should not go.

The Earth's carbon cycle is an example. The cycle consists of
sources and sinks. The carbon dioxide from our fossil energy consumption is overloading the cycle with more carbon than the sinks can
store. The carbon dioxide lingers in the atmosphere along with other
greenhouse gases and causes global warming. The result is climate
change. We might be more careful about the atmosphere's tolerances
if we understood how fragile it is. It's a very thin envelope of gases
that covers the planet and is held in place by gravity. The barely visible
aura around the Earth in the photo on the next page is the atmosphere
in its entirety.

As thin as it is, it has four layers. Our weather takes place in the
layer closest to the Earth's surface, the troposphere. Depending on the

The troposphere contains about 75 percent of the Earth's mass. Most of the gases responsible for climate change are found there. *NASA*

time of year, the troposphere is only 4 to 11 miles thick, the distance you might travel to and from shopping or a movie. It's also the layer where most greenhouse gases linger to produce the greenhouse effect.

We would better appreciate the atmosphere's fragility if we could see it from space, in person, in living color, and in real time. Many astronauts say the experience of seeing the Earth from space permanently changed them. When Apollo astronaut James B. Irwin came back, he recalled, "That beautiful, warm, living object looked so fragile, so delicate, that if you touched it with a finger it would crumble and fall apart. Seeing this has to change a man."[1] But until affordable tickets go on sale for tourist buses in space, the rest of us will have to trust science to tell us what makes the planet fall apart.

The biosphere seems to have its own homeostasis, the ability to maintain fairly stable conditions despite outside changes. But if we push on its limits too hard, bad things happen. Some are happening now.

The Stardust Family

It is simultaneously mind-boggling and off-putting to realize that we are related to all creatures great and small, including bedbugs, cockroaches, and vampire bats. E. O. Wilson, the distinguished biologist whose insights into the human condition I quote from time to time, is not an anthropologist, psychologist, or philosopher. He studies ants, yet many of his insights about the human condition come from those studies. It seems the more we study the more complex animals such as dogs, dolphins, and chimpanzees, the more we find that they understand a lot more than we thought. Chimps and crows make tools. Elephants show empathy. Humpback whales are known to save seals from killer whales. Some birds can talk. There are many examples of animals saving peoples' lives.

All species began as stardust or by a Divine act, depending on our points of view. The planet did not come with an operating manual for those who subscribe to evolution; humankind has studied and learned. Nature is a great teacher because, as one colleague pointed out, it has gone through billions of years of trial and error. For those who subscribe to creation theology, including Christians, Jews, and Muslims, the story of creation and the operating manual are in scripture. All three religions share a similar story of Adam and Eve.[2] Among Christians, there is debate about whether God instructed people to dominate creation or take care of it. There also are tensions between religion and science. Some time ago, during a casual conversation, a Christian minister helped me reconcile the two. "Science," he said, "is God's way of revealing the genius of His creation." For those who subscribe to this belief system, it follows that climate change is God's way of telling us we're messing up.

Whichever perspective we embrace, there are physical realities to deal with, like whether the planet can sustain 10 billion or more people striving for a materialistic middle-class lifestyle in a finite and climate-altered world.[3]

Several groups have tried to identify the planet's critical boundaries. The nonprofit Global Footprint Network calculates the point of the year at which human consumption of natural resources exceeds the planet's ability to replenish them. It calls that point "Earth Overshoot Day." In the 1980s, we reached it in November. In 2019, it happened in July. On our present course, the network says, we will exceed the Earth's regenerative ability every day of every year by mid-century.

A group of renowned scientists set out in 2009 to define the "safe operating spaces" mentioned earlier.[4] They identified nine processes that regulate the biosphere's resilience and stability.

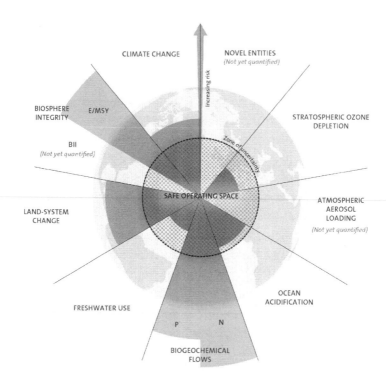

Scientists convened by the Stockholm Resilience Center identified nine planetary systems vital to humanity and the thresholds we cannot cross without undermining our ability to thrive. Humanity remains in safe territory in only three of the nine systems. *J. Lokrantz/Azote based on Steffen et al. 2015*[5]

Then they calculated the points at which humanity would cross into dangerous territory for each of the processes. They warned that crossing those thresholds would cause "large-scale abrupt or irreversible environmental changes." Humanity already has entered four "zones of uncertainty": climate change; the loss biodiversity including the extinction of species; changes in land uses such as deforestation; and biogeochemical flows, the movement of vital chemicals through the biosphere to support life. We already are at high risk of losing biodiversity and causing climate change. Significantly altering either would "drive the earth system into a new state."[6]

We were introduced to another perspective on global limits in 1972 when seventeen researchers ran computer simulations of what would happen to our world of finite resources if there were exponential economic and population growth. Their report, *The Limits to Growth*, sold 30 million copies and, like *Silent Spring*, was translated into thirty languages.[7]

The authors concluded that unless growth trends changed, we would experience a "sudden and uncontrollable decline in both population and industrial capacity." Critics immediately attacked their findings, their computer model, their methodology, and even the authors themselves. They were accused of underestimating the power of technologies and the genius of free markets. But the study confirmed that there were limits past which human activity should not go, a fact that is not consistent with the frontier mindset.

In 1992, the original authors published a sequel, *The Limits to Growth: The 30-Year Update*.[8] They pointed out that sea levels were rising, the income gap between rich and poor was widening, 75 percent of the world's oceans had been overfished, and 38 percent of the world's soils had been degraded.

The Limits to Growth inspired debates that continue today, even as events validate its central conclusion: there are limits to the planet's tolerances and it's a bad idea to exceed them.

Carbon Constraints

The atmosphere is like the Earth's thermostat. It contains nitrogen, oxygen, carbon dioxide, water vapor, dust particles, pollen, plant grains, and small amounts of other elements. We can credit that mixture for the Goldilocks effect—a planet that is not too hot, not too cold, but just right for civilization to flourish. However, we are adding greenhouse gases to the recipe, not only carbon dioxide but also methane, nitrous oxide, ozone, hydrofluorocarbons, perfluorocarbons, and sulfur hexafluoride. Carbon dioxide, methane, and nitrous oxide are of primary concern because they are associated most with human activity.

There are several ways to identify the planet's safe operating space in regard to global warming. One is greenhouse gas concentrations in the atmosphere. The preindustrial concentration was in the range of 260 to 270 ppm (parts per million). We have reached about 415 ppm, and the concentration is climbing. The long-term goal is to bring concentrations back to about 350.

Scientists calculate that we are producing 120 percent more fossil fuels than is safe. If we keep burning the fuels at that level, some say, we will exceed the remaining carbon budget in as little as three years. The IPCC estimated in 2018 there were only twelve years left at today's pollution levels if we want a 66 percent chance of holding global warming to 1.5 degrees C.

The well-regarded policy institute Climate Analytics calculates that the carbon-cutting policies in place around the world right now would result in about 3°C of warming by the end of this century, twice the current international goal. And if all nations ignored global warming, the temperature would climb 4.8 degrees C or more above preindustrial times. The important point is that we are not on a safe trajectory, no matter what measure we use,

The fossil energy sector is being confronted by another limit: the amount of risk that the industry's stakeholders are willing to accept, including investors, shareholders, regulators, and insurers. There are multiple risks including more stringent government regulations, a high

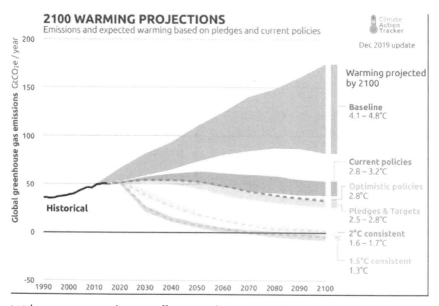

Without a more ambitious effort to reduce CO_2 pollution, the world is headed for about 3°C of warming by 2100. *Copyright 2020 ClimateActionTracker.org*

carbon price (a fee added to fossil fuels to reflect the social costs of carbon), an unflinching international commitment to phase out fossil fuels, and the sector's inability to develop commercially competitive technologies to keep its carbon pollution out of the atmosphere.

Coal, oil, and natural gas are already having trouble competing worldwide with solar energy, wind energy, bioenergy, and other renewable resources. Solar and wind are less expensive than fossil fuels in many places today, and they will soon be less expensive everywhere. If a carbon price is tacked on to fossil fuels, or if they lose their government subsidies, they will be even less able to compete.

Another risk is the flurry of lawsuits that cities have filed against oil companies to hold them liable for damages from sea-level rise, floods, and other adverse climate impacts. As 2020 began, nine states and cities had filed lawsuits against major fossil fuel companies. Some accuse Exxon of fraud because investigations found the company knew as far back as the 1970s that its products were contributing to climate change but hid the knowledge and discredited the same findings by other scientists. Lawsuits by cities in California alone have sought billions of dollars to pay for seawalls and other measures to mitigate climate impacts.

All of these risks are beginning to sink in among the industry's stakeholders. In February 2020, before the pandemic was a factor, Goldman Sachs advised investors to sell their shares in ExxonMobil. Goldman predicted that by 2025, the world's sixth-largest oil company would earn only half the profits it anticipates. Goldman concluded there is no compelling case for people to hold onto ExxonMobil stock.[9]

In November 2019, analysts at Corporate Knights reported that three major state pension funds—two in California and one in Colorado—lost a total of $19 billion over a decade by investing in fossil fuels.[10] The three funds manage pensions for roughly 3.6 million public employees, including retired teachers, police officers, firefighters, correction officers, snowplow drivers, state troopers, and other public employees.

J. P. Morgan economists have advised clients that they "cannot rule out catastrophic outcomes where human life as we know it is threatened" by climate change.[11]

In February 2020, British Petroleum said it plans to be carbon neutral by 2050. In June, the company announced it planned to write off as much

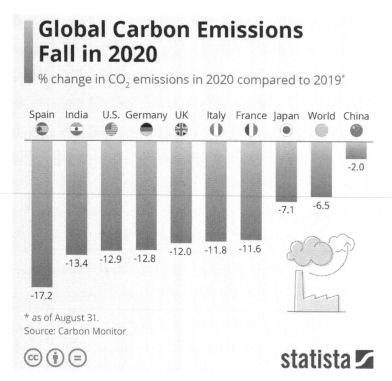

Global Carbon Emissions Fall in 2020

% change in CO_2 emissions in 2020 compared to 2019*

Spain	India	U.S.	Germany	UK	Italy	France	Japan	World	China

-2.0

-7.1   -6.5

-13.4   -12.9   -12.8   -12.0   -11.8   -11.6

-17.2

* as of August 31.
Source: Carbon Monitor

statista

Human-caused carbon emissions leveled off in 2019 after two years of increases. The rising popularity of clean renewable energy was a factor. Carbon emissions have gone down in developed countries, but up in developing nations. *Politico*

as $17.5 billion in the second quarter because of lower demand "in line with a range of transition paths consistent with the Paris climate goals."[12]

"The world's changed," CNBC's Jim Cramer observed. "New money managers want to appease younger people who believe that you can't ever make a fossil fuel company sustainable. . . . You can tell that the world's turned on them, and it's actually kind of happening very quickly."

Despite the many different ways of defining limits, there is one common denominator: by 2050, the global economy should emit no more CO_2 than nature and technology can capture and store. The term is "net-zero carbon." After mid-century, we will have to work our way back to ~350 ppm by taking more CO_2 out of the atmosphere than we put in. That is called "net-negative carbon."

Our belated awareness of the atmosphere's limits raises questions very similar to those we should ask about flood control. If we need new technologies to take carbon out of the air, what will they be? Do we try to manipulate the troposphere like we tried to control rivers, or is there a more harmonious way?

Some researchers are interested in a group of mostly untested ideas called geoengineering. It is the "deliberate large-scale intervention in the Earth's natural systems to counteract climate change." However, we should have learned from the dam-building era that we should not intervene in the Earth's natural systems on any scale without fully understanding the consequences.

Reforestation and afforestation are considered natural geoengineering, but other ideas range from intriguing to dangerous and weird.[13] One set of proposals is called solar radiation management, the idea of reflecting more sunlight back into space. Some of its advocates recommend stationing an aluminum mirror in space, but it would have to be the size of Greenland. Another proposal would use balloons or aircraft to inject reflective sulfate aerosols into the stratosphere. But what effect would blocking sunlight have on the photosynthesis necessary to grow food and the forests and plants that serve as carbon sinks?

More grounded ideas include shinier crops, buildings that reflect sunlight, "microbubbles" that make oceans more reflective, and iron dumped into oceans to stimulate the growth of phytoplankton, a carbon-absorbing single-cell alga. Another idea would deploy huge fans to suck air though filters and trap CO_2. Manufactures would use it to make an array of products.

These ideas require a level of systems thinking we have not seen with other engineered interventions in nature. We must look far beyond the first-order impacts of new technologies to identify how they would influence entire environmental, economic, and social systems.

We will see whether our experience with rivers has taught us anything.

Counting the Uncounted

We might be more inclined to protect nature if we knew its value in measurable and familiar terms. So, ecologist Walter Westman proposed in 1977 that we convert ecosystem values into dollars and cents.[14]

However, to understand the true value of an ecosystem, we must count all of its direct and indirect social, environmental, and economic benefits and costs over its entire lifetime. Without this type of systems thinking and analysis, we have compromised ecosystems without being aware of what we would lose.

It wasn't until 1995 that a group of prominent scholars met in New Hampshire to talk about writing a major book on ecosystem services.[15] They did the book, but the more significant outcome of the meeting was the ambitious idea of computing the dollar value of nature's services at global scale. A team of thirteen researchers led by Robert Costanza, at the time a professor of sustainability at Portland State University, published the result in 1997.[16] The team found that the minimum value for seventeen ecosystem services was $33 trillion per year. It was an astonishing number, twice the global gross national product at the time.[17]

Some in the environmental community thought that $33 trillion was too high, while others felt it was too low. Some people were unhappy because it seemed to imply that everything should be measured by its monetary value rather than its intrinsic worth. Costanza's answer was, "Every time we build homes, schools, and hospitals, which are essential for human wellbeing, we appropriate ecosystems and impact our natural capital. Thus, being more explicit about the value of ecosystem services and natural capital can help society make better decisions in the many cases in which trade-offs exist."[18]

A next step took place from 2001 to 2005. More than 1,360 experts from around the world conducted the Millennium Ecosystem Assessment under the auspices of the United Nations.[19] They evaluated ecosystem conditions, changes, and trends, and what they mean for human well-being. Their conclusions were much like those issued by the Intergovernmental Panel on Climate Change.

The assessment reported that over the previous fifty years "humans have changed ecosystems more rapidly and extensively than in any comparable period of time in human history, largely to meet rapidly growing demands for food, fresh water, timber, fiber and fuel. This has resulted in a substantial and largely irreversible loss in the diversity of life on Earth."

The degradation of ecosystem services is on track to get far worse during the first half of this century. Unless it is reversed, future generations will be deprived of the benefits that past generations have enjoyed. Reversing the degradation will require significant changes in policies, institutions, and practices that are not currently underway.

In 2014, Costanza led another team of researchers to update his 1997 calculation of the value of global ecosystem services.[20] They concluded that in 2011, ecosystem services were worth as much as $145 trillion per year, more than twice global GDP. But they also found that from 1997 to 2011, the world lost as much as $20 trillion worth of ecoservices because of land-use changes such as wetland and forest loss.

The new estimates sparked a flurry of academic research so that by 2017, more than seventeen thousand papers from around the world had been published on the topic. Within five years, a newly launched journal, *Ecosystem Services*, published more than four hundred research review and commentary papers. The work continues today in academia, government, and industry to improve our ability to value ecosystems.

Gross National Happiness

Another example of new math is worth mentioning: what is the value of happiness, and how do we measure it? The Constitution does not guarantee the national cash flow; it guarantees the pursuit of happiness. Yet we haven't known until recently how to verify that society is fulfilling that promise.

In a famous speech he gave while running for the presidency in 1968, Robert Kennedy gave an elegant and widely quoted description of why measuring GDP is not enough:

Our Gross National Product, now, is over $800 billion dollars a year, but that Gross National Product—if we judge the United States of America by that—that Gross National Product counts air pollution and cigarette advertising, and ambulances to clear our highways of carnage. It counts special locks for our doors and the jails for the people who break them. It counts the destruction of the redwood and the loss of our natural wonder in chaotic sprawl. It counts napalm and counts nuclear warheads and armored cars for the police to fight the riots in our cities. It counts Whitman's rifle and Speck's knife, and the television programs which glorify violence in order to sell toys to our children.

Yet the gross national product does not allow for the health of our children, the quality of their education, or the joy of their play. It does not include the beauty of our poetry or the strength of our marriages, the intelligence of our public debate or the integrity of our public officials. It measures neither our wit nor our courage, neither our wisdom nor our learning, neither our compassion nor our devotion to our country, it measures everything in short, except that which makes life worthwhile.

And it can tell us everything about America except why we are proud that we are Americans.

Several nations, international organizations, and US states are using "happiness indicators" to measure Gross National Happiness (GNH) as a supplement to GDP. The nation of Bhutan was the first to develop a method to measure Gross Domestic Happiness (GDH).[21] In 1972, it identified thirty-three indicators including psychological well-being, health, education, leisure, cultural diversity, governance, community vitality, ecological diversity, and living standards. Proximity to nature is another measure of GDH. *Science Daily* published one of many studies about this, reporting that time near green spaces reduces the risks of type II diabetes, cardiovascular disease, premature birth and death, stress, and high blood pressure.[22]

The United Nations General Assembly followed Bhutan's example in 2011, declaring that happiness is a "fundamental human goal." In 2015, the UN's member nations agreed to the requirements of a good life. It endorsed seventeen global sustainable development goals and 169 specific targets, all to be accomplished by 2030. If there is a weakness in this list, it's that human interaction with nature is mentioned only in passing.[23]

In the United States, we have flirted with ecological math for at least twenty years in the context of carbon pollution and climate change. Congress nearly passed legislation in 2009 to put a price on carbon—in other words, a fee added to the prices of fossil fuels to reflect their cost to society, the environment, and the economy. The House of Representative approved a bill that would do this through a so-called cap and trade system, where a firm limit would be set on CO_2 emissions, and polluters would buy emission allowances they could trade with other polluters. The Senate let the bill die.

More recently, there has been talk about a different approach: simply adding a fee to the market prices of coal, oil, and natural gas in hopes that the higher price would encourage the development and use of cleaner fuels. However, Congress has not acted on that idea.

The Obama administration developed another type of ecological mathematics called the social cost of carbon. It was a method for federal agencies to calculate the economic, environmental, and social impacts of CO_2 as part of rulemaking. The Trump administration weakened the formula to significantly underestimate the real costs of CO_2 emissions. President Biden has revived the interagency working group Obama created to compute carbon's social costs and has directed it to update the calculation.

Ecological math is in its infancy. "We still have a long way to go," Costanza says, "especially since policy debates in most countries are still dominated by narrow, mainstream economic ideas and policies." The idea is to keep improving this new math as we understand more about the costs and benefits of things we haven't known how to quantify before.

21

THE RESTORATION ECONOMY

For two hundred years or so, we've been creating the twenty-first century's biggest jobs program. It's to fix all the things we've broken.

—William S. Becker

A FEW OF OUR BEST ENVIRONMENTAL AUTHORS have written that nature is no longer natural and therefore no longer exists. For better or worse, usually worse, our species has modified the biosphere in life-threatening and irreversible ways. Nature has become a human construct, altered by chemicals and plastics and the ability to create life in the laboratory, produce designer babies, and edit the DNA of living things, including ourselves.

The morality of doing these things, the level of judgment they require, and the possibility they will be misused is secondary to the excitement of discovery and the feeling of godlike power. Scientists have transplanted the genes of human brains into monkeys, while others have created "human-animal chimeras"—embryos that are part human, part something else. Because of some perceived or possible benefit, we push science into places it probably should not go simply because we can. For forty dollars, kids can now purchase genetic design "starter kits." For $350, they can step up to a "Bioengineering 101 Beginner Kit—No

Experience Needed." We know how to militarize atoms into bombs and germs into biological weapons, and we are knowingly infusing ourselves and other species with toxins and plastics.

"In the beginning, human beings tended to view nature as a mortal enemy—with wariness, dread, and aggression. The war began before we had even bothered to name our enemy," author Nathaniel Rich has written.[1] "Almost no rock, leaf, or cubic foot of air on Earth has escaped our clumsy signature." It appears that no genome will escape our signature, either. Many of us still think of nature as an enemy, or a savage to be tamed and put into our service, or a treasure chest of inexhaustible resources to which God has given us the key.

Another bestselling author, journalist Elizabeth Kolbert, points out we now develop new technologies to repair the damages other technologies have done, as we fall deeper and deeper into a technological rabbit hole and farther away from the natural world. Nature provides us with trillions of dollars' worth of free services, but we have ignored or destroyed them thinking we could do their jobs better. Flood "control" structures are a perfect example.

Another example, still mostly conceptual, is the family of "geoengineering" technologies. They include some advantageous uses of nature, like planting trees and restoring wetlands. However, others would modify and manipulate natural systems and processes, up to and including the planet's most important life-support systems.

Questioning how we use technology does not make us Luddites. Wondering if we really need to know what a human with a monkey brain would be like does not mean that we disdain knowledge or scientific inquiry. Innovation is universally praised as good, but not all is. Some creates devalue chains; some begin as positives and turn into negatives. From splitting the atom to unearthing carbon, science and industry have endangered the societies they helped to build and the lives they were supposed to improve. Sometimes because of willful negligence, tunnel vision, or insufficient diligence, our technologies produce unintended but foreseeable consequences. So, as Kolbert points out, we have to beget new technologies to fix what we begot. At this moment, for example, scientists and engineers are working on a scheme to cool the planet by spreading glitter in the troposphere to reflect sunlight back into space before it can reach the Earth's surface. But the same sunlight makes agriculture, photosynthesis, solar power, and the sunglass industry possible.

In some cases, we employ our top scientists and engineers to solve political problems. For example, researchers at DOE have been working for twenty-five years to remove the oxymoron from "clean coal." The coal industry wants to remain relevant in a decarbonized world. So, Congress has spent billions of dollars for DOE to develop a way to trap carbon dioxide at power plants before it pollutes the atmosphere. The technology is called carbon capture and sequestration (CCS). People in high places, including the White House and the International Energy Agency, believe the world can't avoid catastrophic climate change without CCS. On close inspection, however, CCS has less to do with preventing climate change than saving coal and natural gas companies from having to leave trillions of dollars of assets in the ground.

CCS strips carbon dioxide from power-plant flue gases. Power plants use steam and electricity to turn the gas into a supercritical fluid—a state between liquid and gas. The hope is that pipelines would carry the fluid to a suitable geologic formation where it would be injected and, if all went well, trapped forever. CCS would allow fossil fuel companies to keep blasting, drilling, and fracturing to unearth carbon until the last cubic foot of gas and ton of coal are gone.

But while a few industries and power plants already use CCS as demonstrations, it is still too expensive for widespread commercialization. Several projects have failed because CCS is hampered by formidable barriers. Power plants have to be much larger and more expensive. They use a significant amount of the energy they produce to decarbonize the electricity they sell. That increases their fuel costs and the price customers must pay for electricity. CCS plants use more water than conventional power plants, which is an issue because thermoelectric power plants already use 40 percent of the fresh water drawn in the US, mostly to cool their equipment.[2]

Solar and wind energy have none of these problems, and they are already less expensive than electricity generated with coal, natural gas, and nuclear power plants. But political leaders like CCS because it helps keep the fossil energy lobby off the warpath about the decarbonization imperative.

CCS is a classic case of reductionist rather than systems thinking. Because so many decades have passed without significant climate action, every molecule of carbon dioxide counts. But CCS doesn't capture all of a plant's carbon pollution and it does nothing for the emissions from extracting, processing, and transporting fossil fuels. In fact, it appears there can be no more investment in or construction of fossil energy power plants and infrastructure if we want to achieve the goals of the Paris climate accord, let alone the more aggressive reductions in greenhouse gas emissions necessary to avoid catastrophic climate changes. Research at the University of California, Irvine found in 2019 that if we used the fossil energy infrastructure in place and planned at that time, it would be impossible to hold global warming to 1.5°C.[3] One of the study's principal investigators reports that the "committed emissions" from existing and planned fossil energy infrastructure grew 9 percent between 2018 and 2019.[4] Yet oil and gas companies are still building pipelines and international banks are still lending them the money. We can expect the fossil-fuel lobby to keep pressuring Congress for more money to repair, replace, and build more new infrastructure.

While work has been underway on CCS and other technical fixes to climate change, the world's "carbon budget"—the amount of greenhouse gases we can emit while still avoiding catastrophic global warming—is getting smaller. Global emissions declined in 2020 during the pandemic, but they were projected to rise in 2021, more than any year on record except 2010. It's clear that CCS cannot contribute to the worldwide effort to keep global warming in check; in fact, it would help make the effort futile.

Heavenly Junk

Long ago, we looked into the night sky to guide our ships, enjoy the beauty of the stars, or contemplate the imponderable infinity of space. Now we look up at a revolving garbage dump filled with millions of pieces of dead satellites, human refuse, and discarded hardware. Space trash endangers astronauts and their crafts. A Japanese company recently launched a janitorial spacecraft to search out and remove some of it, for example by pushing dead satellites into the Earth's atmosphere so they burn up. There is even an intact Tesla up there, presumably with its crash-avoidance software engaged.

But nothing has given mortal man more immortality than plastics. They fill the bellies of sea animals that starve thinking they've eaten, they litter the beaches of island paradises, and they create floating islands of garbage in the oceans. The Great Pacific Garbage Patch in the north Pacific Ocean contained 1.8 trillion pieces of plastic in 2019 and had grown to twice the size of Texas in 2020. The Pacific patch is the most famous, but there are others of significance in the North Atlantic, the South Atlantic, and Indian Oceans. However, a lot of civilization's detritus is closer and more personal.

Toxins Within Us

"We are as gods and might as well get good at it," Steward Brand wrote in 1968. But we have not gotten good at it. Our hubris is ruining oceans, soils, forests, the atmosphere, biological diversity, and ourselves.

If we go to the beach for a Blue Mind experience, we might be disillusioned. On virtually any beach, we are likely to encounter human flotsam coughed up by the seas. We may come across fish strangled by the plastic rings from six packs. More than one million seabirds die every year after choking on plastic straws they thought were food. Whales and dolphins are found dead or dying on beaches with their stomachs full of plastic. By 2050, some predict, plastic in the oceans will weigh more than all the fish. Plastics can be found everywhere on Earth.

But if we want to encounter plastic pollution, we don't have to go to the beach. We don't have to go anywhere because we carry plastic pollution inside us.

Journalist David Ewing Duncan decided to conduct an experiment. He checked into Mount Sinai Hospital in New York City and gave fourteen vials of blood along with a urine sample to test whether he had any contaminants in his body. A few weeks later, the results showed that chemicals infused his body, including some he absorbed when he was in his mother's womb and others he ingested with his mother's breast milk. His blood contained traces of DDT and other pesticides, along with lead and dioxins.

Duncan called this his chemical diary of the previous forty years. The tests raised his awareness that chemicals enter his body every day through his nose, mouth, and skin. They come from phthalates in his shampoo, plastic food wraps, and the dashboard of his car. The dioxins in his blood could have originated at paper mills, incinerators, or chemical factories. Mercury, a neurotoxin, probably came from coal-fired power plants. Duncan figured he ingested it by eating halibut and swordfish from his local market. His body also contained a flame retardant called PBDE, which has been found in polar bears, killer whales, and other species as well as human breast milk. It could have come from the flame retardants the law requires in airplane interiors. "The compounds escape from plastic and fabrics and dust particles or gases that cling to dust," Duncan explained. "People inhale the dust; infants crawling on the floor get an especially high dose."

In sufficient concentrations, these substances cause cancer and impair reproductive health, learning, memory, and behavior. Many chemicals are introduced from products made to solve other problems. The medical professions are still trying to understand their effects. Duncan points out his tests did not cover many thousands of compounds that might be in his blood and urine samples or were "chemical cocktails" made from several chemicals. But as far as his doctor was concerned, Duncan was healthy.[5]

Others aren't so lucky. According to another article, "there are numerous types of pollution from indoor and outdoor sources. Indoor pollution examples include formaldehyde, mold, carbon monoxide, and tobacco smoke. Examples of outdoor pollution include benzene, sulfur monoxide, ozone, and hydrochloric acid from industrial operations. They commonly enter the human body through the skin, eyes, ears, nose and/or mouth. Each of these substances represents a significant threat to human health, causing anything from acute sudden illness to long-term chronic diseases and even death."[6]

Researchers at Columbia University warn, "We are continually exposed to a mixture of pollutants, which lead to changes in our bodies in multiple domains, from conception to old age. They govern gene expression, train and shape our immune systems, trigger physiological responses, and determine well-being and disease."[7]

Plastics are one of the most pervasive. Researchers at Arizona State University studied cadaver organs and found plastic contamination in every lung, liver, spleen, and kidney they examined. More specifically, they found microplastics so small they can be passed from digestive systems into bloodstreams. Plastics do not biodegrade. They break down into microplastics about the size of sesame seeds.

"People who want to avoid ingesting plastic are out of luck, given all of the plastic in the environment," one of the researchers said. "It's impossible to completely protect ourselves from plastic ingestion," another agreed. "Microplastics have been measured in tap water and bottled water, and in the air we breathe." It's difficult to remove them because they are so small. Studies have determined that the average person eats about two thousand microplastics every week, about 5 grams, the rough equivalent of a credit card.

Geologists call plastics a new "mineral" dispersed around the planet so thoroughly that it's one of the reasons for declaring the Anthropocene.

So, there is ample reason to conclude that we have denatured nature. But it does still exist, just as polluted humans are still humans. And not all of the damages our species has caused are irreversible. We should restore as much health to the biosphere as we can. We should still fight to protect biodiversity, ecosystems and their services, and the psychological and spiritual benefits of nature in forests or cities. Many more of us experienced nature's therapeutic effects during the pandemic when we took breaks from quarantine for walks outside. The natural world is simply worth saving, even if it can't be returned to its virgin state.

Each of us is contaminated even before birth. None of us is pristine. No matter how carefully we take care of ourselves, we are filled with toxins and inorganics. Even so, we should not give up trying to be healthier. To the extent we can restore ourselves, we can more fully live the lives we have.

Similarly, those who point out that we have entered the Anthropo-cene would not argue that nature is so far gone that we might as well stop trying to restore, conserve, and protect it. Even profit-obsessed neoliberals should care because environmental restoration is a sig-nificant contributor to the economy and a source of wealth as well as health.

The Restoration Economy

Millions of Americans are engaged in careers to protect and restore the natural world. Environmental restoration is a significant source of jobs and GDP.[8] We don't know precisely how many Americans are employed in the restoration sector because the federal government does not track green jobs. But by the end of 2018, nearly 3.3 million Americans worked in clean energy, energy efficiency, renewable energy, solar and wind energy, and clean vehicles. They qualify as part of the restoration economy because they help restore air and water quality. There were three times as many jobs in clean energy as there were in fossil fuels.[9]

Researchers Lucien Georgeson and Mark Maslin at University Col-lege London concluded in 2019 that the green economy in the United States was generating more than $1.3 trillion annually, or 16.5 percent of the global green economy.[10] They found that low-carbon environ-mental goods and service businesses employed 9.5 million workers. President Trump expected his all-out support for fossil fuels to create four hundred thousand new jobs, but the coal industry lost thirty-seven thousand.[11]

Revenues and employment in the clean energy sector grew 20 per-cent in fiscal years 2012–2013 and 2015–2016 when the Obama administration was developing regulations to control greenhouse gas pollution from vehicles, power plants, and natural gas infrastructure. But after two years of the Trump presidency, clean energy jobs grew only 3.6 percent.[12]

Researchers at the University of North Carolina, Chapel Hill, found in 2015 that the restoration economy employed two hundred thousand people—more than the number of workers in iron and steel mills, coal mining, or logging. It was a $25 billion industry in the United States with positions ranging from scientists and foresters to construction workers, engineers, and heavy-equipment operators.[13]

The Federal Reserve Bank of Boston confirmed these findings in 2016.[14] It found that 221,000 people worked in the restoration economy, producing $24.8 billion in GDP, more than $1 billion in local and state tax revenues, and more than $2 billion in taxes for the federal government. At least twenty-five federal environmental laws had resulted in more than 1,118 restoration projects since 2000, with some in every state, the bank said. This disproves the claim that government regulations are job-killers.

The federal government itself engages in environmental protection and restoration at national parks and on federal lands. It found that every $1 million it invests in ecosystem restoration creates as many as thirty-two full-time jobs and $3.4 million in economic output. The Chapel Hill team concluded that federal restoration work demonstrates that "environmental stewardship and economic development can, in fact, be synergistic, as the process of ecological restoration directly contributes to socioeconomic well-being."[15]

These data are important if we want to know whether a net-zero-carbon economy involves sacrifice or sustainable growth. The data also help us track how the United States is doing in the global green economy. The Georgeson and Maslin research showed that the green economy in the United States is larger than that in other countries, but it could change as green industries expand worldwide. As a report on their research states, "If the US wants to extend economic growth, it should double down on cleaning up the environment and fighting climate change, which are fueling both jobs and revenue."[16]

We will see the green job force grow as the Biden administration reinstates environmental regulations that Trump rescinded. Compliance with those regulations will create a wide variety of jobs, and disprove the myth that the government's environmental rules are job-killers.

Where the Jobs Are

- Reforestation
- Avoided forest conversion
- Improved forest management
- Forest plantations to allow forest regeneration
- Cropland nutrient management
- Conservation agriculture
- Wetland conservation/restoration
- Grazing improvements
- Better animal management/feeds
- Biochar additions to soils
- Grasslands

Restoration puts ecosystems and people back to work. The Costanza study cited earlier found that worldwide ecosystem services were worth $145 trillion in 2011, twice global GDP. The failure to protect them sacrificed services worth $20 trillion.

Revived and healthy ecosystems are also indispensable contributors to stabilizing the climate. Research published by the *Proceedings of the National Academy of Sciences* shows that a suite of twenty "natural climate solutions" implemented between now and 2030 could provide a third of the cost-effective steps the world needs to stabilize warming at less than 2°C above preindustrial levels.[17]

How much is the federal government investing in eco-restoration? According to USGS, federal appropriations were $2.5 billion in one recent year, while public and private investments were nearly $4 billion, and nonprofit investments exceeded $4.3 billion. That's a good start, but we need more ways to finance environmental healing. Organizations such as the World Resource Institute are exploring how restoration can attract more private investment by delivering even higher financial returns.

Some states are working on their own innovative financing. Indiana and Maryland created revolving loans for flood mitigation projects. Maryland's fund has financed nearly $3 million in loans to protect more than 200,000 linear feet of shoreline. Iowa created a fund with local sales taxes. After catastrophic floods in 2010, Minnesota used $50 million in bonds for recovery, leveraged in part with a higher gas tax.[18]

So, here's a radical thought: all who plan and invest in infrastructure should acknowledge that ecosystems are in that category, too, and they provide multiple co-benefits. A highway does not recharge groundwater, or slow floods, or provide habitat for wildlife like a wetland does. The Environmental Protection Agency should ensure that environmental impact statements required by law assess whether government-funded projects reduce or add to ecosystem services and their co-benefits.

Employing the Displaced

The necessary shift to a net-zero carbon economy will be disruptive for some members of society, particularly the workers and communities whose economic security has depended on fossil fuels. Similar disruption occurs with every significant change in technology. What makes the energy transition especially disruptive is the depth and breadth of fossil fuels in the economy and society.

The positive news is that the green economy is replacing old jobs with new jobs. It can create many more jobs as the nation gets more serious about addressing climate change and environmental degradation. The federal government's energy-statistics organization, the Energy Information Administration (EIA), expects renewable energy technologies to provide only 21 percent of America's electricity in 2020. EIA expects that if we continue busines as usual, renewables will generate 42 percent of the nation's power in 2050.[19] But those are very conservative predictions. The world's leading renewable-energy research institution, DOE's National Renewable Energy Laboratory (NREL), says that with the right infrastructure investments, current solar, wind, hydropower, and other renewable energy technologies could generate 80 percent or more of the nation's power by that time.[20]

Before the pandemic began, the US had 344,000 jobs in solar electricity generation, while wind power generation employed 115,000. But many states have much higher jobs potential because they are not yet even close to capturing the full potential of their solar and wind resources.

Onshore wind energy and solar photovoltaics will resume their rapid growth as the US and global economies recover. In fact, global electric production from solar and wind technologies grew 19 and 11 percent respectively in 2020 during the pandemic.[21] They remain the least expensive source of new power generation for two-thirds of the world's population, according to *Bloomberg New Energy Finance.*[22] And in the US, we can expect a boom in offshore wind power, including turbines on floating platforms in deep-water locations.

The ongoing growth of the renewable energy sector opens the door to good jobs for workers displaced from the fossil energy sector. The United Mine Workers' Cecil Roberts is not asking for too much when he petitions Biden for a good transition strategy for his workers. A study four years ago concluded it would have cost less than $2 billion, about 0.0052 percent of the federal budget, for the government to train all of America's coal workers to participate in the transition to zero-carbon energy.[23]

This would help coal and other fossil energy workers shift from declining to rapidly growing industries. One projection is that the global renewable energy market will reach nearly $2 trillion by 2026, another estimates $23 trillion by 2030, but leaders in the solar and wind power industries have reported shortages of skilled workers.[24] After hearing testimony from small business owners in the clean energy sector, the chair of the US House of Representatives' committee in charge of workforce development noted that "as demand for clean energy has risen, small firms have struggled to hire the necessary number of works to keep pace."[25] The shortage is driven in part by the unique skills and certifications required in clean energy industries, he said.

The federal government operates several job-training and apprenticeship programs, but the center-right American Action Forum says that "current federal training programs do not effectively provide workers with the skills that employers require." They need to be "tailored to current and future economic demand."[26]

President Biden's infrastructure plan would help create that demand in a program to reclaim abandoned mines. An estimated 534,000 hardrock mines have been abandoned and require remediation in the United States. More than 7,800 are known to have physical or environmental

hazards and nearly 82,000 have unconfirmed hazards.[27] Some are producing highly acidic water that threatens surface and groundwater. Public safety is an issue because structures at mine sites can be dangerous.
From 2001 to 2017, 278 people died from drowning, falling, or suf-
focating in these mines. Most victims were between the ages of eleven
and twenty.

In 1981, the federal government began requiring mining companies to rehabilitate retired mine sites. Instead, many operators skipped
town, and some mines are now Superfund sites.[28] Reclaiming all of
the abandoned mines would cost as much as $72 billion, according
to the DOI.

Federal law treats coal mines differently. It requires coal companies to post bonds to cover the cost of mine remediation. But this may
become a problem because of the number of coal companies going bank-
rupt. Between 2010 and the first quarter of 2019, more than 546 coal-
fired power plants were retired, according to the US Energy Information
Administration.[29] Journalist Michael Coren writes that some mine owners might simply walk away and abandon their mines.[30]

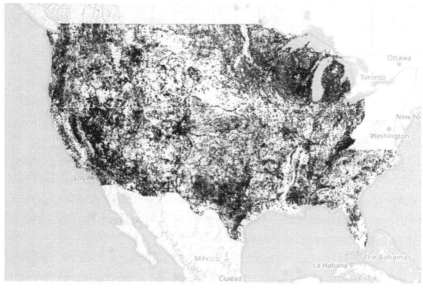

Prospect pits, mine shafts and entrances, quarries, open-pit mines, gravel
and borrow pits in the United States. *US Geological Survey*

He cites the example of a company called ERP Environmental Fund. It reportedly accumulated 160 environmental violations but ignored orders to remedy them. Coren says the company posted $115 million in bonds, but it was not enough to cover the more than one hundred mining permits it had acquired. When the company appeared to run out of cash, West Virginia's environmental agency attempted to be first in line among creditors by putting the mines into receivership. The danger, Coren says, is that other marginal coal companies will follow ERP's example, leaving the state to clean up their mines. This would be an opportunity, albeit unfortunate, to create new remediation jobs.

Tear Down That Dam!

Another emerging opportunity is dam and levee removal to restore watersheds and riparian ecosystems. American Rivers reports that nearly eighteen hundred dams have been demolished since 1912, most of them in the past thirty years. In 2020, sixty-nine dams were taken down because the structures were aging and unsafe or because it became too costly for their owners to maintain them.[31]

Job opportunities in dam removal will grow because so many of the structures are well past their intended reliable lives. "When you begin to look at it on a coldly analytical basis, the shift in the last 40 years has

The Marmot Dam is removed from the Sandy River in Oregon. *NOAA*

been away from dam construction and toward dam removal," according to a former reclamation commissioner, Daniel Beard. He calls this development "inexorable."[32]

At Olympic National Park in Washington, the National Park Service supervised the removal of two dams and reservoirs on the Elwha River. The river flows naturally now so that sediment that was trapped by the dams can rebuild river and shoreline habitats. Native vegetation has returned to the drained reservoirs, and salmon and trout are migrating through the river for the first time in a century.

In Maine, seven conservation organizations, the Penobscot Indian Nation, and area hydroelectric companies are removing two of three dams on the Penobscot River and creating a bypass at a third dam. The objective is to improve access for eleven species of sea-run fish to 1,000 miles of habitat while allowing hydro companies to continue producing clean electricity. Sponsors call it one of the most creative restoration projects in the nation's history.

There are many business, job, and career opportunities in other forms of climate-change adaptation, mitigation, and environmental restoration. The relocation of floodplain homes would create local construction jobs; so would more resources to accelerate the restoration of the Great Lakes, ocean and Gulf coasts, and to revegetate watersheds.

States Lead the Energy Transition

Wind, solar, and other renewable electricity technologies have grown into a $64 billion market in the United States.[33] States deserve a lot of the credit. Half of the national growth of these technologies is the result of states that have diversified their energy mix with renewable resources since the beginning of the 2000s.

In 1983, Iowa became the first state to create what is now called a renewable portfolio standard (RPS). Today, thirty states, Washington, DC, and three US territories have adopted RPSs, requirements that electric utilities generate specific percentages of power with solar, wind, and other renewable fuels. Another seven states and a territory have established renewable energy goals. Fourteen states require that 50 percent or more of their electricity must be generated with renewable resources by specific future dates.[34] Fourteen states and the District of Columbia intend to eventually obtain 100 percent of their energy from renewable resources, or to eliminate 100 percent of carbon emissions from their power sectors.

With the costs of renewable power generation dropping, more than half the states with RPSs have made them more ambitious since 2015. In addition, a growing number of states are establishing targets for energy storage—an important capability for solar and wind because they are intermittent resources. Storage allows utilities to set aside power from sunny and windy periods so the power can be used at night or when the weather is especially cloudy and still.

There is no national standard for renewable energy use or energy efficiency, although many clean energy advocates believe there should be.

Most states have renewable portfolio standards and goals

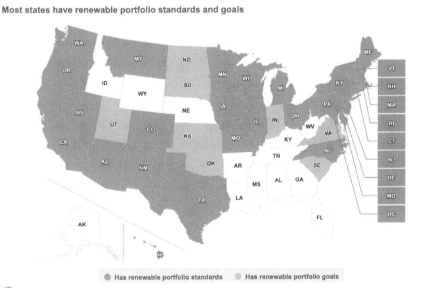

● Has renewable portfolio standards ● Has renewable portfolio goals

eia Source: Database of State Incentives for Renewable Energy & Efficiency®, June 2019

States with renewable energy standards and goals. States with the darkest shading have created renewable energy standards that require electric utilities to produce specific percentages of their power with renewable resources. States with a medium tint, such as Kansas and Oklahoma, have set voluntary goals. The lightest states, such as those in the South, have neither. *US Energy Information Administrations*

The transition to a net-zero-carbon economy is so important that states should resist any temptation to roll back their goals and standards because of problems with the economy in the years ahead. We will not reach the zero-carbon goal without an aggressive and persistent commitment to keep pushing forward.

Consistency is critical at the national level, too. We need a detailed national plan for the transition to clean energy economy, complete with clear milestones and ways to measure progress. As difficult as it may be to reach bipartisan consensus, a national energy plan would reduce false starts, duplication, and wasted resources in what must be the most rapid-ever transformation in how we power our economy. But before a plan, we need a clear vision of the future we want.

22

THE VISION THING

> The first step toward creating an improved future is
> developing the ability to envision it. Vision will ignite the
> fire of passion that fuels our commitment to do whatever
> it takes to achieve excellence.
>
> —Hall of Fame football coach Tony Dungy

THE LATE GEORGE HERBERT WALKER BUSH, the forty-first president of the
United States, was a gentleman of the old school. He was known for his
handwritten thank-you notes. President Bush spent time in the evenings
writing hundreds of them, maybe thousands, during his presidency. It is
one reason that history remembers the elder Bush for his "grace, civility
and social conscience."

However, he is also remembered for a shortcoming. He did not have
a clear concept of where he wanted to take the country, at least not a
concept he could express. He was said to be great with the complexities
of the many issues that presidents deal with, but he didn't have "the
vision thing," as he called it. Ever since, pundits have used that phrase
for politicians who don't articulate a grand aspiration for the country.

On the other hand, President Ronald Reagan's vision was poetic.
He borrowed the idea of America being a "shining city on a hill" from
the Bible. "In my mind," he explained, "it was a tall, proud city built
on rocks stronger than oceans, windswept, God-blessed, and teeming
with people of all kinds living in harmony and peace; a city with free
ports that hummed with commerce and creativity. And if there had to

be city walls, the walls had doors, and the doors were open to anyone with the will and the heart to get here."

Donald Trump borrowed "make America great again" from Reagan, then trademarked it. But phrases that fit on baseball caps rarely qualify as vision. "Great" means different things to different people and, as we have seen, the devil is in the details.

We hear too few substantive and unifying national visions from our leaders. The late environmental scientist and educator Donella Meadows spoke about this, calling vision the most vital step in the policy process. "If we don't know where we want to go, it makes little difference that we make great progress," she said. "Yet vision is not only missing almost entirely from policy discussions; it is missing from our whole culture. We talk about our fears, frustrations, and doubts endlessly, but we talk only rarely and with embarrassment about our dreams."[1]

So, what should the visions be for the future of flood-prone communities or life in a decarbonized and sustainable civilization? A first step is to identify what is pushing and pulling us to change. What is the future we need and want as individuals, families, communities, the nation, and the world? The motivation for moving out of floodplains, for example, should be more than a retreat from danger. It should be the beginning of a future exponentially better than the past.

A World in Search of a Theme

In 2008, I worked as a sustainable development consultant for an international communications company in New York City. The United Nations hired the company to help with an important international climate conference in Copenhagen the following year.[2]

At the same time, the UN was planning an even larger conference four years later in Rio de Janeiro. Its official title was the United Nations Conference on Sustainable Development, but it was nicknamed Rio+20 because it was to be convened on the twentieth anniversary of the historic 1992 Earth Summit in Rio. That was where nations agreed to the UNFCCC, the treaty that established the architecture for the decades of climate negotiations that followed.

Someone mentioned that the UN was having trouble coming up with a tagline for Rio+20. I recalled a phrase that a colleague used in his work with communities: "The Future We Want." I met with the UN's public information officer in his small office deep within the organization's thirty-nine-story headquarters in New York. I suggested that the UN adopt "The Future We Want" as the Rio+20 theme.

Some phrases seem to have superpowers if the timing is right, and Rio+20 turned out be good timing for The Future We Want. It was a phrase, not a vision, but it invited people to think differently about climate change not as an approaching apocalypse, but as an opportunity to build healthier, safer, and more sustainable societies. Global warming invoked images of a dystopian future. Disaster movies like *The Day After Tomorrow* were coming out. The National Geographic Channel aired the *Doomsday Preppers* television series, with families holding disaster drills and building underground bunkers stocked with canned goods. In other words, the images the American people saw were about the future we need to avoid rather than the future we can build.

A focus on dystopia is disempowering. It causes apocalypse fatigue and surrender. In their book about "cultural creatives," Paul Ray and Sherry Ruth Anderson point out: "Today as we are besieged by planetary problems, the risk is that we will deal with them in a pessimistic and unproductive style. . . . Transfixed by an image of our own future decline, we could actually bring it about."[3]

Writer and environmental activist Rob Hopkins wrote about a different dynamic: "It is one thing to campaign against climate change and quite another to paint a compelling and engaging vision of a post-carbon world in such a way as to enthuse others to embark on a journey towards it. We are only just beginning to scratch the surface of the power of a positive vision of an abundant future."[4]

Over several months, The Future We Want tagline inched its way up the UN's chain of command until it reached then Secretary General Ban Ki-moon. He loved it. He decided to adopt it not only for Rio+20, but also for the rest of his term as secretary general.

My partner and I launched a website that encouraged people to send us their "compelling visions."[5] The UN posted a parallel site that reached people worldwide. We invited drawings, essays, poems, songs, anything, and responses came in by the hundreds.

When the conference finally began in Rio, we displayed many of the submissions, including videos of the constructive work people around the world were doing to address social and environmental problems. As the conference began with dignitaries from each nation making speeches, nearly all focused on The Future We Want. The UN began using the phrase in its other initiatives. An international group of children wrote a musical based on the phrase and performed it in Geneva, Switzerland. Groups around the world still use The Future We Want or variations of it in their publications and programs.[6]

There is a caveat, however. While negativity can be immobilizing, positivity can become "happy talk" or substance-free optimism. There are subtleties involved in reaching and sustaining a balance between optimism and pessimism. Self-help author Henry Cloud points out, "We change our behavior when the pain of staying the same becomes greater than the pain of changing. Consequences give us the pain that motivates us to change."[7]

Pain may be the motivation to change, but sustaining the momentum requires both a push and a pull. With climate change, the push is the danger of that dystopian future. The pull is the prospect of a positive and sustainable future. The best place to be is the sweet spot between those two forces, like the fulcrum on a teeter-totter. Knowledge of the negative instills urgency. A vision of the future provides inspiration and direction.

In this time of extraordinary visual technologies, we should be able to help people experience one or more futures that embody their cultures as well as universal values. Either physically or virtually, people should envision the future by walking through it and altering it where they think it should be improved. Astrophysics professor Adam Frank believes "Reaching a good Anthropocene, if such a thing exists, would only happen as a result of millions of people in millions of communities doing experiments. They will be trying millions of ways to alter, adjust and adjudicate the natural processes we already altered by mistake."[8]

Foundations might consider sponsoring projects that give people an opportunity to see what life might be like in sustainable and zero-carbon futures. The experience would demystify abstractions and reduce apprehensions about the transition to a more sustainable world.

Biophilic Cities

Another vision is attracting participation by cities around the world. It is
what cities would look like and what their quality of life would be if they
reintroduced nature into the urban environment. The Biophilic Cities
movement is inspired by the significant body of research showing that
people are happier and healthier in proximity to nature. It's also inspired
by biologist E .O. Wilson's "biophilia hypotheses," the idea he introduced
in the 1980s that humans have an innate tendency to seek connections
with other forms of life.

Several cities around the world, including some in the United States,
are members of an international Biophilic Cities Network. At last check,
the US cities included Austin, Texas; Milwaukee, Wisconsin; Norfolk
and Reston, Virginia; Pittsburgh, Pennsylvania; Phoenix, Arizona; Portland, Oregon; San Francisco, California; St. Louis, Missouri; and Washington, DC.

Biophilic cities share several features, including generous open
spaces and parks, urban forestry, gardens that attract pollinators, and
green roofs. Some cities are creative and experimental. There are 900
linear miles of pavement in the alleys of Los Angeles. The city created
a Green Alleys program several years ago to replace the pavement with
permeable materials, rain gardens, and other absorbent surfaces. Other
cities are turning alleys into mini-parks that invite people to stroll. Seattle, San Francisco, and Chicago have similar initiatives. Austin, Texas,
encourages citizens to grow gardens especially for bees, butterflies, and
other pollinators. Some cities have planted bioswales, long channels
of plants and grasses along roads and parking lots to absorb rain and
catch pollutants in runoff.[9] Methods like these reduce the tax burden of
stormwater infrastructure and treatment. The burden can be considerable: Wilmington, Delaware, found that their annual cost of stormwater
management was more than $4 million, about 43 percent of the city's
total combined sewer costs.

Portland, Oregon, uses a variety of plants to catch and remove pollutants from runoff. For example, phytofiltration uses biological microorganisms to convert pollutants into forms that plants can absorb.
Traffic islands are becoming gardens. So are roofs, where plants collect

as much as 80 percent of the rain that falls on buildings while providing insultation to reduce the costs of cooling the interior.

Urban forestry is a given because of the multiple benefits of trees. They absorb rain or collect it before it reaches the ground, giving it time to evaporate in a process called evapotranspiration. Deciduous trees are capable of reducing surface stormwater by 700 gallons a year, while evergreens can catch up to 4,000 gallons per year. Trees also help purify air, provide wildlife habitat, add beauty to streetscapes, and increase property values.

But because of climate change, the most important benefit of trees is the shade that saves lives in inner-city neighborhoods. Heat-related deaths have been the number-one weather-related killer in the United States. Because asphalt and other dark surfaces absorb heat and buildings block breezes, inner-city temperatures are several degrees higher than those in surrounding areas. On sunny days, roof and pavement temperatures in these urban heat islands can be 50 to 90 degrees Fahrenheit hotter than the surrounding air. Even after sunset, inner-city temperatures can be as much as 22°F warmer than vegetated and less dense suburbs. Shade and evapotranspiration from trees can reduce the heat-island effect by 20 to 45°F. As a bonus, trees and open spaces absorb carbon dioxide.

Every new real estate development, including those created by floodplain relocations, should incorporate biophilia and other elements of sustainable design such as rooftop solar panels or neighborhood-scale solar systems, walkability, electric vehicle charging stations, and plenty of inviting places for informal socializing. I offer some suggestions in appendix 3.

23

THE BIOCENE

We're basically this very young species, only 200,000 years
old. We're one of the newcomers, and we're going through
the same process that other species go through, which is,
how do I keep myself alive while taking care of the place
that's going to keep my offspring alive?

—Janine Benyus

THE IDEA THAT NATURE IS NO LONGER NATURAL has been taken up in
a different form by the world's geologists. Many of them have decided
that the planet we have known for the last ten thousand years is gone. It
has changed and continues to change because of humanity's dominant
and largely negative influence. The geologic community is considering
whether the human influence has been so profound that we have entered
a new epoch in the planet's history, tentatively called the Anthropocene.
The proposal to declare and name this new epoch is climbing slowly up
several strata of world geological organizations.

In its present form, the proposal is incomplete. Geologists, pale-
ontologists, and scientists in related fields organize the Earth's history
into blocks of geologic time. From the shortest to longest, they are ages,
epochs, periods, eras, eons, and supereons. Geologists trace the progres-
sion by studying the Earth's structure on and beneath its surface. They
look for clues like weathering, erosion, sedimentation, and lithification,
the process that compacts sediments under pressure until they become
solid rock.

We have been in the Holocene epoch for the last ten thousand years or so. It began roughly when the last glacial period was ending. With their well-known love of whimsy, some geologists refer to the Holocene as the Goldilocks epoch because it has been neither too hot nor too cold, but just right for us humans to build our civilizations.

But sadly, the Goldilocks epoch has come to an end, not because of natural evolution or the great achievements of homo sapiens, but because of what we have done wrong. Global warming is at the top of the list. The Earth has been inhospitably hot at other times in history, but it did not heat so quickly as now, and humans didn't cause it. This time, the Earth is entering a hot spell because of pollution from fossil fuels. Contemporary global warming is said to be heading to temperatures so high that the human body's defenses, mainly sweating, will not be sufficient to prevent death. One study estimates that nearly 1 percent of the planet's population already lives in these conditions, and 30 percent of the human population could be affected by 2070.[1]

Because carbon dioxide is the primary culprit and because extreme floods and fires have begun earlier than expected, we could call the new epoch the Carbocene, Hydrocene, or Pyrocene. Instead, geologists have recommended calling it the Anthropocene ("anthropo" for man and "cene" for new). The proposal is not without controversy, however, and it has yet to be approved by the larger global geologic community.

Nobel laureate Paul Crutzen is credited with suggesting in 2000 that we had entered a new geologic period in which humans are the driving force on the planet.[2] He was the first to call it the Anthropocene.[3] He believed it began in the late eighteenth century when scientists examined polar ice and found the first evidence that carbon dioxide and methane concentrations were increasing in the atmosphere.

Geologists sped into action on this idea in 2009. They established an Anthropocene Working Group (AWG) to explore whether a new epoch had in fact begun. The AWG, which reports to the Subcommission on Quaternary Stratigraphy, which reports in turn to the International Commission on Stratigraphy, submitted an affirmative preliminary recommendation in 2016 to the International Geological

Congress, an organization sponsored by the International Union of Geological Sciences, which represents more than a million geoscientists from
121 nations. To avoid the appearance of haste, the geology community
may take a year or two more to make a final decision.

We might be flattered at first that the Anthropocene acknowledges
humanity's great influence. It could commemorate how we've decoded
the genome, walked on the moon, and built cars that are smarter than
their drivers. But nothing positive is intended by the proposal. The
AWG decided the new epoch began around the middle of the last century because of these developments:

- Population growth, industrialization, and globalization;
- An order-of-magnitude increase in erosion associated with urbanization and agriculture;
- Global warming, sea-level rise, ocean acidification, and ocean "dead
  zones";
- Rapid changes in the biosphere both on land and in the sea, as a
  result of habitat loss, predation, explosion of domestic animal populations, and species invasions;
- Artificial radionuclides spread worldwide by thermonuclear bomb
  tests in the early 1950s; and
- The global dispersion of concrete, fly ash, and plastics along with the
  myriad "techno-fossils" produced from these and other materials.[4]

The results are altering the trajectory of the Earth system and will
last millennia or longer, the AWG said.

Unpleasant Truths

Geologists are forcing us to confront some unpleasant truths. We may be
the most influential species, but if we continue ruining the planet, we'll
have to stop calling ourselves the most intelligent. We are not only the
planet's dominant species; we are also its most invasive.[5] We have walked
on the moon and hope soon to walk on Mars, but we haven't yet learned
to walk on Earth without leaving a lot of ugly footprints.

Civilization will never be as light afoot as the mythical Shaolin priest who walks on rice paper without leaving a trace. But we can at least learn not to tear it.[6] First, we'll have to shed the weight of believing that greed is good and that we have an unlimited supply of rice paper.

So, why is the AWG's proposal incomplete? The best argument for choosing the word "Anthropocene" is its value-neutrality. It does not imply that we must look forward to ten thousand more years of human hubris and biosphere abuse. Human dominance could be benign and even a blessing for life on Earth. We need not behave like lemmings. It isn't written that humanity will perish by the bang of nuclear annihilation or the whimper of global warming.

The Anthropocene could be the celebrated time when humanity let its better angels prevail, turned itself around, accepted the interconnectedness of everything, and decided not to be "the destroyer of worlds."

When Robert Oppenheimer, the "Father of the Nuclear Bomb," witnessed its first test on July 16, 1945, he quoted the Bhagavad Gita: "Now I am become death, the destroyer of worlds." Unless we are careful, it will be the subtitle of the Anthropocene.

Stewardship

How do we begin a turnaround? We in the developed world can dedicate the rest of this century to fixing what we have broken, insofar as it's fixable, to leaving no ugly traces, and to helping developing nations avoid our mistakes. Geologists could name this century the Biocene. Or we might call it the Atonement, the at-one-ment moment when we fully awakened to our interdependence with other life and realized that for our own good, our proper role is to be the Earth's steward, not its dominatrix.

Biological Bill of Rights

When I use the term "steward," I do not mean humanity should be like the Wizard of Oz, stressing out as we turn dials and pull levers to control all within our domain. I mean humanity as a caretaker of life and the guardian of a Biospheric Bill of Rights. It seems elementary that all species should have the right to drink clean water, breathe clean air, eat clean food, enjoy a climate free of anthropogenic instability, and occupy habitat untainted by toxins and human activity. These are fundamental birthrights, universal common law, that should not need not be formalized by constitutions or statutes.

They do have an anchor in law, however. The Public Trust Doctrine is an ancient principle still found in law today. It establishes that governments must preserve certain natural resources for the use of present and future generations. The doctrine traditionally applied to navigable waterways, but some courts have ruled it also protects air, sea, waters, and forests.

Twenty-one children and young adults invoked this doctrine in one of the more important lawsuits of our time, *Juliana v United States.* They sued the federal government in 2015 for operating a national energy system that causes climate change and violates their constitutional rights to life, liberty, property, and equal protection of the law. They provided the federal judiciary with detailed documentation of climate science and argued that the government violated their right to a "climate system capable of sustaining human life."[7] In January 2020, in a 2-1 decision, a panel of the Ninth Circuit Court of Appeals found that the youth presented sufficient evidence to establish the government was a substantial factor in causing their injuries. But the panel dismissed the case without prejudice, saying "political branches" and voters, not the courts, should decide the issue. At this writing, the youth are seeking a declaratory judgment that the US national energy system is unconstitutional.

As the case made its way through the courts, US Justice Department lawyers used several arguments. One was that there is no substantive due process right to a climate system capable of sustaining human life; another was that the doctrine applies only to the states' ownership of submerged lands, not the atmosphere. But it defies reason that the atmosphere deserves less protection than submerged lands for the use of present and future generations. In ruling that other branches of government should resolve the children's complaint, the courts shirk their responsibility as the third branch of government. It is a system designed to share power with and prevent actions by the other two, like encouraging the use of fossil fuels and the emissions of greenhouse gases.

The Justice Department and the Ninth Circuit panel were wrong. We should hope the children continue their work to establish that government officials have a fiduciary obligation to protect the atmosphere from greenhouse gases and that children more than any other group of citizens have the legal standing to protect their futures against federal policies that "may hasten an environmental collapse."

The Agenda

"I don't think it's sufficient to say that we should do things to reverse the damage that we've done," *Second Nature* author Nathaniel Rich told an interviewer. "Yes, we should try to make the world better. But what world are we trying to create? That's the bigger question."

The goals of the Biocene atonement are not new. They have been debated, defined, developed, and endorsed at the highest levels of government and civil society based on sound science and extensive peer review during decades of study and negotiation. They are commonly known as the Paris climate accord and the United Nation's Sustainable Development Goals.[8] They are not perfect, but they are shovel-ready. They define the objectives for sustaining a livable planet and building a just civilization committed to that "productive harmony" between humanity and nature, or more accurately, humanity's role as part of nature.

The Sustainable Development Goals consist of seventeen specific social, economic, and environmental objectives (see sidebar). Nearly every nation has endorsed the Paris climate agreement, and 190 have approved it so far. It acknowledges that "climate change is a common concern of humankind" and the need to address it with "regional and international cooperation," and to promote it with "universal access to sustainable energy" and the "enhanced deployment of renewable energy." Its principal goals are to keep global warming from advancing more than 2°C, and if possible, no more than 1.5°C above the planet's preindustrial temperature. Each nation submits its own plan to reduce carbon pollution. All nations have promised to increase their plans' ambitions at regular intervals. But so far, their aspirations are far short of what's necessary to achieve the accord's goals.

UN Sustainable Development Goals

No poverty
Zero hunger
Good health and well being
Quality education
Gender equality
Clean water and sanitation
Affordable and clean energy
Decent work and economic growth
Industry, innovation, and infrastructure
Reduced inequalities
Sustainable cities and communities
Responsible consumption and production
Climate action
Life below water
Life on land
Peace, justice and strong institutions
Partnerships for the goals

However, there are requirements not in either agreement. Healing the ecological damage we have done is one. Recognizing and respecting the planet's physical limits is another. A third is to abandon the perverse neoliberal idea that monetary profit should be the sole organizing principle of societies. The organizing principle should be the Biospheric Bill of Rights.

We must also make a simple but fundamental change in our relationship with nature, seeing it as an ally rather than an enemy. There is a difference between forcibly taking nature's resources and simply receiving what it gives freely. For example, nations have developed by drilling, digging, blasting, fracturing, processing, and burning the carbon that nature wisely hid underground. By doing this, we have changed the planet's carbon cycle. We have filled the air not only with carbon dioxide but also with nitrogen oxides, methane, particulates, sulfur dioxide, mercury, carbon monoxide, formaldehyde, benzene, acetaldehyde, and ethylbenzene. The global energy economy has fed itself on finite fuels whose byproducts degrade soil, water, air, and ecosystems essential to our lives and to biodiversity. The Earth has signaled us to stop with air pollution, earthquakes and land subsidence, depleted groundwater, rising seas and dying oceans, monster storms, seemingly endless droughts, uncontrollable wildfires, protracted and bloody military adventures, and much more.

All the while, the energy we needed has been all around us—clean, inexhaustible, and free. Individuals and communities, as well as utilities, can produce it. It generates flexible electricity without carbon dioxide and other emissions. It keeps the carbon cycle in balance. Most of it uses no water. Much of it comes to us from the solar system's greatest power plant, which delivers energy everywhere on Earth in eight minutes from 93 million miles away. We already know how to receive it. We simply need the humility to do so.

Biocene versus Cybercene

I was about to write to the AWG offering my idea about the Biocene at no charge, but I decided first to check on whether anyone else had used the term. It turned out several people have. One is a fellow at NASA who has a very different idea of what the Biocene would mean. His group's literature describes it with words and phrases like the dawn of synthetic life, living machines, nature-inspired artificial intelligence, and the emergence of humans as a "solar system species." In this version, humans would learn from nature not to achieve productive harmony, but to transcend it, make it irrelevant, and "leave it in the dust," as one description puts it.

There is a lot that's artificial there. Would artificial life include fake love, synthetic compassion, virtual empathy, and circuits that mimicked morality? What would the algorithm be for sincerity?

These two versions of the Biocene represent our next great decision in the great acceleration: whether humanity will aspire to what is better called the Cybercene or move into the mostly organic Biocene. There is a possibility on our present course that we will put so many toxic chemicals and plastics into the environment that only the Bots will survive. But we still have time to avoid it.

The Cybercene is the path to the singularity, the point at which artificial intelligence becomes more intelligent than human intelligence, where technological growth becomes uncontrollable, and where the result is "unforeseeable changes to human civilization" and all biologic life. The singularity was once the stuff of science fiction. But organically intelligent people such as the late Stephen Hawking and Ray Kurzweil of Google warn it's coming. "The genie is out of the bottle," Hawking said. "I fear that AI [artificial intelligence] may replace humans altogether."[9] Kurzweil thinks we will reach the singularity by 2045. Artificial intelligence expert Louis Rosenberg thinks it will happen about 2050 and maybe as soon as 2030, unless we "make ourselves smarter, much smarter, and fast" to stay "ahead of the machines."[10]

"To me, the prospect of a sentient artificial intelligence being created on Earth is no less dangerous than an alien intelligence showing up from another planet," Rosenberg writes. "To assume that its interests will be aligned with ours is absurdly naive, and to assume that it won't put its interests first—putting our very existence at risk—is to ignore what we humans have done to every other creature on Earth. . . . We need to assume that this is an existential threat for our species."

In the real Biocene, we would learn from nature to find better and ecologically positive ways to live and work, as advocated by Janine Benyus, the biologist and cofounder of the Biomimicry Institute.[11] She believes

> biomimicry offers an empathetic, interconnected understanding of how life works and ultimately where we fit in. It is a practice that learns from and mimics the strategies used by species alive today. The goal is to create products, processes, and policies— new ways of living—that solve our greatest design challenges sustainably and in solidarity with all life on earth. We can use biomimicry to not only learn from nature's wisdom, but also heal ourselves—and this planet—in the process.[12]

Journalist Dallon Adams offers a few practical examples:[13]

- When Japanese engineers produced the final design of the Bullet Train, they modeled the train's nose after the beak of kingfisher birds, which dive into the water with very little splash. The trains ended up 10 percent faster and consumed 15 percent less energy.
- Researchers at Harvard were curious about why humpback whales were able to lift so high out of the ocean. They figured out that nodules on the whales' fins allowed them to attack the ocean's surface at a 40 percent steeper angle than a smooth fin would. A Canadian company used this information to develop wind turbine blades that generate the same amount of electricity at 10 miles per hour that conventional turbines generate at 17 miles an hour.
- Termites construct intricate networks of air pockets that use convection to ventilate their nests. The engineering firm Arup used this method when it built a shopping center in Zimbabwe. It found that the termite's design used 10 percent less energy than a traditional air-conditioning system.

Another journalist, Mark Sommer, eloquently describes the fork in the road:[14]

The Anthropocene contains within its DNA a fatal hubris, daring us to imagine that we humans are the pinnacle of evolution and masters of the universe. Yet the Cybercene would be an equally unbalanced outcome likely to produce still more dystopian societies. It's time to envision and create a synthesis that merges the wisest of human inventions with our most humane values.

Call it the Biocene, an enduring era of thriving life in which humans finally find our proper place in the great chain of being—no longer dominant but coequal with all creation and in balance with our inventions. That's a long way from where we are today, yet at the warp speed of the present this moment is our decision point. May we choose wisely.

A kinder and gentler relationship with the biosphere does not mean we can't defy natural law in benign ways from time to time. We defy gravity and it still works fine. But our ability to fly to, and perhaps settle on, other planets does not make it OK to ruin this one. We know how to replace diseased organs with artificial substitutes without turning patients into cyborgs. But that doesn't mean we should abuse the organs we have.

The real Biocene requires a different way of perceiving nature. It is the blue mind meeting the blue marble. It is wakefulness and awe about our connections and interdependence with all life. Aware of those connections, we are more careful about our treatment of other species. It is the sustained version of the feeling most of us get after we've been quarantined for weeks because of COVID-19 and step out of the house for the first time into fresh air and sunlight. It is a kind of rebirth.

In economic terms, it is a world driven not by greed but rather by the dedication to that productive harmony with nature. It is humanity that wants to lift life up rather than stomp it down. It is not pantheism. It recognizes the divine in humans as well as everything else, but it does not worship the creation; it worships the genius and generosity of the creator. At the same time, we understand that it is nature's nature to be cruel sometimes, as we think of cruel, and we accept and adapt to what we cannot change.

Technological Nature

In an attempt to split the difference between a Biocene and a Cybercene, we have "technological nature." Larry Schweiger, past president of the National Wildlife Federation, tells the story of being on a flight that passed over the Grand Canyon. A teenager sat next to him in the window seat, focused on his smartphone. One of the world's seven natural wonders was in plain sight below, but the young man never looked out of the window. It was demoralizing for a man who spent his entire adult life fighting to preserve natural wonders like that.

The teenager might have been a frequent flier who was making his one-thousandth flight over the Grand Canyon and found it more entertaining to kill digital enemies and stack up body counts on his iPhone. Or he may have been an example of how virtual experience lures us away from actual experience.

Peter Khan, a professor of psychology at the University of Washington, has examined the difference between our exposure to technological nature and real nature.[15] There is broad agreement that real nature has a wide variety of physical and emotional benefits. Khan says we can get similar benefits from technological nature, to a degree. Exposure to technological nature has been found to reduce violence in prisons. People who watch the television series *Planet Earth* are said to have lower anxiety levels. Workers in offices with scenes of the outdoors are more productive.

But there are important differences between real nature and technological nature. When we walk in a real forest, we enter a symbiotic relationship with it. The trees inhale our carbon dioxide; we inhale their oxygen. Whether we visit the forest or a river or a seashore, we are in the presence of energies we cannot replicate electronically.

Kahn says technological nature is "dumbed down." Real nature teaches us how to take care of ourselves and how to build confidence in our self-sufficiency. To put it simply, if you run into a virtual tree, it doesn't hurt. If you run into a real tree, you learn to pay better attention next time. Starting a good campfire takes more skill than turning up a thermostat. Foraging for food in nature takes more knowledge than foraging at the supermarket.

Khan acknowledges, however, that "we are a technological species. . . . We're drawn to technologies not only because they are foisted on us by corporations, but also because the impetus for them lies within the architecture of our being." It goes back to making and using stone tools 3.3 million years ago, Kahn surmises.[16] But first, we are biological beings living in a biosphere, and we are forgetting the connection. "As care for nature increasingly becomes an intellectual concept severed from the joyful experience of the outdoors, you have to wonder," says author Richard Louv. "Where will future environmentalists come from?" Will there be artificial naturalists? We should hope not because we need an emotional connection to real nature so that we are more likely to take care of it, and that has a lot to do with taking care of ourselves.

Selin Kesebir, an assistant professor of organizational behavior at the London Business School, and Pelin Kesebir, a social psychologist at the University of Wisconsin, Madison, point out that urbanization often is blamed for our nature deficit, but they have doubts. They think technological nature is the greater cause. They found that the rise of television coincides with the decline of references to nature in popular culture, from paintings to songs. Now, the internet and the other devices that offer technological nature are substituting for the real thing. Unfortunately, "this is a time when our children can name more Pokémon characters than wildlife species."[17]

Instead, this should be a time when we put our children in intimate contact with nature. That contact used to be a daily experience; now the human environment, augmented by virtual reality, dominates most children's lives. Our children are poorer for it, and so is nature. If a child learns to experience a river so intimately that he or she can feel it flowing through their veins, they will grow up less inclined to dam it.

The Root of Anthropocentrism

Heather Alberro is a lecturer in political ecology. Writing in the academic journal *The Conversation*, she points out that we suffer from ecological breakdown when we believe we are not part of nature. She traces this back to the transition from paganism to Judaism and Christianity, and the idea that God gave us dominion over the Earth. Terms like "natural capital," "natural resources," and "fish stocks project" perhaps subconsciously tell us "that the Earth's fabric holds no value apart from what it provides us. That leads us to exploit it recklessly."

In the modern world, Alberro notes, the South Asian Kingdom of Bhutan has institutionalized the understanding that humans are members of the natural community. Its constitution requires that at least 60 percent of the nation remain forested. It is one of only two countries that sequesters more carbon than it emits. And, as discussed, it pioneered the idea of "gross national happiness" and developed nine indicators to measure it. One is "ecological diversity and resilience."[18]

Economist Charles Eisenstein proposes that we use a "living planet" narrative in children's education, teaching that the Earth depends on the health of its ecosystems just as we depend on the health of our lungs, heart, and other organs.[19] Environmental education should instill the understanding of how closely human well-being is linked with nature's well-being. The human species is not one entity and nature another. We are connected and codependent physically, emotionally, and spiritually. When we internalize that understanding, we will realize that caring for nature is caring for ourselves. Environmentalism is not interspecies altruism. If our children grew up understanding from the earliest ages that they are members of a living biosphere, environmentalism would not be an issue, a philosophy, or a cause. It would be as natural and essential to our being as breathing.

Making Contact

I've used the term "mindful." In recent years, being in the "now" has been one of the most popular therapies in the United States. Physicians prescribe it for pain, loneliness, anxiety, and burnout.

Mindfulness in nature appears to be especially beneficial. In 2012, a team of researchers in the UK had subjects take twenty-five-minute walks through three environments—two urban and one a green space.[20] The researchers measured the subjects' brain reactions with mobile electroencephalography (EEG), much as Wallace Nichols did to understand his brain's reactions to the ocean. The UK team reported that green space produced its own version of blue mind, the "green mind" if you will, akin to a meditative state.

Here is an exercise in eco-mindfulness. You entered the biospheric world even before you stepped outside. When you stepped into the shower that morning, you inserted yourself into the planet's water cycle. The water cascading down on you may have come from interstellar ice crystals older than the Earth and sun.[21] There is always the same amount of water in the biosphere, but it changes form. It may be ice one day, gas the next day, and the liquid coming through your showerhead the day after that, but the amount of water is always the same. There will never be more or less of it on the planet.

Your breakfast cereal would not exist—in fact, half the food in the supermarket would not exist—without the help of pollinators such as bees, butterflies, hummingbirds, bats, beetles, and flies. With their assistance, fruits and flowers procreate in a process strikingly similar to ours. It's a bit startling to realize that the strawberries in your cereal bowl are actually the plant's ovaries protecting the seeds that contain the genetic code of its species.

The next time you are outside, imagine that all the living things above, around, and below you, from microscopic to big, were making audible sounds. It would be an overwhelming biotic cacophony.

When you walk across your lawn, be aware that a spoonful of the soil under your feet contains more busy microorganisms than there are people on the planet. Bacteria, actinomycetes, fungi, protozoa, and nematodes are at work, each with its own job. Earthworms are sliming around silently beneath the surface, multitasking as they aerate the ground, break down organic matter so plants can use it, and shed casings to fertilize the soil.

Among many other tasks, the hard-working trees are inhaling the carbon dioxide you exhale and exhaling the oxygen you inhale. Seven or eight of them are producing enough oxygen to keep you breathing for a year. You are a player in the carbon cycle. Carbon dioxide is moving continuously through plants, soils, the oceans, the atmosphere, and you.

Lately, some scientists are saying that trees communicate with each other above and below ground. Fungal networks allow them to share water and nutrients and to send out alerts to other trees when they are in distress. The German forester who discovered this network calls it the "wood-wide web."[22]

Someday when your heart stops beating, your body will slowly decompose into elements that are food for other organisms, and life in the biosphere will go on. Students of this process say there is an exception, however. A small part of us becomes helium that floats off into space, where it may be captured by the sun, or another planet, or where it may leave the solar system and drift off into "infinity and beyond."

In the millisecond between life and death, you may discover the answer to the most mysterious question of all: are we humans annuals or perennials? Until that time comes, we all bumble along through a miraculous, mind-boggling array of life serving us and the world around us with the knowledge it has refined through 3.5 million years of evolution.

Remembering Icarus

We don't have to be Luddites to be wary of new technologies. We should control them rather than letting them control us. I can imagine a time when Jeff Bezos is shuttling us to the moon and Elon Musk is selling tickets to Mars. I would buy one if I could afford it, and I'd make the trip in hopes of seeing something that no human has seen before. But assuming my transportation is fast enough, mine would be a round-trip ticket. When I got back to Earth, I would hike a mile through a mountain forest to reach a wild river. I would stand waist-deep in the cold water on a hot summer day and feel the strength of the current trying to sweep me away. I would spend the afternoon casting a line and hoping to trick a trout or two. Whether I did or not, I would be restored.

Yet I know that rivers and creeks will always rise because that's what they do. They are wild and they rage from time to time. When they do, they replenish wetlands, soils, and habitats. They rage with purpose. It's wise to stay out of their way and to let them do their work.

But when they are calm and you pay attention, they flush away your inner babble and strip you clean until all that's left is the vibrant everlasting moment.

Courtesy of Steve Carter

EPILOGUE

There are only two lasting bequests we can hope to give
our children. One of these is roots, the other, wings.

—Johann Wolfgang von Goethe

In the middle of the summer in 2020, a federal agency finally acknowledged what people like Gilbert White pointed out long ago: it is folly to build and rely on dams and levees when avoiding floods is as simple as keeping people out of their way. The agency was the Government Accountability Office (GAO), which conducts research requested by members of Congress.[1]

The GAO agreed with scientists in the US Global Change Research Program that "relocation due to climate change will be unavoidable in some coastal areas" as sea levels rise. The agency's report to Congress focused only on coasts, but the nation's rivers are rising, too, and the areas vulnerable to floods are expanding. Many of the GAO's conclusions and recommendations apply to both types of flood hazards.

GAO pointed out that no federal agency has the authority to lead climate "migration," there is no federal strategy, and government programs are not designed to help communities relocate from floodplains. Insofar as the government has considered helping communities move out of flood hazard areas, the help has been reactive rather than pro-active, responding to tragedies rather than helping communities avoid them.

For those reasons, organized moves out of flood hazard areas are much more disruptive and complicated than they have to be. The agency pointed to a relocation in Alaska that took thirty years and another in Louisiana that took twenty years because the government is not organized to help.

GAO's recommendation was that Congress create a pilot project on how to assist with relocations, but as I hope this book demonstrates, there is no need to experiment. Enough communities have done it, enough organizations have been involved, and enough studies of federal shortcomings have been done for Congress to learn from the pioneers. Seas and rivers are rising now, and so is the impact on taxpayers. Since 2005, the agency pointed out, federal expenditures on natural disasters have been at least $460 billion.

Whether we measure the value of federal disaster policies in money or in misery, it makes no objective sense for governments to encourage people to live in harm's way and to help them remain there after the inevitable happens.

At root, the national approach to flooding has been a symptom of our dysfunctional relationship with nature.

As the fires burned during the Australian summer of 2020, a television newswoman filed her report from a hill overlooking an expanse of charcoal sticks standing naked and upright on ash-covered ground in what used to be a forest. There were no birdsongs, whispering pines, or deer.

Nature had gone silent. The reporter held her microphone out toward the forest. It was as if the mike had gone dead. We were reminded that there are many ways to create a silent spring. The hubris that produces climate change is one of them.

We have created a troubled time in the biosphere. "The health of ecosystems on which we and all other species depend is deteriorating

After the Australian brushfires in 2019. *Photo by Doug Beckers courtesy of Creative Commons Attribution-Noncommercial license*

more rapidly than ever," notes Sir Robert Watson, who led an international study on biodiversity and ecosystem services. "We are eroding the very foundations of our economies, livelihoods, food security, health and quality of life worldwide."[2]

About one million species are threatened with extinction and the rate is accelerating. Three quarters of the land-based environment and two-thirds of the marine environment have been "significantly altered by human actions." More than a third of the world's land and 75 percent of its freshwater are devoted to producing crops and livestock. Some 60 billion tons of renewable and nonrenewable resources are extracted from the planet every year. Nearly a quarter of the world's land surface has been degraded; $577 billion worth of crops are at risk due to the loss of pollinators; and plastic pollution is up tenfold. There are more than four hundred dead zones in the oceans, covering a combined area larger than the United Kingdom. As many as 300 million people face higher risks of floods and hurricanes because coastal habitats have been lost.[3]

This is what Generations X, Y, and Z are inheriting, a world suffering from poverty on one extreme and the rubbish of prosperity on the other. Each new generation is handed the unfulfilled hopes as well as the achievements of its parents. Each old generation counts on the fresh energy, idealism, and hope of its children. But children today are being given an unfair burden including problems that are becoming irreversible and that seriously threaten their futures.

I was born in the first year of the baby boom and have lived on the tip of its spear. Our inheritance included the prospect of nuclear holocaust, another existential threat to civilization. When I was child in a suburb of Chicago, I stood in my backyard and watched commercial jets fly overhead. I worried that they were carrying nuclear bombs to drop on the city. I waited for the explosions, but they didn't happen. Instead, the possibility of a nuclear war cast a shadow on our lives. I was sixteen when Bob Dylan sang a message to the bomb-makers: "You've thrown the worst fear that can ever be hurled, fear to bring children into this world. For threatening my baby unborn and unnamed, you ain't worth the blood that runs in your veins."[4]

Now, nearly seventy years later, the shadow remains. But it is even darker because of climate change. Writer Gracy Olmstead reports that many millennials "wonder whether the children conceived now might face a fate somehow worse than nonexistence in future years—a fate involving planetary apocalypse or catastrophe—and they don't want to bring children into that future."[5]

BuzzFeed contributor Ash Sanders tells that she decided in 2008 not to have a baby. "I did not want to bring a person into this world to generate tons of carbon," she says. "I didn't want to raise a person who would push another animal out of its home, or put island nations underwater. . . . I was supposed to look at a baby and see a child of God, a cooing joy bundle, a future missionary or a father or a grandmother. I was supposed to feel joy. But instead I felt grief. And anger. And nausea."[6]

We have to ask ourselves, and ask each other, why we keep buying from the industries and electing the leaders who make us fear of the most profound and fulfilling human experience. A poll in the fall of 2019 found that 57 percent of teenagers said climate change frightened them, while 52 percent said it made them angry. Fewer than 30 percent of teens were optimistic. There is climate depression, anxiety, stress, and suicide.[7]

Today it's the masters of carbon who traffic in fear.

It doesn't have to be this way. Another baby boom artist, Joni Mitchell, perfectly captured who we are, our problem, and our mission in twenty-five words:

> We are stardust
> Billion-year-old carbon
> We are golden
> Caught in the devil's bargain
> And we've got to get ourselves
> Back to the garden[8]

Lest we make the mistake of thinking this is just pretty hyperbole, know this: We are in fact stardust. More than 90 percent of our bodies are made of it. Twelve percent of our bodies is ancient carbon. We contain hydrogen atoms formed in the Big Bang, and the average-sized person contains about 10 nanoliters of gold.

I have given you my explanation of the devil's bargain. And our reunion with nature by way of the Biocene will get us back to the garden. That leaves the question of who "we" are.

It is customary for each generation to pass the torch to the next, but that custom should not apply today. There is no mandatory retirement age for torch-bearers and Baby Boomers have promises to keep. In Charlton Heston's immortal words, we must carry the torch until it is wrestled from our cold dead hands. When that day comes, as it inevitably will, we should leave our children and children's children with one last thought, handed down to us by the Blackfoot warrior Crowfoot:

> Hold on to what is good, even if it's a handful of earth. Hold on to what you believe, even if it's a tree that stands by itself. Hold on to what you must do, even if it's a long way from here. Hold on to your life, even if it's easier to let go. Hold on to my hand, even if someday I'll be gone away from you.[9]

APPENDIX 1

Climate 101

CLIMATE CHANGE IS A FREQUENT TOPIC in the media these days, as it should be. Even so, decades of denial and misinformation have inhibited public understanding of this complicated phenomenon. Much of the confusion is generated by fossil energy companies that want to continue selling their products, even though pollution from oil, natural gas, and coal is the principal cause of climate change.[1]

To fully appreciate why we need to do something about climate change, it's essential that we understand a few things about the science and also about the politics around the issue. Climate change has been artfully partisanized, but it is not now and never has been an inherently political issue. It's not a matter of belief or nonbelief, either. It is a physical phenomenon that has been investigated and observed by scientists since the 1820s when a French physicist suspected that there must be something besides straightforward sunlight keeping the planet warm.

After a series of breakthroughs in our understanding of the relationship between the Earth's surface temperature and the amount of CO_2 in the atmosphere, climate science progressed far enough by 1988 for nations to recognize that they should be very concerned. So, the World Meteorological Association and the United Nations created an international research program that monitors and periodically reports on the work of climate scientists around the world. It is called the Intergovernmental Panel on Climate Change.

It was clear that nothing short of a global effort would stabilize the climate. In 1992, international leaders gathered to create the United Nations Framework Convention on Climate Change. It established the underlying architecture for negotiating and reaching agreements among nations on specific steps to reduce their fossil energy emissions. The UNFCCC was blessed by the US Senate and ratified by President George H. W. Bush.

It took twenty years of talks before the world's nearly two hundred countries agreed unanimously in 2015 to take voluntary steps to reduce the pollution from fossil fuels. That agreement is the Paris Agreement. During his last two years in office, President Obama created a climate action plan for the United States to comply with the accord. It included several major initiatives, but two were especially historic. One was a regulation to control carbon emissions from power plants for the first time. The second set aggressive federal efficiency standards for vehicles.

Shortly after taking office in 2017, President Trump notified the United Nations that the United States would drop out of the Paris accord, and he began rescinding the climate action plan, including the power plant and vehicle rules.

Because of disinformation from the fossil energy sector and its advocates in politics, the American people have been slow to accept that climate change is real. But there has been a sharp increase recently in the proportion of Americans who acknowledge global warming, driven in large part by the violent weather they are witnessing.[2] In March 2019, Gallup found that although there is still a definite difference of opinion between Democrats and Republicans, 66 percent of Americans accept that human activity causes global warming, close to an all-time high. Nearly 60 percent acknowledge that it has already begun.[3]

The following are answers to several of the most common questions about climate change:

What is causing it?

The planet has gone through cycles of global warming and global cooling throughout its history due to natural influences. But now the Earth is warming more rapidly than ever before. Science has confirmed that the principal reason is the carbon released when we burn oil, natural gas, and coal.

These fuels consist mostly of carbon. When they burn, their carbon is released into the atmosphere where it combines with oxygen to produce carbon dioxide. Carbon dioxide is the most important of several gases that linger in the atmosphere, some of them for hundreds or thousands of years. They allow sunlight to pass through to the Earth's surface, but they keep some of it from reflecting into space. The trapped solar energy makes the Earth's surface warmer—ergo, global warming.

For that reason, they are called "greenhouse gases," and CO_2 is the most consequential. It is responsible for more than 80 percent of human-caused global warming today.

What are the other greenhouse gases?

They include water vapor, methane, ozone, nitrous oxide, and chlorofluorocarbons. Organic wastes produce methane. Natural gas consists mainly of methane. Some escapes when the fuel is extracted, transported, stored, and used. Ozone comes from a reaction between sunlight and nitrogen oxide from car exhaust, coal power plants, and factories along with emissions (volatile organic compounds) from gasoline, paints, and many cleaning solvents. Aerosol sprays, foams, solvents, and refrigerants use chlorofluorocarbons. Each gas has different characteristics that determine how much heat it traps and how long it stays in the atmosphere.

What is the foundation of the claim that scientists are in virtual agreement about climate change?

Six independent studies confirm that 97 percent of the scientists who have published research on global warming agree that it is real and human caused.[4] The consensus is highest among researchers with the most climate expertise.

Carbon is essential to life, so why is more of it bad?

It's true that most living things are made of carbon and need it to live, grow, and reproduce. But too much carbon, like too much of almost anything else, turns it from healthy to dangerous.

Carbon cycles continuously through the biosphere—the space on and near the Earth where land, water, and air support all life. Carbon moves through soils, oceans, and plants. Each absorbs it for a time, then releases it to continue in the cycle. The ecosystems that absorb it (the ocean, wetlands, forests, and soils) are called "carbon sinks." When soils are disturbed or plants die, their carbon reenters the cycle. When carbon is released and absorbed in equal measure, the carbon cycle is in balance, and all is well.

However, a substantial amount of carbon was kept out of the cycle hundreds of millions of years ago. The US Department of Energy explains that fossil fuels formed "when prehistoric plants and animals died and were gradually buried by layers of rock. Over millions of years, different types of fossil fuels formed—depending on what combination of organic matter was present, how long it was buried, and what temperature and pressure conditions existed as time passed."

As we and other advanced nations industrialized, we extracted and burned these deposits for energy (see chart below). The resulting CO_2 transfers the carbon from deep within the Earth to the air. That has thrown the carbon cycle out of balance. The imbalance has grown worse not only because of using fossil fuels but also because human activity has destroyed carbon sinks with deforestation, the loss of grasslands and wetlands, and poor soil health.

CO_2 also enters the atmosphere from sources other than fossil fuels. In addition to its release from organic material like dying plants, volcanoes and forest fires release the gas. To a point, the presence of CO_2 in the atmosphere is beneficial. It has kept the planet at temperatures that have supported life for many thousands of years. But our use of fossil fuels has overloaded the atmosphere.

Atmospheric CO_2 and other greenhouse gases have caused the Earth's average surface temperature to rise steadily since 1880.[5] The warming has triggered significant changes in our climate—changes that generally

History of energy consumption in the United States, 1775-2009

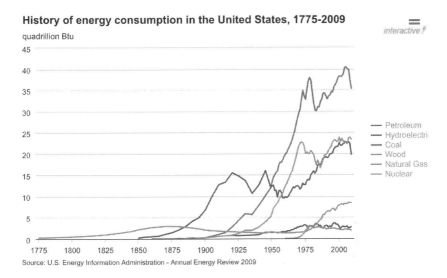

quadrillion Btu

Legend: Petroleum, Hydroelectri, Coal, Wood, Natural Gas, Nuclear

interactive

Source: U.S. Energy Information Administration - Annual Energy Review 2009

The United States has used fossil fuels since the middle of the nineteenth century. They soon dominated the nation's energy mix. Fossil fuels' share of energy consumption in the United States peaked at 94 percent in 1966; although the use of carbon-free fuels such as wind and solar power has proliferated in recent years, 80 percent of the nation's energy still came from coal, oil, and natural gas in 2018. *US Energy Information Administration*

make weather and its secondary impacts more extreme. Floods are the most common weather disaster, and they are getting more destructive. Some regions are experiencing prolonged droughts, which threatens food production and increases wildfire danger. Heatwaves, hurricanes, and tropical storms are getting stronger, too.

What do scientists mean when they talk about parts per million (ppm), and why is it important?

PPM indicates the concentration of a pollutant in the air. In the context of global warming, it refers to the atmosphere's concentration of greenhouse gases. Higher concentrations increase the greenhouse effect, which means more warming.

Before the industrial era, the atmosphere contained 278 ppm of CO_2, a level at which the carbon cycle was in balance. Scientists generally agree that 350 ppm is the safe upper limit. But in 2013, carbon concentrations exceeded 400 ppm, the highest ever measured and believed to be the highest in more than three million years.[6] In 2017, the atmospheric concentration of CO_2 reached more than 410 ppm. In May 2019, it passed 415 ppm, a level never before experienced by our species.

What can we do to mitigate climate change?

Nations agreed in Paris that we must achieve a net-zero-carbon global economy by mid-century. In other words, we will put no more CO_2 into the atmosphere than carbon sinks can remove. In the second half of the century, we must remove enough CO_2 from the air to restore the carbon balance. In other words, we will remove more carbon from the atmosphere than we put in. That is called a net-negative-carbon economy.

Both goals require that we stop burning fossil fuels.[7] Both require that we restore and conserve natural carbon sinks. To get to net-negative carbon, we will need the help of new carbon-removal technologies.[8]

Why are sea levels rising?

Oceans have absorbed about 90 percent of the heat from human-caused warming. When water gets warmer, it expands. At the same time, land-based glaciers and ice sheets are melting and adding water to oceans.

The good news is that the oceans' role as a heat sink has kept terrestrial warming from accelerating even more rapidly. The bad news is that rising seas threaten to inundate lowlands and significant parts of coastal cities. Rising seas also increase coastal erosion and produce storm surges that penetrate farther inland. Sea-level rise is also responsible for "nuisance" or "sunny day" floods during high tides, where floods occur in coastal communities even when the weather is good. Nuisance floods are happening between 300 and 900 percent more often than fifty years ago.[9]

What impact does warming have on sea life?

Coral provides shelter and spawning grounds vital to 25 percent of ocean fish. Warmer water temperatures cause coral to turn white and die (called coral bleaching). That affects food supplies and commerce for millions of the world's people. Also, as oceans absorb CO_2, it reacts with seawater to make it more acidic (called ocean acidification). That reduces the ability of sea life to produce skeletons and shells.

Why are hurricanes more intense?

When tropical storms and hurricanes pass over warm water, they gain energy. Remarkably, the heat oceans have absorbed since 1997 is equal to the energy generated if a bomb the size of the one that struck Hiroshima exploded every second for seventy-five consecutive years.

At what point would global warming become intolerable?

International scientists warn that we must hold the average temperature of the Earth's surface to no more than 1.5 degrees Celsius (2.7 degrees F) above preindustrial temperatures. The Earth already has warmed nearly 1.1 percent Celsius, and records keeping falling. The warmest decade ever recorded was 2010 to 2019, 2015 to 2019 were the five warmest years on record, and sixteen of the last seventeen years were the warmest on record. We have to act quickly before global warming becomes catastrophic.

Why do such small temperature changes have such significant impacts?

Although these temperature changes seem minuscule compared to what we experience in everyday weather, the more apt comparison is what happens to the human body when its temperature rises above normal. Only a few degrees are a fever; more than a few degrees can cause death.

Why do we see more torrential rains?

Warmer air and surface waters cause more water to evaporate from the Earth's surface. The result is more substantial and sustained rains inland and during coastal storms. Precipitation is growing 1 to 2 percent every decade in dry as well as wet locations.[10] It will continue to increase as global warming gets worse.

Not all parts of the United States will experience this the same way. Some places will get the same amount of yearly precipitation but in deluges rather than many smaller storms. We already see a larger percentage of precipitation in the form of extreme one-day events.[11] Large floods have become more frequent in the Northwest, Pacific Northwest, and northern Great Plains, and floods have become more intense in rivers and streams in the Northeast and Midwest.[12]

NOAA predicts that the worst floods we see today will be routine by mid-century. Recent research at the University of Central Florida projects that by 2050, coastal floods with a 1 percent chance of happening in a given year will be 50 or 100 times more likely than they are today.

In May 2019, an unusual "bomb cyclone" dumped vast amounts of precipitation in the Midwest and northern states over short periods.[13] One meteorologist compared it to a "1,000-mile-wide hurricane plopped

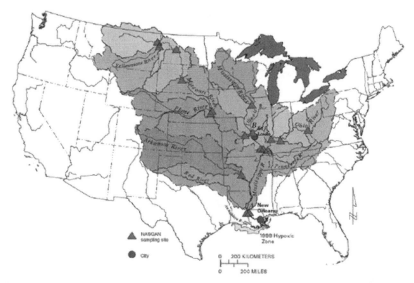

The Mississippi River Basin, where record floods have occurred, spans 40 percent of the continental United States. The 2019 flood may have been its longest, but it was far from the first. The river also flooded in 1543, 1734, 1788, 1809, 1825, 1851, 1858, 1859, 1874, 1882, 1883, 1884, 1890, 1893, 1897, 1903, 1908, 1912, 1913, 1916, 1922, 1927, 1928, 1929, 1931, 1932, 1935, 1937, 1944, 1945, 1950, 1973, 1975, 1979, 1983, 1997, 2002, 2011, 2016, 2017, and 2018. *EPA*

in the middle of the Central Plains." The Mississippi River produced its most significant flood in history in 2019, with several rounds of flooding and continuous storms over 140 days. For the first time, the entire Mississippi River Basin, which covers 40 percent of the continental United States, was at flood stage. In September 2019, several high plains states including parts of the Dakotas and Wyoming received more than 200 percent of normal precipitation, while several locations in North Dakota received between 400 and 800 times their normal precipitation.[14]

Scientists from the federal agencies in the USGCRP anticipate that more frequent and intense weather extremes will "continue to damage infrastructure, ecosystems and social systems that provide essential benefits to communities."

What have the impacts been so far?

During the last three decades in the United States, there were 254 weather disasters that each caused more than $1 billion in losses. A recent study found that more than 1.1 million people were displaced by disasters during 2016 alone, placing the United States fifth in the world.[15]

Because of climate change, we must deal with weather disasters differently than we did in the twentieth century. Engineered structures like dams, levees, and seawalls have saved millions of lives and billions of dollars' worth of buildings and infrastructure. But the enormous investment we have made to subdue rivers and tame waves has failed to reduce weather- and climate-related fatalities and property damages. We should not expect to be safer if we keep trying the same failed approaches we used in the past.[16]

How do we know that climate change is really contributing to extreme weather?

Until recently, scientists acknowledged that they couldn't attribute single weather events to climate change. Now, a new branch of knowledge known as attribution science allows experts to calculate how much climate change has added to the strength of extreme weather. For example, scientists determined that when Hurricane Harvey stalled over Texas in 2017, climate change intensified precipitation by as much as 19 percent.

What are we doing to keep climate change from getting worse?

Far too little. Climate change is well underway worldwide. The Earth's average surface temperature has already increased more than 1.5°C in some locations. If we stopped greenhouse gas pollution today, climate change still would continue for hundreds or even thousands of years because that is how long some of the greenhouse gases persist in the atmosphere.

There also is a "lag effect," in which the planet takes several decades to respond to increases in CO_2. We will not feel the full effect of today's pollution for forty years or so. Scientists sometimes use the analogy of water on a stove to explain this. When you put a pan of water on a gas stove, the flame is extremely hot, but it takes several minutes before the water reaches the boiling point. The heat of the flame does not instantly heat the water.

We should feel a sense of urgency about this. Scientists said in 2018 that we had only twelve years to reverse course on greenhouse gas pollution if we hope to keep warming to no more than 1.5°C above preindustrial levels. It will require rapid and revolutionary changes in many parts of our lives—changes that we have not yet seen society willing to make. We have to stop producing, using, and subsidizing fossil fuels and replace them with zero-carbon energy from resources such as sunlight and wind. We need to help workers in the oil, coal, and gas industries get training for jobs in post-carbon industries. We need to drive vehicles powered by electricity, hydrogen, and other clean fuels. We need to build more efficient buildings and equip them with their own solar energy systems.

Instead, we are moving in the opposite direction. In the United States and worldwide, momentum is pushing us in the direction of a much more violent and less livable planet. Zero-carbon and inexhaustible energy from sunlight and wind is cheaper than fossil fuels today. Yet, the US Department of Energy projects that with current policies, petroleum will remain our dominant source of energy in 2050, and while renewable resources will provide 42 percent of US electricity, double their contribution now, fossil fuels will provide 47 percent.[17] These are disappointing projections in light of the international goal and President Biden's objective for the United States to achieve a net-zero-carbon economy by mid-century and to rely heavily on "clean" electricity.

POLITICO
DATAPOINT
ON ENERGY

Nov. 22, 2019

Fossil fuel production plans are far outside climate targets

The world's governments are on track to produce about 120 percent more fossil fuels than levels needed to avoid the worst effects of global warming, according to a collaborative assessment by a group of research and academic institutions and experts, who based their analysis on recent government plans and projections for fossil fuel production. The report recommended countries close the production gap by limiting exploration and extraction, eliminating fossil fuel subsidies and aligning future production plans with climate goals.

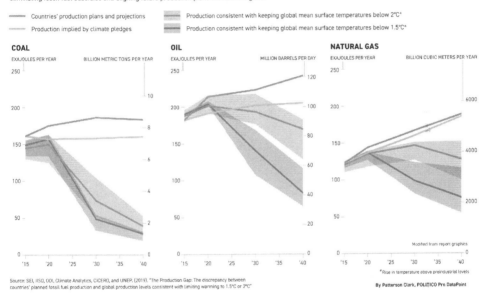

Source: SEI, IISD, ODI, Climate Analytics, CICERO, and UNEP. (2019). "The Production Gap: The discrepancy between countries' planned fossil fuel production and global production levels consistent with limiting warming to 1.5°C or 2°C"

By Patterson Clark, POLITICO Pro DataPoint

The world is producing 120 percent more fossil fuels than the amount required to avoid the worst impacts of global warming. *Politico*

Why aren't we doing better?

Societal inertia is one reason. It is much easier to do nothing than to take the disruptive steps we know are necessary. Besides, politicians are more concerned about losing the lucrative support of oil companies than the support of voters. To delay the transition to zero-carbon energy, oil and gas companies spent more than $112.5 million to lobby the United States Congress during 2020.[18] The industry had 680 lobbyists, two-thirds of them former government employees. During the 2020 election cycle, oil and gas companies contributed nearly $40 million to congressional campaigns, including $30.5 million to Republicans.[19]

To be clear, the objective of a net-zero-carbon economy is not to put oil and gas companies out of business; it's to have them change their business models from producing fossil fuels to producing and distributing zero-carbon energy. Market forces are moving in that direction; energy companies should, too. The International Energy Agency predicts that renewable electric capacity, led by solar energy, will grow 50 percent worldwide by 2024. With more push, the growth could be 26 percent higher.

The analysis firm Bloomberg New Energy Finance projects that solar and wind power, combined with batteries to store the power, will provide nearly half of the world's electricity by mid-century and will attract $10 trillion in investment.[20] Another prominent research company, Deloitte, projects that solar and wind power will provide nearly 97 percent of America's new electric generating capacity in 2020.[21] As I mentioned earlier, NREL has shown that 80 to 90 percent of our electricity could come from renewable resources by mid-century using technologies available today. However, we will have to invest in modern electric infrastructure to achieve that goal.

In short, without a radical correction in national and international energy and water policies, the long-term weather forecast is a 100 percent chance of unprecedented disasters, including a deluge of climate migrants and refugees within the United States and on its borders, international crises and conflicts, many billions of dollars in lost and damaged infrastructure, frequent flooding along rivers and on coasts, many lost lives, competition for freshwater supplies, poor air quality and related illnesses, rising insurance premiums, sinking land, parts of our major cities disappearing under oceans, unprecedented heat waves, and so on.

But unlike our usual weather forecasts, we can change this one if we move quickly enough to zero-carbon emissions. At the same time, we must become better prepared to deal with the extreme weather that already is in the pipeline.

APPENDIX 2

Recommendations

THE PRESIDENT OF THE UNITED STATES should create a **National Flood Avoidance Task Force** with members that represent the US Army Corps of Engineers, the Federal Emergency Management Agency, the National Association of State Dam Safety Officers, the National Association of State Floodplain Managers, the National Conference of Mayors, and the National Academy of Sciences to refine the following recommendations, designate the appropriate organizations and agencies to implement them, and to estimate the costs of implementation for each.

Equip states for a national climate-change/dam-safety audit

Immediately provide states with the resources to hire sufficient numbers of qualified dam safety inspectors. Make the funds contingent upon state participation in a national dam-safety inspection program that assesses the ability of nonfederal high-hazard and significant-hazard-potential dams to protect lives and property during 100-, 500-, and 1,000-year flood events. Determine whether intensive programs of ecosystem restoration and managed retreats would be more cost-effective than repairing, upgrading, or building structural measures.

Deal immediately with deficient dams

Request that dam safety inspectors in states where deficient dams have been identified to assess the cost of repairs, replacement, demolition, or replacement with nonstructural flood avoidance such as floodplain relocations, river restoration, and other "soft" alternatives. Develop a plan and appropriate sufficient funds to immediately mitigate the risks posed by the nearly 2,200 deficient high-risk dams. Alternatively, or additionally, require dam owners to pay all or part of the repairs.

Fully fund levee safety

Appropriate and release all of the nearly $400 million it authorized in the National Dam Safety Act of 2014 for a national levee safety program.

Expand and expedite "living" coastal restoration projects

Allocate additional resources to fund projects along the Great Lakes, the Atlantic Ocean, and the Gulf of Mexico. In a recent report on the "living shorelines" approach to reducing coastal erosion and floods, the National Wildlife Federation concludes, "Although there has been progress in the adoption of these softer approaches in some states, the rate of living shoreline installation is still low relative to the amount of hardened shoreline protections."[1]

Decarbonize US fiscal policies

Request that the National Academy of Sciences identify federal fiscal policies that directly or indirectly result in greenhouse gas emissions. The Congressional Budget Office, the Government Accountability Office, or the Internal Revenue Service should then assess the economic and environmental impacts of eliminating these perverse incentives.

Prioritize relocation in national water policy

Make the relocation of property out of floodplains the first objective of national water policy over the next decade.

Develop a strategy for using disaster management funds

The GAO has recommended several times that presidential administrations develop a strategic plan for the use of disaster management funds. FEMA should comply and integrate this plan with the audit of deficient and high-hazard potential dams proposed previously. FEMA and the GCRP should inform the strategy by applying the probable maximum precipitation (PMP) methodology to identify the highest priority regions based on the anticipated regional impacts of climate change.[2]

Mitigate danger to vulnerable hazard sites

GAO reported in October 2019 that about 60 percent of all nonfederal Superfund sites classified as high priorities are in areas vulnerable to floods, storm surges, wildfires, and sea-level rise. These sites have released hazardous substances or may present a danger of release. The GAO concluded that the EPA is ignoring climate change in its risk-management process for the sites. In addition, assess and mitigate the risks associated with power plants, coal-waste sites, and other sensitive facilities to 1,000-year flood events and PMP sea-level rise, coastal erosion, storm surges, and coastal storms.

Institute tough-love water policy

Federal flood insurance subsidies and disaster recovery assistance have the perverse effect of encouraging people to remain in floodplains. These policies make taxpayers who choose to live in safe places pay for the problems of those who don't. This transfer of resources will become substantially larger and more politically sensitive as weather worsens. Shift the liability for disaster damages back to private insurance, communities that permit floodplain development, or real estate developers that build in floodplains to take advantage of cheap land.

There are mixed signals from private insurers on whether they are ready to take over flood coverage again. One opinion is that the industry now has sufficient reserves and the ability to more accurately model risks. However, the market is complicated by other climate-related disasters—wildfires, for example—as well as FEMA's outdated floodplain maps and the role of subsidized state insurance programs of last resort in about thirty states. Over the transition decade, work with states and the property/casualty industry to try to deal with these barriers.

Meanwhile, the following changes should be made to national water policy.

- Phase out the NFIP over ten years except for low-income households, while shifting to risk-based insurance premiums to smooth homeowners' transition to private insurers.
- During the decade, make communities ineligible for federal disaster recovery funds after two disasters.
- Ramp up FEMA's buyout program to encourage managed retreats from floodplains. To encourage early relocations, provide 100 percent federal funding for buyouts during the first half of the decade, rather than the current 75 percent.

Assign highest priority to managed retreats

Direct the US Army Corps of Engineers to assign highest priority to managed retreats in flood avoidance planning.

Reduce red tape

Significantly reduce the bureaucratic paperwork and time required to approve buyouts. Encourage buyouts at floodplain rather than building scale.

Encourage pre-disaster planning

Encourage flood-prone communities to develop buyout and relocation plans prior to another disaster. The plans should include zoning ordinances, building codes, and other ordinances that would go into effect immediately after the next disaster, as well as incentives for floodplain homeowners to relocate inside the community. Research shows that because federal disaster assistance is not place based, many disaster victims who take buyouts are likely to take the money and run. This has been the pattern since FEMA was created in 1978. While this still reduces the number of people living in disaster zones, it results in the loss of social networks and tax bases.

Encourage community development outside floodplains

Encourage communities to identify and purchase property outside the floodplain at sufficient size to accommodate the relocation of floodplain properties. Coordinate with FEMA to locate its temporary housing at the site and to provide permanent rather than temporary infrastructure there.

Align priorities of greatest risk and adequate accessibility

Require communities to develop buyout strategies that prioritize homes in greatest danger of flood damages and that provide sufficient low-income housing to accommodate all low-income floodplain residents.

Restore ecosystems

Require communities to incorporate ecosystem restoration in their flood-avoidance plans to reduce the size of floodplains.

Require infrastructure investment

Encourage permitting agencies to require that (a) the owners of proposed new dams provide proof of the ability to maintain the structure over its design life, and (b) have an acceptable emergency plan in case of structural failure.

Remove incentives to develop floodplains

Make communities ineligible for federal disaster relief if they allow any further development in floodplains.

Identify our most vulnerable regions

Direct FEMA to work with the US Global Change Research Program and NOAA to use best available science to identify regions most vulnerable to extreme floods. Update the information as science's ability improves to predict climate-change impacts at local scale.

Use the best science for risk assessment

Direct the EPA to include the best available climate change information in its risk management work. The GAO reports that the EPA is not doing this at present.

Provide federal assistance for local greenhouse gas reductions

Determine whether new federal assistance is needed to empower states, cities, and businesses to accomplish their greenhouse gas reduction goals.[3]

Expand grants

Expand the range of state activities eligible for formula and/or competitive grants in the State Energy Program.

Develop a national energy policy plan biannually

Direct the secretary of energy to develop a national energy policy plan every two years, consistent with the requirements and procedures in the Department of Energy Organization Act and designed to help the nation achieve a net-zero-carbon economy by 2050. Include specific timelines, milestones, and performance measures.

Develop a national plan for flood-control structures

Develop a comprehensive national plan to repair, upgrade, supplement, or replace the nation's flood control structures to meet 1,000-year flood standards and projected sea-level rise. Estimate the costs of the proposed measures and prioritize them based on best available projections of climate-change impacts, the level of structural risks, and the benefits and costs of nonstructural alternatives based on life-cycle analysis. Nonstructural measures should include reforestation of watersheds, restoration of wetlands, reconnections of rivers with floodplains, buyouts of at-risk properties, and urban floodproofing such as permeable surfaces and additional open space.

Assess the potential for an economic bubble

Direct the Council of Economic Advisors to assess the potential for an economic bubble created by the fossil energy industry's overinvestment in exploration, production, and infrastructure in view of the industry's growing climate-related risks.

Ensure the role of science in policy

Ensure public access to government research, restore the role of science in policy, protect science integrity, establish baseline qualifications for political appointees to science and science-administration positions, and fill vacant science positions in government. In a study of the federal government's science capabilities, the Union of Concerned Scientists (UCS) found that science has been attacked and politicized for many years under presidential administrations regardless of political party.[4] According to the UCS, during its first three years in office, the Trump administration "stunted or stalled scientific research, retaliated against government scientists, weakened and disbanded science advisory committees, left appointed scientific positions vacant, and undermined career staff at many agencies." Yet science is indispensable if leaders are to make informed decisions and laws. Nearly thirty federal agencies have scientific integrity policies, but enforcement varies and none have been put into national law. President Biden is rebuilding the government's sciences capabilities, but to prevent future presidents from abandoning or manipulating science, Congress should pass legislation that codifies the role of sciece and scientists in the executive branch.

Create a State of the Nation's Environment address

Deliver a nationally televised address each Earth Day on the State of the Nation's Environment. Include a situation report on climate change in the United States and a progress report on the nation's clean energy and carbon-reduction goals. The address should also include reports on other environmental indicators such as air and water quality, freshwater resources, forest health, wildlife habitat, endangered species, biodiversity, and so on.

Use full-cost accounting in planning

Determine whether federal agencies are using state-of-the-art full-cost accounting, including the social costs of carbon in their benefit-cost analyses and budget planning.[5] If necessary, the president should issue a directive requiring the use of this methodology. All benefit-cost analyses and environmental impact statements related to floodplain management should be based on the full life-cycle costs of what is proposed, including the social costs of carbon.[6]

Study extreme Probable Maximum Precipitation

Commission a study by the National Academies of Science, Engineering, and Medicine (NASEM) to identify the current best options for estimating extreme Probable Maximum Precipitation (PMP). This would help USACE, FEMA, and others determine up-to-date PMPs for disaster avoidance strategies.

Improve national planning

Direct the appropriate agencies to prepare the following plans:

- A **national ecosystem restoration plan** that sets goals for maintaining or restoring wildlife habitat, freshwater supplies, healthy soils, wetlands, afforestation, river and coastal protections, fisheries, and so on. The plan should give highest priority to ecosystems that reduce flood dangers and that sequester carbon dioxide.
- A **climate-resilient national infrastructure plan** for adapting critical infrastructure to climate change, including requirements that new or substantially improved infrastructure be fortified against anticipated weather-related disasters.
- A **national coastal protection plan** that builds on the Great Lakes, Gulf Coast, and other ongoing coastal restoration projects with

an emphasis on "soft" protections against erosion, storm surges, and sea-level rise. The plan should proactively promote buyouts among private property owners whose property values are falling because of sea-level rise, storm surges, extreme coastal weather, and floods.[7] It should prioritize the most threatened areas. The long-term goal should be to create continuous publicly owned and protected coastlines on the Gulf, the Atlantic Ocean, and the Great Lakes by converting seashore and lakeshore properties into national conservation areas, national recreation areas, or national seashores. The plan should include options for compensating coastal and lakeshore jurisdictions for an estimated $1.5 billion in lost property-tax revenues.

Designate climate sanctuary cities

Climate change is expected to result in a substantial migration inland as homeowners and businesses flee sea-level rise, beach erosion, more violent storms, rainfall, and so on. The Department of Housing and Urban Development should propose a plan that designates cities with declining populations and tax bases as "climate sanctuary cities" (CSCs) that are willing to welcome US climate migrants. Census data show that nearly a fifth of all states have experienced declining populations in recent years.[8] Congress and HUD should provide CSCs with economic development assistance to create clean energy manufacturing hubs and to train workers to help fill the skills gaps in renewable energy and energy efficiency industries.

Integrate climate-change information with risk management

Direct that federal agencies base their decisions and programs on current climate-change impact information and the national goal of reducing greenhouse gas emissions. This information is especially important for the EPA, FEMA, USACE, Bureau of Land Management, and any other federal agencies that permit, build, own, or manage coastal or riverine flood-control structures and devices. This is necessary in view of reports that "EPA officials do not always have clear direction to ensure that they consistently integrate climate change information into site-level risk assessments and risk response decisions."

Standardize data

Direct FEMA and the USACE to work with ASCE to generate and standardize data on deficient, high-risk, and significant-risk dams and costs of recommended maintenance and repairs.

Boost FEMA Corps

Provide AmeriCorps with funds necessary to increase compensation and incentives for young Americans to enroll in FEMA Corps, specifically to help communities restore ecosystems with multipurpose benefits, including flood avoidance and climate-change resilience.

Strengthen the "polluter pays" principle

With Congress and the executive branch failing to act on climate change, courts have become the last resort for penalties and cost recovery. Strengthen the "polluter pays" principle for citizens and communities to obtain court-ordered compensation from fossil energy companies for climate damages and adaptation expenses. Establish that attribution science is admissible in determining liability and authorize "special circumstances" penalties against companies that knew but withheld their knowledge that their products were contributing to climate change.[9]

Codify the Trust Doctrine

Put the Public Trust Doctrine into US law. It establishes that public officials have a fiduciary duty to protect certain natural resources for the benefit of all people, present and future. This principle, established in ancient law, usually applies to resources like fish, wildlife habitat, and recreation. Congress should make clear that the atmosphere also must be held in trust.

Fund displaced-worker transitions

Congress should create and fund a transition assistance program for workers and communities displaced by the transition to zero-carbon energy. The training should include a focus on jobs related to zero-carbon energy, managed retreats (construction), ecosystem services, and other environmental restoration fields.

Deploy relocation planning assistance teams to localities

Create and deploy expert teams that provide on-site consultation to communities planning a significant retreat. Offer lessons learned from other managed retreats, urban designs that reduce infrastructure demand, the use of gasoline-powered vehicles, and energy demands while promoting sustainability and community-scale distributed solar energy systems.

Set mandatory national standards for new dams

Develop compulsory federal standards for dam and levee design, construction, and maintenance taking anticipated future climate-change impacts into account.

Estimate floodplain populations

Adopt the methods and technology that researchers at the University of Bristol used when they determined that 43 million Americans, 254 million homes, and $1.2 trillion in assets are currently at risk of floods in the lower forty-eight states.

Map extreme flood risks

Provide flood-prone communities with maps showing the areas at risk from 500-year and 1,000-year floods, and areas that would be affected if nearby dams or levees failed.

Improve the buyout program

Proactively promote and encourage the use of buyouts for managed retreats. Significantly simplify and shorten the buyout process. Encourage communities to create and obtain government approvals of buy-out plans before the next disaster. To promote buyouts, pay 100 percent of fair market value of floodplain homes for five years before returning to a federal share of 75 percent.

Standardize data

Data on the number of dams, degrees of deficiency, cost of repairs, and so on are inconsistent among the several different governmental and nongovernmental organizations involved in dam safety. Convene these agencies and organizations to reach an agreement on standardized data.

Establish minimum requirements for dam owners

Federal and state agencies with jurisdiction over dam safety and permitting should require every dam owner to have an approved emergency action plan. When permitting or approving the construction of new dams, agencies with jurisdiction should require proof that the owner has sufficient resources to properly maintain the structure.

Set national standards for estimating rainfall

Provide NOAA clear direction on the development of twenty-first century national standards for estimating extreme rainfall including PMP standards. PMP standards have long been used for regulation and design of high-hazard potential infrastructure including dams and nuclear power facilities. Those standards are used to bring consistency between federal agencies, state agencies, and the private sector professional design community. Federal leadership is needed to update these standards.

Extend the "compensatory mitigation" model

Currently, if a developer wants to build a housing project that will damage a wetland, stream, or river, it must obtain a permit from the USACE. The permit requires the developer to avoid damage to the wetland, stream, or river. If the damage is unavoidable, the developer must invest in creating or restoring a comparable natural resource elsewhere. This requirement has resulted in a market for "wetland credits." Private investors can put their money into wetlands restoration, earn credits, and sell them to developers.

Budget for disaster management

Comply with the series of recommendations by the GAO over several years that the administration develop a strategic plan to prioritize how federal funds will be spent on disaster management.

Create a single agency to coordinate federal grant programs

There are currently many layers of bureaucracy to apply for flood disaster prevention, response, and recovery. The single agency should also weight funding toward prevention.

Quantify the benefits of ecosystem services

Develop guidelines for agencies and localities on how to quantify the benefits of ecosystem services for benefit-cost analyses. Require the USACE to include those monetized benefits in its environmental impact statements.

Accurately determine annual flood damages

Request that the interagency Federal Floodplain Management Task force determine average annual flood damages in the United States. Despite a few databases from generally reliable agencies like NOAA, there is not a consistent, credible database of average annual flood damages. For example, the damages from hurricanes do not accurately separate the damage from wind versus flood.

Accurately calculate the people and property at risk of flood damage

Develop consensus data on the number of people and amount of property vulnerable to floods and likely to be vulnerable in the future. For example, researchers at the University of Bristol estimate that 41 million Americans are located in 100-year riverine floodplains in the lower forty-eight states, while FMEA estimates that 13 million Americans are at risk.[10]

The First Street Foundation calculates that 14.6 million properties are in danger from 100-year floods, far more than 8.7 million properties it says are shown on federal flood maps.[11] The New York University Furman Center indicates that an average of 15 million Americans lived in 100-year floodplains from 2011 to 2015, and 30 million lived in combined 100- and 500-year floodplains during the same period.[12]

Direct the BLS to begin counting green jobs again

If necessary, have the National Academies help the Bureau of Labor Statistics define green jobs and direct the BLS to begin reporting them again.

Include ecosystem services in infrastructure plans and investments

For example, floodplains, wetlands, marshes, and reefs help reduce flood damages. Urban open spaces and natural drainage swales help reduce the cost of stormwater systems.

Launch a national biophilia initiative on Earth Day

The initiative should include actions to "green" cities with urban forestry to cool heat islands, open spaces, gardens, green roofs, natural drainage swales, and permeable surfaces. Use biophilic cities as models of innovative ways to incorporate nature into urban environments.

Encourage nonstructural alternatives for levees

The USACE repairs and reconstructs damaged levees. Federal taxpayers end up paying 80 percent to 100 percent of the costs. Direct levee owners and the USACE to consider nonstructural alternatives to replace levees or to reduce wear and tear.

Promote pre-disaster mitigation programs

Research shows that a dollar spent to mitigate floods produces at least $6 of savings. Congress passed legislation in 2018 to require that 6 percent of

FEMA's disaster costs are set aside each year for a pre-disaster mitigation program. Determine whether the funds are well-spent and sufficient to meet demand. If demand is low, direct FEMA to do a better job promoting the program.

Recommendations from the House of Representatives Select Committee on the Climate Crisis

As the 116th session of Congress began in January 2019, House Speaker Nancy Pelosi created a Select Committee on the Climate Crisis to recommend what Congress should do to address global climate change. The Committee issued its suggestions in June 2020. They include the following in regard to floods:

- Increase funding to address the ecological effects of dams and to repair high-hazard dams; to fully fund the national levee safety program; to have USACE develop consistent levee-safety standards for development behind levees; to assess the nation's levees taking climate change into account; and to address the climate risks identified by the assessment.
- Direct the USACE to identify repeatedly damaged levees and engage in pre-disaster planning for levee repairs including nonstructural options, and provide technical assistance to communities, levee owners and operators on managing the risks associated with these structures.
- Ensure that the USACE considers the full range of options for reducing flood losses including buyouts and relocations of willing property owners and communities, restoring ecosystems and setting levees back further from rivers to reduce the speed and force of floodwaters.

APPENDIX 3

Tips for Relocation Facilitators

WHEN WE HELPED COMMUNITIES PLAN RELOCATIONS from floodplains or helped them incorporate sustainable development principles in their more conventional plans, several colleagues and I learned a few things. Facilitating a relocation takes a gentle touch, a willingness to listen to everyone in the community, and skills in helping to keep the momentum alive. Here are a few of the most important tips.

The first step is to get the blessing of the community's elected leadership. If you are not from the community, mayors, city council members, and Indigenous planners will be wary about inviting strangers into town to create wild expectations and promises that community leaders may not want or be able to deliver. You'll have to gain the local leaders' trust and their permission to seriously consider, if not commit to, the ideas that emerge from the planning process.

You'll also need to win the trust of the "planning elite" that is present in most communities. They might include elected officials, city engineers and architects, officers of regional planning associations, or especially influential citizens. When you engage the entire community in the planning process, they may feel as if their influence is usurped. It's good practice to help them feel as if they own the project by involving them in the planning process, asking for their guidance, and so on. Unless they feel that sense of ownership, they are likely to hijack the plan when you leave town, even to the point of violating assurances to citizens that they are, in the final analysis, the architects of their future. The sweet spot is to help them feel an investment in the outcome of relocation, while they share control of that income with the entire community.

The idea is to build citizens' sense of ownership, too, so that they stick to their vision through thick and thin. There will be inevitable delays, disagreements, legal issues, and funding lapses that will test peoples' resolve. But people are more likely to persist and to defend the plan if they helped create it.

Spend time in the community before you meet with citizens. Drive around and study it. Make friends and ask questions at a local tavern. Your credibility will increase if you show you know things about the community and its issues.

Before work is done, identify a committed local "champion" who has the mayor's and city council's blessing to keep the project on track. Citizens may want to snap back into traditional thinking, denial, and rationalizations if there is no progress. This is the role that Tom Hirsch filled in Soldiers Grove. Celebrate progress, however small, to show movement. Keep citizens informed. The art of leadership in disruptive projects like relocation is to keep citizens on the fulcrum I mentioned earlier—the point of balance between the negative situation they must leave and the positive situation they can create. If the champion is not familiar with sustainable designs and technologies, offer to remain available to him or her as a technical resource.

The tools to help a community visualize life after relocation can be as simple as paper and markers, or as sophisticated as virtual reality. The most appropriate tool depends on the community. People who are not very familiar with computers and software or state-of-the-art presentation tools can be alienated by them.

It may seem obvious, but visualization of life after relocation should be visual. People can process visual information sixty thousand times faster than words, and they remember visuals better. We've been in communities that cleared a big space on the floor and used cardboard boxes to represent buildings, then moved them around to negotiate where each building would go in the new development.

A step up from cardboard boxes is a visual preference survey in which people are shown before and after images of how a relocated neighborhood could look. The community is asked to vote on which image they prefer. Their options can be obvious, like those shown here. Or they might be two very desirable but different visions. Those who have used visual preference surveys usually have been surprised at the level of agreement.

Visual preference surveys use photographs like these for before-and-after visualizations of sustainable development projects. *Compliments of Steve Price, Urban Advantage*

It's useful to ask local teachers to have their students draw pictures of what they'd like to see in the new development. We hung drawings on the walls where the town meetings were held to remind people that in a development that should last for generations, they were rebuilding more for their children than themselves.

When relocation gets to the point where the site is chosen and lots are to be assigned, you are likely to see competition for the choicest lots. This can get ugly. Some towns have organized assigned lots by lottery, so the process is transparent and fair. Let people trade with one another if they'd like.

This tip is especially important. Encourage flood-prone communities to plan and implement relocation *before* rather than after the next flood or storm. If the community has a history of flooding, people can be sure it will happen again. After the disaster has taken place, people will be overwhelmed with basic needs and financial stresses; they'll be anxious to simply get their lives back to normal, and "normal" means the way things were. A pre-disaster relocation can be done much more thoughtfully.

FEMA can make funding available for pre-disaster "mitigation assistance" when state and local governments have developed and adopted hazard mitigation plans.[1] The agency's grants are used primarily to reduce or eliminate the risks of repetitive flooding of buildings insured by the National Flood Insurance Program.

There is a tradeoff here, however. People who have not experienced a flood for a while may not be as motivated to go through the disruption of a pre-disaster relocation. As time goes on, flood victims often slip into denial that another flood will happen. In these cases, the best approach is to emphasize the social, economic, quality of life, and environmental benefits of rebuilding outside the floodplain.

The next-best option is to *prepare* pre-disaster for a post-disaster relocation. Communities can get through the process of holding public hearings; identifying, purchasing, and preparing the relocation site; and approving provisional zoning ordinances and building codes that will take effect immediately after the next flood.

If all of this must be done post-disaster, there will be a small window of opportunity where people will be receptive to relocation because they never want to go through another flood. But again, floodplain amnesia will soon set in where people only remember the good parts of the disaster, like how everyone in the community came together to help one another. The facilitator and local leaders' challenge is to extend that sense social cohesion and goodwill all the way through relocation.

Look for and promote opportunities for co-benefits from the move. These are benefits that piggyback on parts of a project. For example, a relocation might include moving a municipal well or water treatment plan out of the floodplain to prevent contamination during floods. Those who rebuild their homes can rebuild them for this century rather than the past. They can incorporate better insulation, more modern appliances, rooftop solar systems, and so on. Some opportunities include:

- Permeable street and parking surfaces that absorb rain where it falls.
- Well-positioned trees to reduce temperatures during heat waves by shading homes without blocking another building's access to sunlight.
- Rooftop solar panels to generate electricity or neighborhood-scale solar arrays that serve several houses, including those where shade or orientation are not conducive to rooftop solar.
- Energy-efficient building envelopes and appliances. Buildings should achieve efficiency levels far above the current national model energy building code. In fact, it is possible now to build net-zero energy homes that produce as much as or more energy than they consume.
- Natural drainage swales to help handle stormwater during intense rains.
- Streets with segregated lanes for pedestrians and bicyclists.
- Informal social gathering places such as sidewalk tables at a coffee shop, or benches at small green spaces in the downtown.
- Urban designs where people are a fifteen-minute walk or less from grocery stores, schools, churches, mass transit, and other critical services.
- Access to high-speed internet.
- Modern affordable housing for low-income residents. A new development should include at least one affordable housing unit for every low-income family that is displaced. Retail establishments should consider including apartments above their stores, giving elderly and

low-income residents the opportunity to live close to things like shopping and church services.

Most towns have a local curmudgeon or two who have complaints and want to be heard. They have been shut down in city council meetings. People don't respect their opinions. Many times, the curmudgeon just wants a chance to speak his or her peace. As a facilitator, you need to make a decision whether to ignore the curmudgeons or take their questions and even give them the floor to get things off their chests. I've found times when these people turn out to be the most involved and creative in the crowd when they know they will be heard and their opinions respected.

A lot of things will come up, some of them off topic. Have a tablet and easel to put those things in a "parking lot" so they are recognized but set aside for the moment to take up later or at another meeting, or to simply turn over to city officials for their consideration.

Many people will expect you to tell them how to design the new neighborhood. Make clear to the townspeople that you're not there for that. They will design the development. Your role is to help them record it and to expand their menu of options with some things they may not be familiar with, like solar energy. We often started the meeting with something called a "treasures exercise." Set up two tablets. On one, record everyone's thoughts about what they didn't like in the old neighborhood. On the other, record the things they loved. The result is a list of criteria or attributes for the new neighborhood. When finished, tell them that they've just taken a big first step in designing the new place.

Finally, one of most current resources for communities that want to consider managed retreats has been released by the Georgetown Climate Center. It's the Managed Retreat Toolkit, the first comprehensive resource of its kind to offer tips on best practices, legal and policy tools, and case studies.[2]

APPENDIX 4

Ecosystem Restoration Resources Compiled by the Environmental and Energy Study Institute

EPA Clean Water Act Nonpoint Source Grants (Section 319)

Description: Section 319 of the Clean Water Act awards grants for projects that manage nonpoint sources of water pollution. Section 319 grants may only be used for water management activities that do not directly implement a National Pollutant Discharge Elimination System permit. Eligible nature-based solutions include wetland and riverbank restoration and protection, infiltration basins (vegetated depressions used to manage stormwater runoff), green roofs, and landscape swales.

    Eligible to apply: States, territories, and tribal agencies.

    Example: In 2010, a Clean Water Act Section 319 grant provided $910,753 to restore the Watts Branch watershed in Washington, DC, which had been eroded by excessive stormwater runoff. Restoration efforts involved planting trees, creating floodplain benches to reduce stormwater energy, and regrading stream banks to control stream flow.

EPA Clean Water State Revolving Fund (CWSRF)

Description: The CWSRF uses federal and state funds to provide low-interest loans for water infrastructure projects. States contribute a 20 percent match of the federal funding and are responsible for operating and implementing the projects. Nature-based solutions for habitat restoration, pollution management, and other projects are eligible for CWSRF funding.

   Eligible to apply: All fifty states, Washington, DC, and US territories.

   Example: In 2015, Bellingham, Washington, restored Squalicum Creek to natural conditions using $2.5 million in CWSRF funding. The project reconnected the creek to a floodplain, which improved water quality, restored habitat for salmonid species, and expanded recreational opportunities. Squalicum Creek's surrounding wetlands and forests are now able to absorb higher flows, which has reduced flooding in the region.

EPA Great Lakes Restoration Initiative (GLRI)

Description: The GLRI protects and restores the Great Lakes and the surrounding region by funding the abatement of toxic substances, removal of invasive species, and reduction of nonpoint source pollution harmful to humans and ecosystems. The GLRI prioritizes nature-based solutions, including wetland restoration and green stormwater infrastructure.

   Eligible to apply: Agencies, states, tribes, local governments, universities, nongovernmental organizations.

   Example: In 2019, the GLRI funded a $475,000 project to reconnect Ohio's Cuyahoga River to 105 acres of river floodplains. This nature-based solution will help the Cuyahoga River area be more resilient by reducing erosion during flood events and enhancing habitats. Healthy floodplains slow floodwaters, improve water quality, protect people and property from floods, and recharge groundwater.

EPA Greening America's Communities Program

Description: The Greening America's Communities program supports green infrastructure and sustainable design projects in cities and towns across the United States. The EPA provides design and technical assistance to help implement these projects.

Eligible to apply: Cities and towns.

Example: In 2016, Greening America's Communities assisted Oklahoma City, Oklahoma, to address flooding and city connectivity issues. The program redesigned five parts of the city to incorporate pervious pavers, bioretention planters, riparian restoration, and bioswales to reduce stormwater runoff.

EPA Superfund Redevelopment Initiative (SRI)

Description: The SRI supports the cleanup and redevelopment of sites that are contaminated with hazardous waste by providing "site owners, businesses, local governments and lenders with the tools and information resources they need to make reuse happen." Creating resilience to climate change is incorporated into Superfund site cleanup. Many Superfund sites can be redeveloped to include nature-based solutions that prevent flooding, erosion, and transport of contaminants.

Eligible to apply: Government agencies, site owners, responsible parties, community members, developers, nonprofit agencies, and other partners.

Example: In 2011, SRI funding helped restore Bayou Verdine in Lake Charles, Louisiana, which had been contaminated by industrial activities. The project removed contaminated soils, reinforced parts of the bayou's shorelines to prevent flooding, and created a drainage bioswale.

EPA Urban Waters Small Grants Program (UWSG)

Description: UWSG uses small grants, up to $60,000, to fund individual projects that improve urban water quality. The projects must also provide additional community benefits (i.e., economic, recreational, and employment opportunities), engage underserved communities, and foster partnerships. Water quality issues can often be addressed with green infrastructure to manage runoff and reduce flooding.

Eligible to apply: States, local governments, tribes, public and private universities and colleges, public or private nonprofit institutions/organizations, intertribal consortia, and interstate agencies.

Example: Denver, Colorado, received a $60,000 UWSG in 2015 to restore 80 acres of land around Heron Lake. This project reduced runoff pollution and improved habitat.

FEMA Flood Mitigation Assistance (FMA) Grant Program

Description: The FMA grant program provides resources "to reduce or eliminate the risk of repetitive flood damage to buildings and structures insurable under the National Flood Insurance Program." FMA funds projects that reduce flood damage and make communities more resilient to future flooding. Stormwater management, wetland restoration or creation, and floodplain and stream restoration projects are eligible for FMA funding.

Eligible to apply: States, territories, and federally recognized tribes can submit applications on behalf of homeowners, businesses, and private nonprofits.

Example: Sebastian County, Arkansas, secured a $25,000 FMA grant in 2015 to update their Flood Hazard Mitigation Plan. The plan identified several nature-based solutions such as planting trees around buildings and parking lots and installing green roofs to mitigate extreme heat.

FEMA Pre-Disaster Mitigation (PDM) Grant Program

Description: FEMA PDM grants allow participants to develop resilient infrastructure to reduce the impacts of natural disasters, such as floods, earthquakes, droughts, and wildfires, before a disaster occurs. The current PDM program will be replaced by FEMA's new Building Resilient Infrastructure and Communities program, which is currently under development. The goal of both iterations of the funding source is to direct more resources for projects, including nature-based solutions, that prevent or reduce disaster impacts. Increased investment in pre-disaster mitigation should also reduce the cost of federal assistance for disaster response and recovery.

Eligible to apply: States, tribes, territories, and local communities.

Example: Chelsea, Massachusetts, received a PDM grant to update its 2014 Hazard Mitigation Plan. The Hazard Mitigation Plan identifies several high-priority hazard mitigation strategies, such as implementing green infrastructure best management practices and updating floodplain zoning and conservation regulations, to reduce flooding.

HUD Community Development Block Grant (CDBG) Program

Description: HUD administers the CDBG program to support a range of community needs, including affordable housing, neighborhood stabilization, and economic development. Green infrastructure for stormwater management and urban tree planting are eligible for CDBG funding because they create jobs, mitigate flooding in communities, and increase economic activities.

Eligible to apply: States, cities, and counties.

Example: In 2014, Detroit, Michigan, received an $8.9 million CDBG to demolish abandoned properties, plant trees on two hundred vacant lots, and install a bioretention basin. This project improved stormwater management and the vibrancy of the neighborhood.

NOAA Community-Based Restoration Program

Description: The Community-Based Restoration Program funds coastal and marine habitat restoration projects, such as restoring coral and oyster reefs, removing dams, and rebuilding coastal wetlands. The program provides grants and technical assistance for "restoration projects that use a habitat-based approach to rebuild productive and sustainable fisheries, contribute to the recovery and conservation of protected resources, promote healthy ecosystems, and yield community and economic benefits."

Eligible to apply: Institutions of higher education; nonprofit organizations; for-profit organizations; foreign public entities and foreign organizations; and state, territory, local, and tribal governments.

Example: The Save the Redwoods coalition was awarded $603,375 through the Community-Based Restoration Program in 2017 to restore 18 acres of wetland habitat in Humboldt County, California. The project restored floodplain access and increased resilience to severe weather.

USDA Urban and Community Forestry (UCF) Program

Description: The UCF Program works with states to provide technical, financial, research, and educational services so communities can conserve, restore, and enhance their urban forests. The program funds projects that improve human health, educate communities on urban forestry, and increase the resilience of urban forests. Urban forests help manage storm-water runoff and reduce building energy use by moderating temperatures (which also reduces the public health impact of heat waves) and mitigate climate change by sequestering carbon.

Eligible to apply: Local governments, nonprofit organizations, community groups, educational institutions, and tribal governments.

Example: In 2019, the UCF Program provided $590,622 to Oregon's Department of Forestry (ODF) to improve their urban forests. ODF used the funds for public education on invasive species and to provide technical assistance to thirty-five citizens and twenty-five schools, colleges, and public entities.

US Fish & Wildlife Service Coastal Program

Description: The Coastal Program provides technical and financial assistance for conservation and habitat restoration projects on private or public land that improve the resilience of coastal ecosystems. On average, the Coastal Program leverages eight dollars from partners for every one dollar spent by the Coastal Program itself.

Eligible to apply: Federal agencies, state agencies, local and tribal governments, businesses, conservation organizations, and private landowners in the twenty-four priority coastal areas along the Atlantic and Pacific Oceans, Gulf of Mexico, Great Lakes, and the Caribbean.

Example: Shipping channels, oil and gas facilities, and road construction have all taken a toll on the Salt Bayou in Texas. In 2013, the Salt Bayou Watershed Restoration Plan, created with help from the Coastal Program, restored the marsh and protected it from future damage.

ACKNOWLEDGMENTS

TOM HIRSCH HAS MY UNDYING ADMIRATION for the work he did as the relocation coordinator at Soldiers Grove. Larry Larson, formerly the executive director of the Association of State Floodplain Managers and a vital ally in the project, has remained a patient mentor all these years as I've pestered him with questions about national water policy. Thanks to Kathy Fairchild and Kate Walter for their help with the relocation, the *Kickapoo Scout*, and some of my writings over the years.

Dr. Michael MacCracken, the chief scientist for Climate Change Programs at the Climate Institute, was invaluable in helping me with the climate-change tutorial at the end of the book. Any mistakes are not Mike's but rather mine as I tried to simplify some of the more molecular-level input he provided.

Mary Louise Becker has given me all the time I needed to write this book. She spent endless hours busying herself with crafts (probably treasuring her solitude) while I hammered away at the keyboard. Kendall Rauch assisted with research.

I am thankful for all the colleagues around the world who are so dedicated to the often-frustrating work of getting their countries to accept and act against the harsh realities of global climate change. There are far too many to list here, and that is a good thing. Many have served at one time or another as unpaid members of the several successive national advisory committees for my day job with the Presidential Climate Action Project (PCAP).

I am especially grateful to Michael Northrop of the Rockefeller Brothers Fund for his unflinching support of PCAP since its inception in 2007. I don't know anyone who has done more than Michael to help people across the country push the envelope on climate action, sustainable development, and the transition to clean energy.

NOTES

Foreword

1. "Summary of the National Environmental Policy Act," US Environmental Protection Agency, https://www.epa.gov/laws-regulations/summary -national-environmental-policy-act.

Introduction

1. Dalbyul Lee and Juchul Jung, "The Growth of Low-Income Population in Floodplains: A Case Study of Austin, TX," *KSCE Journal of Civil Engineers* (January 1, 2014), https://www.researchgate.net/publication/259636751 _The_growth_of_low-income_population_in_floodplains_A_case_study _of_Austin_TX.

2. "One-Third of the Lower 48 Faces Risk of Flooding This Spring, Weather Service Says," *Washington Post*, March 19, 2020, https://www.washingtonpost .com/weather/2020/03/19/spring-flood-outlook-nws/. Population estimates are illusive because coastal populations are rising so rapidly that census data are quickly outdated. Flood hazard zones are increasing with the intensity of precipitation events. Technology plays a role, too. Estimates of populations vulnerable to river flooding range from 13 million by FEMA to 41 million by British researchers who used more advanced technology. As I write this, the most current estimates are that 118 million Americans live in counties adjacent to the coasts (2013 data cited by the Fourth National Climate Assessment); 24 million people (on the East and Gulf Coasts) are vulnerable to storm

surges (2010 worst-case projection by the National Hurricane Center, https://www.nhc.noaa.gov/nationalsurge/).

3. Matthew Cappucci, "One-Third of the Lower 48 Faces Risk of Flooding This Spring, Weather Service Says," *Washington Post*, March 19, 2020, https://rb.gy/i2kf1q.

1. The Kickapoo Valley

1. I highly recommend a book by the late Ben Logan, *The Land Remembers*, for anyone interested in a profoundly beautiful description of growing up in the Kickapoo Valley. A reviewer for the *New York Times* said it best when he wondered how the book could make him nostalgic for things that never happened to him. Then he realized, "It's not nostalgia for my own past *The Land Remembers* made me feel; it's nostalgia for a world [Logan] makes me wish I'd known."

3. The Dam

1. Marc Reisner, *Cadillac Desert: The American West and Its Disappearing Water*, Revised Edition (New York: Penguin Books, 1987).

4. The Soft Path

1. Because the value of the old buildings generally was too low to provide owners with sufficient funds for down payments on mortgages for their new buildings, the village determined fair-market value based on unflooded buildings in the region.

2. Passive solar energy systems heat buildings without mechanical components, while "active" systems include fans to distribute the heat or, in the case of solar systems that produce electricity, solar panels, power converters, and batteries to store electricity if the system is not connected to the conventional power grid.

3. When communities use FEMA's buyout program to remove buildings from floodplains, they must leave the land undeveloped in perpetuity. However, some uses are permitted including grazing, nature reserves, community gardens, wildlife habitat, outdoor recreation, and parks. Depending on a community's needs, relocations can provide opportuni-

ties to move municipal wells and water treatment plants out of the flood-plain; improve stormwater management; build streets and parking lots at the new site(s) with permeable materials so that rain is absorbed where it falls; reroute streets to avoid the floodplain so that first responders are not cut off from parts of the community during floods; upgrade internet access; and so on. Most relocations will increase the local tax base to support municipal services.

5. The Battle of La Farge

1. This is a condensed version of her much longer letter.

2. Louis A. Goth, "Obituary of a River and the Life It Shared," *New York Times*, February 11, 1973, https://rb.gy/knwcyj.

7. Mní wičhóni (Water Is Life)

1. Jesse Newman, "The Water Wars that Defined the American West Are Heading East," *Wall Street Journal*, December 2, 2019. https://rb.gy/canzur.

2. Christina Chen, "Nuclear vs. Climate Change: Feeling the Heat," Natural Resources Defense Council, August 12, 2019. https://rb.gy/zksgbf. Water issues will lead to more electric generation from renewable resources such as sunlight and wind because their equipment does not require cooling water.

3. Wallace J. Nichols, "Why Our Brains Love the Ocean: Science Explains What Draws Humans to the Sea," excerpted from Wallace J. Nichols, "Blue Mind," *Salon*, July 20, 2014, https://rb.gy/cb7xpd.

4. Nell Greenfieldboyce, "Study: 634 million people at risk from rising seas," National Public Radio, March 28, 2007, https://rb.gy/mp4zkx.

5. Beth Harpaz, "Hannibal, Missouri, a window into Mark Twain's Process," *Detroit News*, November 16, 2014, https://rb.gy/mb0kud.

6. Alexis Madrigal, "What We've Done to the Mississippi River: An Explainer," *Atlantic*, May 19, 2011, https://www.theatlantic.com/technology/archive/2011/05/what-weve-done-to-the-mississippi-river-an-explainer/239058/.

7. Alexis Madrigal, "What We've Done to the Mississippi River: An Explainer," *The Atlantic*, May 19, 2011, https://www.theatlantic.com/technology/archive/2011/05/what-weve-done-to-the-mississippi-river-an-explainer/239058/.

8. How the Federal Role Began

1. "A Chronology of Major Events Affecting the National Flood Insurance Program," American Institutes for Research, December 2005, https://rb.gy /ecjw6k.

2. Typical of older floods, accounts differ about the cost, size, and number of fatalities.

3. Robert W. Adler, "Addressing Barriers to Watershed Protection," *Environmental Law* 25(973) (1995): 1013–1014, https://rb.gy/k5dtbb.

4. Martin Reuss, "Coping with Uncertainty: Social Scientists, Engineers, and Federal Water Resources Planning," *Natural Resources Journal* 32 (Winter 1992), https://rb.gy/xwyvds.

5. White founded and directed the Natural Hazards Research and Applications Information Center. Before his death in 2006, he became one of the nation's most respected proponents of nonstructural flood prevention.

6. James M. Wright, "The Nation's Responses to Flood Disasters: A Historical Account," *A Report by the Association of State Floodplain Managers*, April 2000, https://rb.gy/mxu2w0.

7. In 2018, Congress took a good first step by passing legislation that allows as much as 6 percent of federal disaster assistance funds to be spent on pre-disaster mitigation, including the elevation of buildings, wetland restoration, and buyouts for people who agree to move out of the floodplain.

8. Kelsey Ramirez, "1 in 4 Homeowners in At-Risk Areas Made No Preparations for Hurricane Season," *Housing Wire*, August 23, 2019, https://rb.gy /sdm7ki.

9. Galloway and Brody, et al., "The Growing Threat of Urban Flooding: A National Challenge," University of Maryland College Park and Texas A&M University, 2018, https://rb.gy/ftpttc.

10. James Elliot, Phylicia Lee Brown, and Kevin Loughran, "Racial Inequalities in the Federal Buyout of Flood-Prone Homes: A Nationwide Assessment of Environmental Adaptation," *SAGE Journals* (February 12, 2020), https://rb.gy/pvmfco.

11. "10 Years after Katrina, Many New Orleans Residents Permanently Displaced," Amnesty International, n.d., https://rb.gy/9yjq7m.

12. Gary Rivlin, "White New Orleans Has Recovered from Hurricane Katrina. Black New Orleans Has Not," *Talk Poverty*, August 29, 2016, https://rb.gy/9yjq7m.

13. "Who We Are," Lower Ninth Homeowners Association website, https://www.l9wha.org/about.

14. Cesar Alfonso, "PTSD and Suicide After Natural Disasters," *Psychiatric Times*, April 24, 2018, https://rb.gy/ipcnvd.

15. Hurricanes are rated according to sustained wind speeds and based on the Saffir-Simpson Hurricane Wind Scale. The scale is 1 to 5, with 5 being the most severe. Category 3 and higher are major storms with the potential for significant fatalities and damage. The most dangerous, a Category 5 event, has sustained wind speeds of 157 miles per hour or higher, meaning that catastrophic damage will include the destruction of framed homes, long-term power outages, and areas left uninhabitable for months.

16. M. Taherkhani et al., "Sea-Level Rise Exponentially Increases Coastal Flood Frequency," *Scientific Reports* 10, Article 6466, April 16, 2020, https://rb.gy/3i9cxm.

17. Hurricane Katrina is often called a Category 5 event, reflecting its maximum strength over the Gulf of Mexico. It was rated as a Category 3 event when it made landfall in Louisiana and Mississippi.

18. *Fourth National Climate Assessment*, Chapter 8, "Coastal Effects," US Global Change Research Program, Fall 2018, https://rb.gy/znlevy. The estimate includes population living in shoreline counties including along the Great Lakes and Pacific and Caribbean Islands.

19. "Defining American's Flood Risk," First Street Foundation, n.d., https://firststreet.org.

20. "Military Installations and Sea-Level Rise," Congressional Research Service, July 26, 2019, https://rb.gy/rsqso2.

21. "Report on Effects of a Changing Climate to the Department of Defense," Office of the Under Secretary of Defense for Acquisition and Sustainment, July 2019, https://rb.gy/03uirp.

22. Phil Briggs, "Former SECNAV predicts Naval Station Norfolk will be under water within our lifetime," *Radio.com*, July 8, 2019. https://rb.gy/duymwe.

23. "Climate Resilience: DOD Needs to Assess Risk and Provide Guidance on Use of Climate Projections in Installation Master Plans and Facilities Designs," Government Accountability Office GAO-19-453, June 2019. https://rb.gy/liamdt.

9. Problems with Structures

1. "A look at how safe dams are across Michigan," WLX 10 Radio, May 21, 2020, based on US Army Corps of Engineers data, https://rb.gy/cb1yto.

2. "The Midland Dam Break, Green Ooze and Why Regulation Isn't All Bad," *Detroit Free Press* editorial board, May 28, 2020, https://rb.gy/azrvur.

3. This is the count used by the National Inventory of Dams. There are different numbers of dams in the literature. The 2021 inventory by the American Society of Civil Engineers reports more than 91,000 dams, including 15,600 rated as high-hazard.

4. David Lieb, Michael Casey, and Michelle Minkoff, "At Least 1,680 Dams across the US Pose Potential Risk," Associated Press, November 11, 2019, https://rb.gy/9xuqvv.

5. "Dam Safety Overview and the Federal Role," Congressional Research Service report R45981, October 24, 2019, https://fas.org/sgp/crs/homesec/R45981.pdf.

6. AECOM, "The Impact of Climate Change and Population Growth on the National Flood Insurance Program through 2100," prepared for the FEMA Climate Change and Coastal Studies Project, June 2013, p. ES-6, http://www.acclimatise.uk.com/login/uploaded/resources/FEMA_NFIP_report.pdf.

7. Several other federal agencies and organizations also build and operate flood-control structures. They include the Bureau of Reclamation in the Department of the Interior, which operates multipurpose water projects in seventeen western states; the Tennessee Valley Authority, which has multipurpose dams; the International Boundary and Water Commission, which operates US–Mexico border dams and levees; the Bureau of Indian Affairs; and the four federal land management agencies: Bureau of Land Management, National Park Service, US Fish and Wildlife Service, and US Forest Service.

8. "Ten Facts about Flooding," *American Rivers*, n.d., https://rb.gy/5si7r0.

9. Andrew Boryga, "King Tides Are a Glimpse into Future with Rising Seas. For Many, Flooding Is the New Normal," *South Florida Sun-Sentinel*, October 25, 2019, https://rb.gy/4ndjkx.

10. National Ocean Service, "2019 State of US High Tide Flooding with a 2020 Outlook," NOAA Technical Report NOS CO-OPS 092, July 2020, https://rb.gy/hjbsx2.

11. "2018 State of the Beach Report Card," Surfrider Foundation, December 13, 2018, rb.gy/da3ezk. Lost property includes land and structures.

12. These data come from chapter 1, "Floods and Floodplains," in a FEMA instruction text. At the time the chapter was published in 2001, the federal government had spent $25 billion on flood-control projects, "hundreds of millions of dollars" on flood disaster relief and recovery, and more than $100 million annually to provide flood-prone communities with technical and planning assistance.

13. "2.5 Million Homes, Businesses Totaling $1 Trillion Threatened by High Tide Flooding," Union of Concerned Scientists, June 18, 2018, https://rb.gy/re6ozv.

14. "Billion-Dollar Weather and Climate Disasters," National Centers for Environmental Information at NOAA, 2020, https://rb.gy/idbqbx.

15. "Expected Costs of Damage from Hurricane Winds and Storm-Related Flooding," Congressional Budget Office, April 10, 2019, https://rb.gy/sedoza.

16. Linda Lam, "A Concerning Trend: Flooding Deaths Have Increased in the US the Last Few Years," *The Weather Company*, November 8, 2018, https://rb.gy/3utf1z.

17. Heather Smith, "People Are Still Living in FEMA'S Toxic Katrina Trailers —and They Likely Have No Idea," *Grist*, August 27, 2015. FEMA eventually deployed 140,000 trailers along the Gulf Coast after Katrina, costing nearly $3 billion from sixty different companies. It turned out that many trailers contained unsafe formaldehyde levels. That resulted in a $3.4 million exercise in which the Centers for Disease Control tried to find and track the health of families that had lived in the trailers. Seven years later, a federal judge approved a nearly $43 million settlement between the companies that made the trailers and people who reported they had been exposed to hazardous fumes.

10. Sound the Retreat

1. Cary Funk and Meg Hefferon, "US Public Views on Climate and Energy," Pew Research Center, November 25, 2019, https://rb.gy/iykvmf.

2. OpenSecrets.org, "Oil & Gas Long-term Contribution Trends," n.d., https://rb.gy/msut4p.

3. OpenSecrets.org, "Oil & Gas Lobbying 2020," n.d., https://rb.gy/fbnx5r.

4. Joshua Axelrod, "Oil and Gas Leasing Is Off the Rails," Natural Resources Defense Council, October 9, 2020, https://rb.gy/vnovi5.

5. Renewables 2020: Analysis and Forecast to 2025. International Energy Agency, November 2020, https://rb.gy/ouz8og.

6. WPED Staff, "2019 was the US wind industry's third strongest installation year," *Windpower Engineering & Development*, January 30, 2020, https://rb.gy/8plwxq.

7. "Global Energy Review 2021," International Energy Agency, April 2021, https://rb.gy/tdufqg.

8. OCI Team, "Banking on Climate Change 2021: Fossil Fuel Finance Report Card," *OilChange International*, March 2021, https://rb.gy/nrskit.

9. Jillian Ambrose, "Renewable energy growth must speed up to meet Paris goals, agency says," *Guardian*, March 15, 2021, https://rb.gy/fg8cql.

10. Multi-Hazard Mitigation Council, "Natural Hazard Mitigation Saves Lives," National Institute of Building Sciences, December 2019, https://rb.gy/iuvcif.

11. In the *Fourth National Climate Assessment* federal scientists said it is more difficult to discern the influence of climate change on inland floods. Extreme precipitation is an obvious factor, they concluded, but it is compounded by other factors such as land use, land cover, and water management. "Human induced warming has not been formally identified as a factor in increased riverine flooding," the assessment said, "and the timing of any emergence of a future detectable human-caused change is unclear." USGCRP, *Climate Science Special Report: Fourth National Climate Assessment, Volume I*, D. J., Wuebbles, D. W. Fahey, K. A. Hibbard, D. J. Dokken, B. C. Stewart, and T. K. Maycock (eds.) (Washington, DC: US Global Change Research Program, 2017), doi: 10.7930/J0J964J6. In 2014, however, the *Third National Climate Assessment* acknowledged that "heavy downpours are increasing nationally," and the heaviest rainfall events have become heavier and more

frequent in the Northeast, Midwest, and upper Great Plains. https://rb
.gy/ozsnb9.

12. Adam Smith, "2010–2019: A landmark decade of US billion-dollar weather
and climate disasters," National Oceanic and Atmospheric Administration,
January 8, 2020, https://rb.gy/udgje6.

13. "U.S. Climate Resilience Toolkit," US Global Change Research Program,
March 25, 2020. The USCGRP consists of scientists from thirteen fed-
eral agencies. It is responsible for issuing the periodic *National Climate
Assessments*.

14. US Global Change Research Program, "Reducing Risks Through Adaptation Actions," *Fourth National Climate Assessment* Chapter 28, November
23, 2018, https://rb.gy/zappys. This chapter contains excellent guidance on
assessing and implementing climate change adaptation strategies, including
relocations.

15. James Kossin, Kenneth Knapp, Timothy Olander, and Christopher Velden,
"Global Increase in Major Tropical Cyclone Exceedance Probability of the
Past Four Decades," *Proceedings of the National Academy of Sciences of the
United States of America* (June 2, 2020), https://rb.gy/xibycq.

16. Union of Concerned Scientists, "Underwater; Rising Seas, Chronic Floods
and the Implications for US Coastal Real Estate," June 2018, https://rb
.gy/7t6bqb.

17. "Climate Change: Potential Economic Costs and Opportunities to Reduce
Federal Fiscal Exposure," Government Accountability Office, Report GAO-
20-338T, December 19, 2019, https://rb.gy/2zsakp. In addition to coastal and
inland floods, climate change will result in more cases of heat-related mortality in the Southeast and Midwest, changes in water supply and demand in
the West, and decreased agricultural yields in the southern Great Plains and
Southwest.

18. Zack Colman and Katy O'Donnell, "Borrowed Time: Climate Change Threatens US Mortgage Market," Politico, June 7, 2020. Politico reports that by 2018,
there were 7 million mortgages for homes in floodplains. The number of tax-
payer-backed flood insurance politics peaked in 2006, and then dropped to
5.2 million in 2018. https://rb.gy/xqzd1w.

19. "What We Don't Know About State Spending on Natural Disasters Could
Cost Us," Pew Charitable Trusts (June 19, 2019), https://rb.gy/fob6xe.

20. Marlene Lenthang, "More People Are Leaving California than Ever Before, Driven out by Worsening Wildfires, Politics and the Skyrocketing Costs of Living," *Dailymail.com*, September 13, 2020, https://rb.gy/4eyavy.

21. Christopher Flavelle, "US Flood Strategy Shifts to 'Unavoidable' Relocation of Entire Neighborhoods," *New York Times*, August 26, 2020, https://rb.gy /j4v8lm. In the past, FEMA's regulations have required that buyouts be strictly voluntary.

22. Kevin Crowe and Dinah Voyles Pulver, "Flood Model Relies on Decades of Climate Data," *USA Today*, June 29, 2020, https://rb.gy/kn2gip. The Flood Factor app is available at https://floodfactor.com/.

23. University of Maryland, Center for Disaster Resilience, and Texas A&M University, Galveston Campus, *The Growing Threat of Urban Flooding: A National Challenge* (College Park: A. James Clark School of Engineering, 2018), https://rb.gy/ftpttc.

24. Katharine Mach et al., "Managed Retreat Through Voluntary Buyouts of Flood-Prone Properties," *Science Advances*, October 9, 2019, https://rb.gy /na7q41.

25. National Public Radio reported in 2019 that "disasters, and the federal aid that follows, disproportionately benefit wealthier Americans. The same is true along racial lines, with white communities benefiting disproportionately" (Rebecca Hersher and Robert Benincasa, "How Federal Disaster Money Favors the Rich," National Public Radio, March 5, 2019, https:// rb.gy/uagnl3). Education and homeownership versus renting also made differences in how FEMA distributes funds after disasters. Nearly four in ten housing units located in 100- and 500-year floodplains were rentals, according to a study in 2017 (Stephanie Rosoff and Jessica Yager, "Housing in the US Floodplains," NYU Furman Center, May 2017, https://rb.gy /x1cxhr). On the one hand, landlords who don't live in floodplains may be less inclined to retrofit their rental properties with flood mitigation measures; on the other hand, renters may find it easier to relocate since they are less likely than owners to be financially or emotionally tied to their housing.

26. Anonymous, "Barriers to Equity in Flood Mitigation Buyouts," *Ralph Bunche Journal of Public Affairs*, Manuscript 1042, n.d., https://rb.gy/sunvg0.

27. See appendix 3 for more tips on making a relocation project successful.

28. For example, see Kimberly M. S. Cartier, "Equity Concerns Raised in Federal Flood Property Buyouts," *Eos*, October 9, 2019, https://rb.gy/zb01se.

29. Anna Weber and Rob Moore, "Going Under: Long Wait Times for Post-Flood Buyouts Leave Homeowners Under Water," *Natural Resources Defense Council*, September 12, 2019, https://rb.gy/ba2n0o

30. In a phone conversation, a FEMA spokesperson explained that one reason for the drop-off in buyouts was the spike that took place after the Great Mississippi River Flood in 1963.

31. Anna Weber and Rob Moore, "Going Under: Long Wait Times for Post-Flood Buyouts Leave Homeowners Underwater," NRDC, September 12, 2019, https://rb.gy/vmkbp6.

32. "In Town Hard-Hit by Katrina, Buyouts Offer Opportunity—For Lucky Few," National Public Radio, August 21, 2015, https://rb.gy/elguv4.

33. Christopher Flavelle, "America's Last-Ditch Climate Strategy of Retreat Isn't Going So Well," *Bloomberg*, May 2, 2018, https://rb.gy/yatiob.

34. Andrew G. Simpson, "Federal Flood Insurance Premiums Far From Keeping Up With Expected Losses," *Insurance Journal*, March 8, 2021, https://rb.gy/xxukpx.

35. See guidelines published by the International Association of Impact Assessment for examples of what should be included in a social impact assessment, https://rb.gy/4gq188.

36. While most of America's dams were built for water storage, irrigation, recreation, and other reasons unrelated to flood control, real estate development has taken place below dams designed to protect lives. The result is that structures not designed to protect people have acquired that mission. People below those dams should also be considered for buyouts and relocations.

37. First Street Foundation, "Highlights from 'The First National Flood Risk Assessment,'" June 29, 2020. The foundation says its research indicates that nearly 6 million property owners are not aware of their flood risks because FEMA does not identify them as being in flood hazard zones, https://rb.gy/bwzdno.

38. Oliver Wing et al., "Estimates of Present and Future Flood Risk in the Conterminous United States," *Environmental Research Letters*, February 28, 2018, https://rb.gy/4bloc3.

39. NYU Furman Center, "Population in the US Floodplains," December 2017, https://rb.gy/a8kzin.

40. One study of US tax subsidies for fossil energy put them at $27.4 billion annually. However, the International Monetary Fund estimated that tax subsidies combined with the impact of fossil fuels on society totaled nearly $650 billion in 2015. In regard to weather and climate disasters, NOAA reports they have cost more than $1.75 trillion since 1980, an average of more than $58 billion yearly.

41. "Expected Costs of Damage from Hurricane Winds and Storm-Related Flooding," Congressional Budget Office, April 2019, https://rb.gy/ocaxbo. The CBO did not separate the cost of hurricane winds from storm-related floods.

42. Kris Al Johnson et al., "A Benefit-Cost Analysis of Floodplain Land Acquisition for US Flood Damage Reduction," *Nature Sustainability* 3: 56–62, December 9, 2019, https://rb.gy/lvla6f.

43. Eric Roston, "Americans Are Paying $34 Billion Too Much for Houses in Flood Plains," *Bloomberg Green*, March 2, 2020.

44. *Natural Hazard Mitigation Saves 2019 Report*, National Institute of Building Sciences, December 2019, https://rb.gy/e1exxk.

45. "State by State Analysis: Property Value Loss from Sea Level Rise," First Street Foundation, August 8, 2019, https://rb.gy/incx6n.

46. Miyuki Hino and Marshall Burke, "Does Information About Climate Risk Affect Property Values?" National Bureau of Economic Research working Paper 2687, February 2020, https://rb.gy/pdubxn.

11. Natural Solutions

1. Aria Bendix, "7 American Cities That Could Disappear by 2100," *Insider*, April 3, 2019, https://rb.gy/iyp12v.

2. "Deputy Secretary for Ecosystems Restoration," Florida Department of Environmental Protection, n.d., https://floridadep.gov/eco-rest.

3. "A New Meaning for Restoration: Strengthening the Battered Gulf Coast Gives Young People Real Jobs and a Path Forward," The Nature Conservancy, February 6, 2019, https://rb.gy/brgbeu.

4. "ECOS Environmental Conservation Online System," US Fish and Wildlife Service, n.d., https://rb.gy/duxu8o.

5. "Listing and Critical Habitat – Frequently Asked Questions," US Fish and Wildlife Service, updated January 30, 2020, https://rb.gy/de9gwu.

6. "Zero Draft of the Post-2020 Global Biodiversity Framework," Convention on Biological Diversity, February 2020, https://rb.gy/nxl3wn.

7. University of Maryland Center for Environmental Science, "Climate of North American Cities Will Shift Hundreds of Miles in One Generation," *Science Daily*, February 12, 2019, https://rb.gy/zx34ug.

8. "United States Mid-Century Strategy for Deep Decarbonization," The White House, November 2016, https://rb.gy/cysuik.

9. "A Platform for the Trillion Tree Community," World Economic Forum, n.d., https://www.1t.org.

10. As of April 30, 2020, FEMA reported that it expected to have a balance of more than $74 billion in the fund at the end of fiscal year 2020, including $53.7 billion for major disasters declarations and $454 million for pre-disaster mitigation. FEMA, "Disaster Relief Fund: Monthly Report," May 7, 2020, https://rb.gy/ylpa52.

11. Under the act, federal regulators review the lending practices of community banks to determine how well they are serving the needs of low- and moderate-income communities. The scores are considered when banks apply for mergers, charters, acquisitions, deposit facilities, and branches.

12. Early Adopters

1. Kris A. Johnson et al., "A Benefit-Cost Analysis of Floodplain Land Acquisition for US Flood Damage Reduction," *Nature Sustainability* 3 (January 2020), https://rb.gy/lvla6f. However, the authors also found that nearly 40 percent of the 100-year floodplains in the coterminous United States have not been mapped by FEMA, limiting the ability to identify and protect these areas from development.

2. As noted earlier, floodproofing can involve elevating a residential building, sealing the home to prevent water from entering (dry floodproofing), modifying the building to protect parts from flooding while allowing water to enter other parts during flood events (wet floodproofing), or finishing the residence with materials able to withstand prolonged exposure to floodwaters.

3. Cassie Ringsdorf, "20 Years Later: A Resilient Recovery after Catastrophe," FEMA blog, https://rb.gy/qkwpl1.

4. Timothy Meinch, "Iowa town takes flooding in stride," *USA Today*, May 31, 2013, https://rb.gy/zcrtyh.

13. The Next Mass Migration

1. University of Exeter, "Cultural Dimensions of Climate Change Are Underestimated, Overlooked and Misunderstood," *Science Daily*, November 11, 2012, https://rb.gy/upnnsf.

2. "Tuscarora: Drawing on Traditional Teaching to Confront a Changing Climate," Northern Arizona University, n.d., https://rb.gy/uqqzfl.

3. Thanks to Naveena Sadasivam at *Grist* for the story that alerted me to this. Naveena Sadasivam, "Indigenous Tribes Are at the Forefront of Climate Change Planning in the US," *Grist*, February 4, 2020, https://rb .gy/sjotqb. The University of Oregon lists tribal adaptation plans at https:// rb.gy/63yruk.

4. Garrit Voggesser et al., "Cultural Impacts to Tribes from Climate Change Influences on Forests," *Climate Change*, March 29, 2013, https://rb.gy /wpvbv9.

5. Institute for Economics & Peace, "Ecological Threat Register 2020: Understanding Ecological Threats," September 2020, https://rb.gy/pfah2q.

6. "World Migration Report 2020," International Organization for Migration, 2019, https://rb.gy/vijgr0

7. Tom Dart, "'New Orleans West:' Houston Is Home for Many Evacuees 10 Years after Katrina," *Guardian*, August 25, 2015, https://rb.gy/mv9e7x.

8. Tim McDonnell and Amanda Shendruk, "It's Time to Prepare Cities for People Uprooted by Climate Change," *Quartz*, September 1, 2020, https://rb .gy/nqizdr.

9. Lucy Dadayan, "COVID-19 Pandemic Could Slash 2020-21 State Revenues by $200 billion," Tax Policy Center, Urban Institute & Brookings Institution, July 1, 2020, https://rb.gy/zt9wzv.

10. Linda Poon, "Cities That Were Poised to Absorb Climate Migrants Face a New Challenge," *Bloomberg City Lab*, October 5, 2020, https://rb.gy/ezmxfr.

11. Jesse Keenan et al., "Climate Gentrification: From Theory to Empiricism in Miami-Dade County, Florida," *Environmental Research Letters*, April 23, 2018, https://rb.gy/hiuggu.

12. Caleb Robinson et al., "Modeling Migration Patterns in the USA under Sea Level Rise," *PLOS One*, January 22, 2020. https://rb.gy/ojvq3p.

13. Qin Fan et al., "Climate Change, Migration, and Regional Economic Impacts in the United States," *Journal of the Association of Environmental and Resource Economics* 5, No. 3, July 2018, https://rb.gy/dzjl0i.

14. Fourth National Climate Assessment, *Global Change Research Program*, US government, November 2018, https://rb.gy/tun7jj.

15. J. Bamber et al., "Ice Sheet Contributions to Future Sea-Level Rise from Structured Expert Judgment," *Proceedings of the National Academy of Sciences of the United States of America*, May 20, 2019, https://www.pnas.org/content/116/23/11195.

16. Mathew E. Hauer, "Migration Induced by Sea-Level Rise Could Reshape the US Population Landscape," *Nature Climate Change*, April 17, 2017, https://tinyurl.com/yyk3ywg7.

17. Samuel Stebbins, "America's Fastest Shrinking Cities," *24/7 Wall St.*, May 2, 2019, https://rb.gy/pkqonh.

18. John Cromartie and Dennis Vilorio, "Rural Population Trends," Economic Research Service, US Department of Agriculture, February 15, 2019, https://rb.gy/zltgtz.

19. For example, the US Department of Housing and Urban Development has Empowerment Zone, Enterprise Community, and Renewal Community programs that offer tax credits to businesses that are located in distressed urban and rural communities. At this writing, the tax credits were allowed until the end of 2020. Congress would have to extend the programs for them to continue. Tax Credit Group, "WOTC at Work in Empowerment Zones and Renewal Communities," Tax Credit Group, Inc., January 28, 2020, https://rb.gy/ig3wxm.

20. Heidi Garrett-Peltier, "Green versus brown: Comparing the employment impacts of energy efficiency, renewable energy, and fossil fuels using an input-output model," *Economic Modelling*, 61, Feb. 2017. https://rb.gy/ce4niz.

21. W. Neil Adger, Jon Barnett, Katrina Brown, Nadine Marshall, and Karen O'Brien, "Cultural Dimensions of Climate Change Impacts and Adaptation," *Nature Climate Change*, November 11, 2012, https://rb.gy/3ah0al.

22. Anthony Oliver-Smith, "Disasters and Large-Scale Population Dislocations: International and National Responses," *Oxford Research Encyclopedia of Natural Hazard Science*, June 2018, https://rb.gy/kqnmbb.

23. "Implications of Climate Change for the US Army," United States Army War College, 2019, https://rb.gy/wjuijd.

24. David Biello, "Climate Change May Mean More Mexican Immigration," *Scientific American*, July 26, 2010, https://rb.gy/3jifwe.

25. "How Climate Change Is Driving Emigration from Central America," *PBS News Hour*, September 8, 2019, https://rb.gy/4o45jo.

26. "Activities of Selected Agencies to Address Potential Impact on Global Migration," General Accountability Office, GAO-19-166, January 2019, https://rb.gy/v9vmec.

27. Gretta Pecl et al., "Biodiversity redistribution under climate change; Impacts on ecosystems and human well-being," *Science*, March 31, 2017, https://rb.gy/ritf2x.

28. Craig Welch, "Half of All Species Are on the Move—and We're Feeling It," *National Geographic*, April 27, 2017, https://rb.gy/lpbtsw.

14. Revisiting Soldiers Grove

1. Chris Hubbuch, "Soldiers Grove; Relocated Town Spared Heavy Flood Damage; Former Site Inundated," *La Crosse Tribune*, June 22, 2008, https://rb.gy/ghqhzm.

2. Eric Roston, "FEMA May Have to Buy Millions of US Homes, Due to Climate Crisis," *Aljazeera*, October 9, 2019, https://rb.gy/xqcix6.

3. Linda Poon, "Where America's Climate Migrants Will Go As Sea Level Rises," *Bloomberg CityLab*, February 3, 2020, https://rb.gy/zyqbi7.

15. Introducing the Biocene

1. The Editors of Encyclopedia Britannica, "Do Lemmings Really Commit Mass Suicide?" *Britannica website,* n.d., https://rb.gy/kppukj. The account here comes from the editors and a fact-check of the lemming myth by David Mikkelson on Snopes.

2. "Summary of the National Environmental Policy Act," *US Environmental Protection Agency,* n.d. https://www.epa.gov/laws-regulations/summary-national-environmental-policy-act.

3. *Sustainable Development Report 2019,* United Nations, June 28, 2019. One study ranked the US last among 193 countries in making progress toward these goals, https://rb.gy/wiyhvx.

4. *World Happiness Report 2020,* March 20. In collaboration with this report, Gallup conducts surveys in more than 160 countries. Its latest research showed that 62 percent of the world's people prioritize environmental protection over economic growth, but only half are satisfied with environmental protection in their countries. See C. Krekel and G. MacKerron, "How Environmental Quality Affects Our Happiness," *World Happiness Report 2020,* https://rb.gy/ezq0rp.

5. Z. A. Wendling, J. W. Emerson, A. de Sherbinin, D. C. Esty, et al. *2020 Environmental Performance Index,* Yale Center for Environmental Law and Policy, 2020, epi.yale.edu. The index ranks 180 nations in 11 categories related to environmental health and the vitality of ecosystems.

6. Caleb Silver, "The Top 20 Economies in the World," *Investopedia,* March 18, 2020, https://rb.gy/ulzrmw. The rankings are based on data from the International Monetary Fund.

16. The Devalue Chain

1. "Toxic Air: The Price of Fossil Fuels," Centre for Research on Energy and Clean Air, Greenpeace, February 2020, https://rb.gy/ubuc0l.

2. "The State of the Air 2020," American Lung Association, April 21, 2020, http://www.stateoftheair.org/key-findings/.

3. In 2019 and 2020, before the onset of the COVID-19 pandemic, Appalachia's poverty rate was 16.3 percent compared to 14.6 percent for the nation as a whole, according to the Appalachian Regional Commission. "ARC Announces County Economic Status Designations for Fiscal Year 2020," ARC, June 2019, https://rb.gy/bwqy1a.

4. One of those writers is Jeff Biggers, whose book *The United States of Appalachia* (Berkeley, CA: Counterpoint, 2007) should be required reading.

5. Elizabeth Payne, "Owning the Mountains: Appalachia's History of Corporate Control," *Appalachian Voice*, February 18, 2016, https://rb.gy /opzsdg.

6. Readers who want to learn more about the "cynical" experiment in Appalachia will find a detailed but concise account in the article "The 100-Year Capitalist Experiment That Keeps Appalachia Poor, Sick, and Stuck on Coal" by Gwynn Guilford, published by *Quartz* on December 30, 2017, https://rb.gy/2ige5o. It is a sad example of the corporate greed touched upon later.

7. Melissa Ahern and Michael Hendryx, "Cancer Mortality Rates in Appalachian Mountaintop Coal Mining Areas," *Journal of Environmental and Occupational Health* 1(2) (2012): 63–70, https://rb.gy/g8tpcj.

8. James Bruggers, "Appalachia's Strip-Mined Mountains Face a Growing Climate Risk: Flooding," *Inside Climate News*, November 21, 2019, https://rb.gy /uxryqb.

9. Phil McKenna, "EPA Rejects Civil Rights Complaint Over Alabama Coal Ash Dump," *Inside Climate News*, March 7, 2018, https://rb.gy/p1pszy.

17. The Four Alarms

1. History.com editors, "Earth Day 2021," A&E Television Networks, https:// www.history.com/topics/holidays/earth-day.

2. My accounts of the two oil crises are greatly simplified. A variety of other factors, including economic policies and price controls, were also in play. For more complete analyses, see https://www.federalreservehistory .org/essays/oil_shock_of_1978_79 and https://www.csis.org/analysis /arab-oil-embargo%E2%80%9440-years-later.

3. "How Much Petroleum Does the United States Import and Export?" Energy Information Administration, updated March 3, 2020, https://www.eia.gov /tools/faqs/faq.php?id=727&t=6.

4. An important point: An oil addiction is an oil addiction, no matter where the oil comes from. Under its business-as-usual scenario, the Energy Information Administration expects petroleum to remain the most-consumed fuel and the largest source of US carbon dioxide emissions through 2050. https://rb .gy/bnrgis.

5. "Restoring the Quality of Our Environment," *Environmental Pollution Panel,* President's Science Advisory Committee, November 1965. https://rb.gy/2vf5gp.

6. Since the US Senate gave its "advice and consent" in 1992 to the United Nations Framework Convention on Climate Change, Congress has rejected or failed to act on bills dealing directly with climate change. In general, state and local governments have led any progress the United States has made on addressing this existential crisis.

7. The principal federal tax incentives for renewable energy are the Production Tax Credit (PTC) that began in 1992 and the Investment Tax Credit (ITC) that began in 2006. While fossil energy tax incentives are permanent parts of the US tax code, the PTC and ITC have been temporary, requiring Congess's reauthorization every few years. Congress has allowed these incentives to lapse several times before renewing them, causing uncertainty.

8. NASA published this story in 2012, and I drew heavily from its account. "Apollo Astronaut Shares Story of NASA's Earthrise Photo," NASA, March 29, 2012, https://rb.gy/b48omy.

9. "Statement by President Trump on the Paris Climate Accord," The White House, June 2, 2007, https://rb.gy/fxszob.

10. Marshall Burke, "The Cost of Paris Withdrawal," deputy director of the Center on Food Security and the Environment, Department of Earth System Science, Stanford University, G-Feed, n.d., https://rb.gy/5krepn.

11. Justin Worland, "The Pandemic Remade Every Corner of Society. Now It's the Climate's Turn," *Time,* April 26/May 3, 2021, https://rb.gy/kuyuzh.

12. "Preserving Coal County: Keeping America's Coal Miners, Families and Communities Whole in an Era of Global Energy Transition," United Mine Workers of America, u.d., https://rb.gy/h5isnb.

13. This seems like an overstatement, but it is not. Because the United States produces more greenhouse gas pollution than any other nation except China, because it has the world's largest economy, and because other nations traditionally look to America as an example, the international response to climate change will not be sufficient without the United States.

14. "As Economic Concerns Recede, Environmental Protection Rises on the Public's Policy Agenda," Pew Research Center, February 13, 2020, https://rb.gy/8w3h7q.

15. Alec Tyson and Brian Kennedy, "Two-Thirds of Americans Think the Government Should Do More on Climate," Pew Research Center, June 23, 2020, https://rb.gy/dzbpz0.

18. Frontierism

1. Verlyn Klinkenborg, "Why Was Life So Hard for the Pilgrims?" as published by Historynet from the December 2011 issue of *American History*, https://rb.gy/t8vedz, and Jed Kaplan et al., "The Prehistoric and Preindustrial Deforestation of Europe," *Elsevier*, September 24, 2009, https://rb.gy/tilcig.

2. Kamala Doršner, "Essentials of Environmental Science," licensed under CC BY 4.0. Modified from the original by Matthew R. Fisher.

3. Ray Allen Billington, "How the Frontier Shaped the American Character," *American Heritage*, April 1958, https://rb.gy/pcv3z5.

4. Gilbert King, "Where the Buffalo No Longer Roamed," *Smithsonian Magazine*, July 17, 2012, https://rb.gy/a2chzt.

5. Elizabeth Prine Pauls, "Trail of Tears," *Encyclopedia Britannica*, n.d., https://rb.gy/zhcffg. For a soldier's eyewitness account, go to https://n9.cl/e3jk.

6. There is an ongoing discussion about whether we should call it global climate change or global warming. Technically, greenhouse gases are causing global warming, and global warming is causing the climate to change. To avoid redundancy, though to the discomfort of scientists, I will use the terms interchangeably.

7. Center for Responsive Politics, "Oil & Gas," OpenSecrets.org. Campaign contributions were during the 2019–2020 election cycle as of September 21, 2020. Eighty-five percent went to Republican candidates and 15 percent to Democrats, https://rb.gy/apukoz.

8. Center for Responsive Politics, "Oil & Gas."

9. Karin Kirk, "Fossil Fuel Political Giving Outdistances Renewables 13 to 1," Yale Climate Connections, January 6, 2020, https://yaleclimateconnections.org/2020/01/fossil-fuel-political-giving-outdistances-renewables-13-to-one.

10. Robert Hine, John Mack Faragher, and Jon Coleman, *The American West: A New Interpretive History*, 2nd ed. (New Haven, CT: Yale University Press, 2000), https://tinyurl.com/yydb3c9n.

11. Hine, Faragher, and Coleman, *The American West*.

12. Keri Blakinger, "A Look Back at Some of the Coolest Attractions at the 1939 World's Fair," *New York Daily News*, April 30, 2016, https://rb.gy/geuplo.

13. I did not make this up.

14. Much of this history is drawn from an account by Alex Davies in 2017. See Alex Davies, "The World's Fair Future of 1939 and the Quest for Our Next Utopia," *Wired*, December 31, 2017, https://rb.gy/kh4mnn.

15. Devin Garofalo, "Teaching *Silent Spring* in Wisconsin: A Guide for Educators," Great World Texts, University of Wisconsin–Madison Center for the Humanities, 2017, https://rb.gy/lxsa5d.

16. Alexis de Tocqueville Quotes. BrainyQuote.com, BrainyMedia Inc, 2020, accessed October 5, 2020, https://rb.gy/ympmlh.

19. Avarice

1. G. William Domhoff, "Power in America: An Investment Manager's view on the Top 1%," Who Rules America?, posted July 2011, https://whorulesamerica.ucsc.edu/power/investment_manager.html.

2. J. Horowitz, R. Igielnik, and R. Kochhar, "Trends in Income and Wealth Inequality," Pew Research Center, January 9, 2020, https://www.pewsocialtrends.org/2020/01/09/trends-in-income-and-wealth-inequality/.

3. Chuck Collins, "Update: Billionaire Wealth, US Job Losses and Pandemic Profiteers," Inequality, April 15, 2021, https://rb.gy/moaxh9.

4. "National: Public Troubled by 'Deep State,'" Monmouth University poll, March 19, 2018, https://www.monmouth.edu/polling-institute/documents/monmouthpoll_us_031918.pdf/. The poll queries a random sample of more than eight hundred adults.

5. Frank Sammartino and Eric Toder, "How Did the Tax Cuts and Jobs Act Change Tax Expenditures," Tax Policy Center, January 22, 2020, https://www.taxpolicycenter.org, via the House Committee on the Budget, https://budget.house.gov/sites/democrats.budget.house.gov/files/documents/2017%20Tax%20Law%20Impacts%20FINAL_1.pdf.

6. David Coady et al., "Global Fossil Fuel Subsidies Remain Large: An Update Based on Country-Level Estimates," International Monetary Fund, May 2, 2019.

7. Andrew Blasko, "Reagan and Heritage: A Unique Partnership," Heritage Foundation, June 7, 2004, https://rb.gy/1py5bg.

8. Jonathan Mahler, "How One Conservative Think Tank Is Stocking Trump's Government," *New York Times Magazine*, June 20, 2018, https://rb.gy/7dpjuh.

9. "Trump Administration Embraces Heritage Foundation Policy Recommendations," Heritage Foundation, January 23, 2018, https://rb.gy/5njjgn.

10. The Charles Koch Foundation and the David H. Koch Foundation were created by brothers Charles and David Koch to support conservative and libertarian causes. They owned the majority of Koch Industries, an oil, gas, paper, and chemical conglomerate that is the United States' second-largest privately held company. David Koch died in 2019. "Mont Pelerin Society: A Window into Ideological Heart of Kochtopus Climate Denial," DeSmog, January 27, 2014, https://rb.gy/qiupn5.

11. David Harvey, *A Brief History of Neoliberalism* (New York: Oxford University Press, 2007), quoted by George Monbiot, "How Did We Get Into This Mess?", Monbiot.com, August 28, 2007, https://rb.gy/jqjket.

12. "Rachel Carson," Wikipedia, n.d., https://en.wikipedia.org/wiki/Rachel_Carson.

13. "Rethinking the Rachel Carson Legacy," Competitive Enterprise Institute, May 21, 2007, https://cei.org/content/rethinking-rachel-carson-legacy.

14. Rebecca Harrington, "The EPA Has Only Banned These 9 Chemicals Out of Thousands," *Business Insider*, February 10, 2016, https://www.businessinsider.com/epa-only-restricts-9-chemicals-2016-2.

15. "Fast Facts," Centers for Disease Control and Prevention, reviewed November 15, 2019.

16. H. S. Karagueuzian et al., "Cigarette Smoke Radioactivity and Lung Cancer Risk," *Nicotine and Tobacco Research* Vol. 13, Issue 1 (January 2012), https://rb.gy/raicuf.

17. Thomas Carr, "Who Is Really Benefiting from the Tobacco Settlement Money," American Lung Association, February 3, 2016, https://www.lung.org/blog/who-benefit-tobacco-settlement.

18. Melissa Healy, "Who's to Blame for the Nation's Opioid Crisis? Massive Trial May Answer That Question," *Los Angeles Times*, Septem-

ber 18, 2919, https://www.latimes.com/science/story/2019-09-17/opioid-lawsuit-who-is-to-blame.

19. "HR 4069 – Ensuring Patient Access and Effective Drug Enforcement Act of 2013," MapLight, n.d, https://rb.gy/bxsuoi.

20. R. deShazo et al., "Backstories on the US Opioid Epidemic. Good Intentions Gone Bad, and Industry Gone Rogue and Watch Dogs Gone to Sleep," *American Journal of Medicine* 131(6) (June 2018): 595–601, https://rb.gy/s5vbr8.

21. Matthew Taylor and Jillian Ambrose, "Revealed: Big Oil's Profits Since 1990 Total Nearly $2tn," *Guardian*, February 12, 2020, https://www.theguardian.com/business/2020/feb/12/revealed-big-oil-profits-since-1990-total-nearly-2tn-bp-shell-chevron-exxon.

22. Shannon Hall, "Exxon Knew About Climate Change Almost 40 Years Ago," *Scientific American*, October 26, 2015, https://www.scientificamerican.com/article/exxon-knew-about-climate-change-almost-40-years-ago/.

23. Directional drilling allows oil companies to reach oil deposits horizontally as well as vertically from a single well; hydraulic fracturing injects a mixture of sand, water, and chemicals under pressure to break underground shale formations and release trapped gas.

24. "US Becomes World's Largest Crude Oil Producer and Department of Energy Authorizes Short Term Natural Gas Exports," Department of Energy, September 13, 2018. https://rb.gy/cuztwe.

25. Republican Party Platform 2016, Republican Party Platform Committee, n.d., https://rb.gy/fypin1.

20. Safe Operating Spaces

1. Elizabeth Howell, "James Irwin: Eighth Man on the Moon," Space.com, April 8, 2013. https://rb.gy/zllhid.

2. Sulayman Nyang, "The Origins of Life: A Muslim View," NPR/CPR News, August 8, 2005, https://rb.gy/oq5kwi.

3. Visit the Worldometer to see the world population growing in real time. https://www.worldometers.info.

4. "The Nine Planetary Boundaries," Stockholm Resilience Center, n.d., https://rb.gy/zdlso4. The team included eighteen scientists from a variety of institutions including the Scripps Institution of Oceanography, the Stockholm

Resilience Center at Stockholm University, the Center for Macroecology, Evolution and Climate at the University of Copenhagen, and the Potsdam Institute of Climate Impact Research.

5. Will Steffen et al., "Planetary Boundaries: Guiding Human Development on a Changing Planet," *Science* Vol. 347, Issue 6223, February 13, 2015, https://rb.gy/an7rkt.

6. Robert Monroe, "Earth Has Crossed Several 'Planetary Boundaries,' Thresholds of Human-Induced Environmental Change," UC San Diego and Scripps Institution of Oceanography, January 15, 2015, https://rb.gy/ava6xu.

7. *The Limits to Growth* was commissioned by the Club of Rome and authored by Donella H. Meadows, Dennis L. Meadows, Jørgen Randers, and William W. Behrens III. Using computer models, they evaluated the exponential growth of five variables: population, food production, industrialization, pollution, and consumption of nonrenewable natural resources. They concluded, "If the present growth trends in world population, industrialization, pollution, food production, and resource depletion continue unchanged, the limits to growth on this planet will be reached sometime within the next one hundred years. The most probable result will be a rather sudden and uncontrollable decline in both population and industrial capacity." Donella H. Meadows, Dennis L. Meadows, Jørgen Randers, and William W. Behrens III, *The Limits to Growth* (Falls Church, VA: Potomac Associates, 1972).

8. D. Meadows et al., *A Synopsis: Limits to Growth: The 30-Year Update*, Academy for Systems Change, https://rb.gy/tmnxfm.

9. Julia Conley, "Divestment Fever Spreads as 'Eco Radicals at Goldman Sachs' Downgrade Exxon Stock to 'Sell' Status," *Common Dreams*, February 3, 2020, https://rb.gy/qwu8ri.

10. Sharon Kelly, "Fossil Fuels Investments Cost California and Colorado Pension Funds Over $19 Billion, Report Finds," *DESMOG*, November 5, 2019 https://rb.gy/6yx4jv.

11. Tom Espiner, "JP Morgan Economists Warn of 'Catastrophic' Climate Change," *BBC News*, February 21, 2020, https://rb.gy/bjrasc.

12. OGJ Editors, "BP to Write Down up to $17.5 Billion in Second Quarter, Lowers Oil Price Expectations to 2050," *Oil & Gas Journal*, June 5, 2020, https://rb.gy/xvt11w.

13. The website Business Insider offers a good explanation of geoengineering ideas. See tiny.cc/x8d6jz.

14. Walter E. Westman, "How Much Are Nature's Services Worth?" *Science* 197(4307) (September 2, 1977): 960–964, https://rb.gy/9e54vu.

15. Jane Lubchenco, Stephen Carpenter, Paul Ehrlich, Gretchen Daily, Hal Mooney, Robert Costanza, and others.

16. Other members of the team were Ralph d'Arge of the University of Wyoming, Rudolf de Groot of Wageningen Agricultural University in the Netherlands, Stephen Farber of the University of Pittsburgh, Monica Grasso, Bruce Hannon of the University of Illinois at Champaign-Urbana, Karin Limburg of the Institute of Ecosystem Studies, Shahid Naeem of the University of Minnesota, Robert V. O'Neill of Oak Ridge National Laboratory, Jose Paruelo from the University of Bueno Aires, Robert G. Raskin of the Jet Propulsion Laboratory, Paul Sutton of the University of California at Santa Barbara, and Marjan van den Belt of Ecological Economics Research and Applications Inc.

17. R. Costanza, R. d'Arge, R. de Groot, et al. "The Value of the World's Ecosystem Services and Natural Capital," *Nature* 387 (1997): 253–260, doi:10.1038/387253a0.

18. The world's stocks of natural assets including geology, soil, water, and all living things.

19. Millennium Ecosystem Assessment Overview, December 2005, https://www.millenniumassessment.org/en/About.html#2.

20. Costanza et al., "Changes in the Global Value of Ecosystem Services," *Global Environmental Change* 26 (May 2014): 152–158, https://doi.org/10.1016/j.gloenvcha.2014.04.002.

21. "Bhutan's Gross National Happiness Index," Oxford Poverty and Human Development Initiative, University of Oxford, n.d. https://rb.gy/trhvqy.

22. Caoimhe Twohig-Bennett, "It's Official—Spending Time Outside Is Good for You," University of East Anglia, *Science Daily*, July 6, 2018, https://rb.gy/hdoubz.

23. There is strong evidence that one of the criteria for human happiness is contact with nature, yet most Americans spend little time in touch with it. Researchers led by Howard Frumpkin at the University of Washington found that Americans typically spend 90 percent of their time in buildings and vehicles, and adults spend more than 10.5 hours daily consuming media,

while outdoor activities have declined substantially. Groups such as the National Institute of Environmental Health Sciences (Nate Seltenrich, "From Intuitive to Evidence Based: Developing the Science of Nature as a Public Health Resource," *Environmental Health* Perspectives 125[11] [November 2017]: 114002, https://rb.gy/nj6zhd) contend that nature is a public health resource. "Doctors nationwide have already begun giving their patients 'park prescriptions,' instructions to improve their health by spending more time outdoors," the institute reports. "A growing body of evidence suggests that nature, whether the green leaves of a city park or the natural sounds of a back-country wilderness, may help us think better, feel better, and possibly even live longer."

21. The Restoration Economy

1. Nathaniel Rich, *Second Nature: Scenes from a World Remade* (New York: Macmillan, 2021).

2. Cities, farms, energy producers, and householders all compete for America's freshwater. One result that needs more attention is how water withdrawals in several parts of the US have caused lands to subside. On the East Coast, subsidence leaves affected properties more vulnerable to floods and sea-level rise. In other words, the continental United States is shrinking and sinking, leaving less for us to sing about from sea to shining sea.

3. Dan Tong et.al., "Committed emissions from existing energy infrastructure jeopardize 1.5°C climate target," *Nature*, July 1, 2019, https://rb.gy/1wsf2k.

4. April 24, 20021, email communication with Steven J. Davis, a principal investigator in the UC, Irvine study.

5. David Ewing Duncan, "Chemicals Within Us," *National Geographic*, n.d., https://rb.gy/yburss.

6. Ban Alonzo, "The Effects of Pollution on the Body," *Sciencing*, updated April 25, 2017, https//rb.gy/ebbwuo.

7. Andrea Baccarelli et.al., "Eight ways chemical pollutants harm the body," *ScienceDaily*, March 5, 2021, https://rb.gy/won9nr.

8. Catherine Cullinane Thomas et al., "Estimating the Economic Impacts of Ecosystem Restoration—Methods and Case Studies," USGS, Report 2016-1016, 2016, https://rb.gy/r3apyt.

9. "Clean Jobs in America 2019," Environmental Entrepreneurs (E2), March 13, 2019, https://rb.gy/v41tiq.

10. Lucien Georgeson and Mark Maslin, "Estimating the Scale of the US Green Economy Within the Global Context," *Palgrave Communications* 5, Article 121, 2019. https://www.nature.com/articles/s41599-019-0329-3.

11. The American Petroleum Institute says oil and gas contribute 7 percent of the US GDP. The more important number would be net GDP, i.e., 7 percent minus direct and indirect fossil-fuel subsidies. The International Monetary Fund calculates that direct and indirect US subsidies for oil, gas, and coal were $649 billion in 2015. But subsidies probably are more since then due to Donald Trump's America First energy policy to support a significant increase in fossil energy production.

12. "Clean Jobs in America 2019."

13. T. BenDor et al., "Estimating the Size and Impact of the Ecological Economy," *PloS One* 10(6): e0128339, https://doi.org/10.1371/journal.pone.0128339.

14. S. Kelmenson, T. BenDor and T. W. Lester, "The Economic Impacts of the US Ecological Restoration Sector," Federal Reserve Bank of Boston, June 2, 2016, https://www.bostonfed.org/publications/communities-and-banking/2016/summer/the-economic-impacts-of-the-us-ecological-restoration-sector.aspx.

15. Kelmenson, BenDor, and Lester, "The Economic Impacts."

16. Eri Roston, "America's 'Green Economy' Is Now Worth $1.3 Trillion," *Financial Advisor*, October 15, 2019. https://rb.gy/so8c02.

17. B. W. Griscom et al., "Natural Climate Solutions," *Proceedings of the National Academy of Sciences of the United States of America* 114(44) (October 31, 2017): 11645–11650, https://doi.org/10.1073/pnas.1710465114.

18. "Mitigation Matters: Policy Solutions to Reduce Local Flood Risk," Pew Charitable Trusts, November 19, 2019, https://www-aws.pewtrusts.org/de/research-and-analysis/articles/2019/11/19/mitigation-matters-policy-solutions-to-reduce-local-flood-risk.

19. "EIA Projects renewables share of US electricity generation mix will double by 2050," US Energy Information Administration, February 8, 2021, https://rb.gy/sjqfyh.

20. "Renewable Energy Futures Study," National Renewable Energy Laboratory, US Department of Energy, 2012, https://rb.gy/zydcfj. The study was a col-

laboration between NREL and 100 contributors from 35 organizations including other national laboratories, industry, universities, and non-government organizations.

21. "Global Electricity Review 2020," Ember, March 2020, rb.gy/jgeovx.

22. "BNEF Says Solar and Wind Are Now Cheapest Sources of New Energy Generation for Majority of Planet," Renewable Energy World, April 28, 2020, https://rb.gy/7acsta.

23. Edward Louie and Joshua Pearce, "Retraining Investment for US Transition from Coal to Solar Photovoltaic Employment," *Energy Economics* 57 (June 2016), https://www.researchgate.net/publication/303977030 _Retraining_Investment_for_US_Transition_from_Coal_to_Solar_Photovoltaic _Employment.

24. "Renewable Energy Market by Product Type (Bioenergy, Geothermal Energy, Hydroelectric Power, Solar Energy, and Wind Power) and By End Use (Industrial, Commercial, Residential, and Others)," Global Industry Perspective, Comprehensive Analysis, and Forecast, 2020–2026, March 2021, https://rb.gy /foknyf; Mark Vogel, "Fighting Labor Shortages: Strategies for Recruiting, Training and Retaining in the Solar Industry," Solar Power World, October 21, 2019, https://rb.gy/reibho.

25. Representative Jason Crow, "Crow Looks to Close Skills Gap in the Clean Energy Sector," House Small Business Subcommittee on Innovation and Workforce Development, October 29, 2019, https://rb.gy/6ucdyn.

26. Jacqueline Varas and Aaron Iovine, "The State of Federal Worker Training Programs," American Action Forum, September 1, 2017, https://rb.gy /rvm94e.

27. "Abandoned Hardrock Mines: Information on Number of Mines, Expenditures and Factors That Limit Efforts to Address Natural Hazards," Government Accountability Office report GAO-20-238, March 2020, https://rb .gy/2shgbu.

28. Thanks to Rachael Bale of the Center for investigative reporting and her article "The Problem with American's Abandoned Mines," *Reveal News*, October 21, 2014, https://rb.gy/jhjj3p.

29. "More US Coal-Fired Power Plants Are Decommissioned as Retirements Continue," US Energy Information Administration, July 26, 2019, https://rb .gy/k3n52s.

30. Michael Coren, "Coal's Collapse Could Lead to Landscape of Abandoned Mines," *Quartz*, April 23, 2020, https://rb.gy/odnpad.

31. "Map of US Dams Removed Since 1912," American Rivers, n.d., but data loaded in 2020, https://rb.gy/1pxtot.

32. As quoted in Jeremy Jacobs, "Risks Soar, Bills Come Due as 20th Century Dams Crumble," E&E News, March 6, 2017, https://rb.gy/rlaxfo. This is not to imply that the corps no longer does big structural projects. North Dakota and Minnesota are building a $2.2 billion flood diversion project with the ACE to prevent flooding in the Fargo-Moorhead area by redirecting floodwater through 30 miles of channels. Also in the Midwest, in compliance with federal requirements on restricting combined sewer overflows, Chicago is constructing the $4 billion Deep Tunnel, also known by its bureaucratic name, the Tunnel and Reservoir Plan, or TARP. When completed in 2029, Deep Tunnel will connect 109 miles of tunnel with three massive reservoirs that can contain a combined 20.6 billion gallons of water.

33. "State Renewable Portfolio Standards and Goals," National Conference of State Legislatures, April 17, 2020. https://rb.gy/eubtps.

34. "State Renewable Portfolio Standards and Goals."

22. The Vision Thing

1. Donella Meadows, "Envisioning a Sustainable World," Academy for Systems Change, u.d., https://rb.gy/alm2fd.

2. COP 15, the next of the annual conferences in which nations hoped to reach an agreement on combatting climate change.

3. P. H. Ray and S. R. Anderson, *The Cultural Creatives, How 50 Million People Are Changing the World* (New York: Harmony Books, 2000).

4. Rob Hopkins, *The Transition Handbook* (White River Junction, VT: Chelsea Green Publishing, 2008).

5. Jonathan Arnold of Arnold Imaging in Kansas City, Missouri, https://arnoldimaging.com.

6. "Future We Want – Outcome Document," United Nations, June 22, 2012, https://rb.gy/t9ca4t.

7. Dr. Henry Cloud, Goodreads, u.d. https://rb.gy/zichpz.

8. Adam Frank, "'Under a White Sky' examines what it might take for humans to continue to exist," NPR, February 8, 2021, https://rb.gy/p06jzj.

9. "Biofilters for Stormwater Discharge Pollution Removal," State of Oregon Department of Environmental Quality, 2003, https://rb.gy/ubc3ru.

23. The Biocene

1. Deanna Conners, "Will large parts of the Earth be too hot for people in 50 years?" *EarthSky*, June 23, 2020, https://rb.gy/upu2q9.

2. Paul J. Crutzen, "Geology of Mankind," *Nature* 415(23) (January 3, 2002), https://doi.org/10.1038/415023a.

3. For the background on how the term was born, see Nicola Davison, "The Anthropocene Epoch: Have We Entered a New Phase of Planetary History?" *Guardian*, May 30, 2019. https://rb.gy/xudq3a.

4. "Results of the Binding Vote by AWG," Working Group on the 'Anthropocene', Subcommission on Quaternary Stratigraphy, May 21, 2019. https://rb.gy/g8u5zi.

5. The National Oceanic and Atmospheric Agency defines invasive species as "an organism that causes ecological or economic harm in a new environment where it is not native. . . . Invasive species are capable of causing extinctions of native plants and animals, reducing biodiversity, competing with native organisms for limited resources, and altering habitats."

6. Those who are old enough will remember the television series *Kung Fu*, in which the Shaolin master tells his student, "Your tread must be light and sure, as though your path were upon rice paper . . . This rice paper is the test. Fragile as the wings of the dragon fly, clinging as the cocoon of the silk worm. When you can walk its length and leave no trace, you will have learned."

7. *Juliana v. United States*, 947 F.3d 1159, 1164 (9th Cir. 2020). The Ninth Circuit Court ruled on the Justice Department's appeal of a decision by a District Court judge that supported the children's case. The children argued that the government violated their constitutional right "under the Due Process Clause of the Fifth Amendment to a 'climate system capable of sustaining human life.'"

8. "The Paris Agreement," United Nations Climate Change, reached on December 12, 2015, and entered into force on November 4, 2016, https://rb.gy

/ozp6oy; "17 Goals to Transform Our World," United Nations, n.d., https://rb.gy/ebjhrw.

9. Dom Galeon, "Stephen Hawking: 'I Fear That AI May Replace Humans Altogether,'" *Futurism*, November 4, 2018. https://rb.gy/pltekx.

10. Dom Galeon, "Separating Science Fact from Science Hype: How Far off Is the Singularity?" *Futurism*, https://rb.gy/wfkq8j.

11. https://biomimicry.org/history.

12. https://biomimicry.org/what-is-biomimicry/.

13. Dallon Adams, "The Best of Biomimicry: Here's 7 Brilliant Examples of Nature-Inspired Design," Digital Trends, January 29, 2017, https://rb.gy/bzeyiz.

14. Mark Sommer, "Cybercene or Biocene: Which Future Will We Choose?" *Medium*, June 7, 2019.

15. Drawn from an interview with Peter Kahn by Adrienne Matei published by *Quartz*, August 8, 2017, https://rb.gy/9mutij.

16. Rebecca Morelle, "Oldest Stone Tools Pre-date Earliest Humans," *BBC News*, May 20, 2015. https://rb.gy/xlfdlf.

17. Selin Kesebir and Pelin Kesebir, "How Modern Life Became Disconnected from Nature," *Greater Good Magazine,* September 20, 2017, https://rb.gy/hjoa8q.

18. "Bhutan's Gross National Happiness Index," Oxford Poverty and Human Development Initiative, n.d., https://ophi.org.uk/policy/national-policy/gross-national-happiness-index/.

19. See "Signs That Humanity Is Returning to Loving a Living Earth," a video interview with Charles Eisenstein, May 20, 2019, https://rb.gy/aqfqmg.

20. Peter Aspinall et al., "The Urban Brain: Analyzing Outdoor Physical Activity with Mobile EEG," *British Journal of Sports Medicine* 49(4) (March 6, 2013), https://rb.gy/rnptus.

21. L. Ilsedore Cleeves et al. "The Ancient Heritage of Water Ice in the Solar System," *Science* 345(6204) (September 26, 2014), https://rb.gy/c32kkn.

22. Richard Grant, "Do Trees Talk to Each Other?" *Smithsonian Magazine*, March 2018.

Epilogue

1. "CLIMATE CHANGE – A Climate Migration Pilot Program Could Enhance the Nation's Resilience and Reduce Federal Fiscal Exposure," GAO-20-488, Government Accountability Office, July 2020.

2. "UN Report: Nature's Dangerous Decline 'Unprecedented': Species Extinction Rates 'Accelerating,'" Intergovernmental Science-Policy Platform on Biodiversity and Ecosystem Services, May 2019, https://rb.gy/zoh4pe.

3. "UN Report: Nature's Dangerous Decline."

4. Bob Dylan, *The Freewheelin' Bob Dylan*, 1963 by Warner Bros. Inc.; renewed 1991 by Special Rider Music.

5. Gracy Olmstead, "Don't Let Climate Change Stop You from Becoming a Parent," *New York Times*, September 19, 2019.

6. Ash Sanders, "I Chose Not to Have Kids Because I'm Afraid for the Planet," *BuzzFeed News*, July 24, 2019. https://rb.gy/kscs5x.

7. Jason Plautz, "The Environmental Burden of Generation Z," *Washington Post Magazine*, February 3, 2020, https://rb.gy/ry40fr. Also, Michelle Horton, "Stanford Researchers Explore the Effect of Climate Change on Suicide Rates," *Stanford News*, March 29, 2019. https://rb.gy/tmfvwq.

8. Joni Mitchell, "Ladies of the Canyon," A&M Studios April 1970.

9. Sources attribute this quote variously to Crowfoot (1830–1890) and to a traditional Pueblo prayer. https://rb.gy/zhjynr.

Appendix 1: Climate 101

1. An investigation by *Inside Climate News* (N. Banerjee et al., "Exxon: The Road Not Taken," September 16, 2015, https://insideclimatenews.org /content/Exxon-The-Road-Not-Taken) and a peer-reviewed study at Harvard University (G. Supran and N. Oreskes, "Assessing ExxonMobil's Climate Change Communications [1977–2014]," *Environmental Research Letters* 12(8), https://rb.gy/j1ygec) found that ExxonMobil's scientists warned company executives as early as 1977 that fossil fuels would cause global warming. Nevertheless, the company kept that conclusion secret. In 1989, Exxon and Shell Oil organized the Global Climate Coalition to spread doubt about climate science and to lobby against policies that would result in less use of their products. Other early members and collaborators in the Global Climate

Coalition included the National Association of Manufacturers, Amoco, the American Forest & Paper Association, American Petroleum Institute, Chevron, Chrysler, Cyprus AMAX Minerals, Ford, General Motors, Texaco, and the United States Chamber of Commerce.

2. A. Gustafson et al., "A Growing Majority of Americans Think Global Warming Is Happening and Are Worried," Yale Program on Climate Change Communication, February 21, 2019, https://rb.gy/cfmm2k.

3. Lydia Saad, "Americans Concerned as Ever About Global Warming," Gallup, March 25, 2019, https://rb.gy/yyfcyw.

4. J. Cook et al., "Consensus on Consensus: A Synthesis of Consensus Estimates on Human-Caused Global Warming," *Environmental Research Letters* 11(4) (April 13, 2016), https://rb.gy/zzykep.

5. "This Graphic Puts Global Warming in Full Perspective," Climate Central, April 19, 2017, https://rb.gy/nzj23m.

6. "Climate Milestone: Earth's CO_2 Level Passes 400 ppm," *National Geographic*, March 29, 2019, https://rb.gy/3o1imu.

7. The fossil energy industry promotes carbon capture and sequestration at the point of combustion, but decades of research and demonstrations have not produced a market-ready result. Also, fossil fuels produce carbon emissions not only when they are combusted but also during extraction, processing, and transportation. Finally, the high cost of carbon capture will make it difficult for fossil fuels to compete with clean, renewable energy.

8. Many new ideas for collecting and sequestering carbon dioxide involve exotic forms of geoengineering, such as blocking some sunlight from reaching the Earth's surface and seeding oceans with iron to produce more algae. However, many of these ideas would have high potential for unintended consequences.

9. "Is Sea Level Rising?" National Ocean Service, NOAA, updated October 9, 2019, https://oceanservice.noaa.gov/facts/sealevel.html.

10. Linda Lam, "A Concerning Trend: Flooding Deaths Have Increased in the US the Last Few Years," The Weather Channel, November 8, 2018, https://rb.gy/kwexzc.

11. "Climate Change Indicators: Heavy Precipitation," EPA, updated August 2016, https://rb.gy/hlg5sg. The EPA has published a consolidated report on climate change indicators at https://www.epa.gov/climate-indicators.

12. "Climate Change Indicators: River Flooding," EPA, updated August 2016, https://rb.gy/f9zpki.

13. In a bomb cyclone, a storm intensifies so rapidly that the barometric pressure drops 24 millibars in 24 hours.

14. "National Climate Report – September 2019," NOAA National Centers for Environmental Information. https://rb.gy/rjbmdh.

15. "Disasters and Large-Scale Populations Dislocations: International and National Responses," Anthony Oliver-Smith, Oxford Research Encyclopedia of Natural Hazard Science, June 2018, https://rb.gy/pbbpgv.

16. This book focuses on floods, but there are many other impacts of global warming. They include more intense heat waves (the deadliest type of weather disaster in the United States), drought, and the danger of "positive feedback loops"—i.e., incidents like the melting of permafrost that result in self-perpetuating warming. Secondary impacts include the introduction of disease vectors into new areas of the country, more intense wildfires and longer fire seasons, crop losses, longer pollen seasons, more asthma, decreases in the productivity of outdoor workers, freshwater shortages, the migration of climate refugees across national borders, international instability resulting in state failures, and so on.

17. "Annual Energy Outlook 2021 with projections to 2050," Narrative, US Energy Information Administration, February 2021. https://rb.gy/bnrgis. These are EIA's reference case projections based on current policies and expert analyses.

18. "Oil & Gas: Lobbying, 2020," Center for Responsive Politics, n.d., https://rb.gy/avxk5o.

19. "Oil & Gas: Money to Congress," Center for Responsive Politics, n.d., https://rb.gy/9dmkvb.

20. "Energy transition investment reached a half a trillion dollars in 2020," BloombergNEF 2021 Executive Factbook, BloombergNEF, March 2, 2021. Energy transition investments include renewable energy, electrified transport, electrified heat, energy storage, hydrogen, and carbon capture and storage. https://rb.gy/e6axl3.

21. "2020 Renewable Energy Industry Outlook, Exploring Renewable Energy Policy, Innovation and Market Trends," Deloitte, n.d., https://www2.deloitte.com/content/dam/Deloitte/us/Documents/energy-resources/us-2020-renewable-energy-industry-outlook.pdf.

Appendix 2: Recommendations

1. C. Hilke et al., "Softening Our Shorelines: Policy and Practice for Living Shorelines along the Gulf and Atlantic Coasts," National Wildlife Federation, 2020, https://rb.gy/zobhua.

2. PMP is a theoretical concept used by hydrologists to estimate probable maximum floods (PMF) for designing flood control structures.

3. As determined by the Climate Action Tracker. It reports that as of December 2019, 22 states, 550 cities, and 900 companies with operations in the United States had made commitments that, if achieved, would put the United States within "striking distance" of the America's goal under the Paris Agreement: a 17 to 24 percent reduction in emissions below 2005 levels by 2025. See https://rb.gy/awowgc. Also see "Greenhouse Gas Emissions Reduction Targets and Market-Based Policies," a recent report on state goals compiled by the National Conference of State Legislatures, https://rb.gy/bqkgl0.

4. "Presidential Policy Recommendations for 2020," Center for Science and Democracy, Union of Concerned Scientists, January 2020, https://rb.gy/knpvs1. Contains many specific recommendations.

5. The social cost of carbon is a calculation of the social, environmental, and economic impacts of the CO_2 produced by an action.

6. See Johnson et al. "A Benefit-Cost Analysis of Floodplain Land Acquisition to Reduce Flood Damages in the US," 2019. The authors conclude that by 2070, acquiring undeveloped flood-prone lands and conserving them for nature would cost less than paying for flood damages in 100-year floodplains. In large areas, the savings from avoided damages would be at least 5 to 1.

7. The market value of coastal buildings already is declining because of sea-level rise. A study by the Union of Concerned Scientists found that more than 300,000 coastal homes and 14,000 commercial properties are at risk of chronic inundation by 2045. Their combined market value is $136 billion. "Underwater: Rising Seas, Chronic Floods, and the Implications for US Coastal Real Estate," Union of Concerned Sciences, n.d., https://rb.gy/c0icrk.

8. In a study of 382 metro areas, *24/7 Wall St.* has identified the US cities with the greatest population losses between 2012 and 2017. See S. Stebbins, "These 25 Cities Are Losing More Residents than They Are Gaining as Population Declines," *USA Today*, March 21, 2019, https://rb.gy/ughhlj.

9. Attribution science is a new branch of climate research that can determine how much climate change contributed to an extreme weather event.

10. Oliver Wing et al., "Estimates of present and future flood risk in the conterminous United States," Environmental Research Letters, February, 28, 2018. The university says its high-resolution data allow it to identify floodplains along smaller streams and rivers. https://rb.gy/4bloc3.

11. "Highlights from 'The First National Flood Risk Assessment,'" First Street Foundation, June 29, 2020. The foundation says its research indicates that nearly 6 million property owners are not aware of their flood risks because they are not identified by FEMA as being in flood hazard zones. https://rb.gy/bwzdno.

12. "Population in the US Floodplains," NYU Furman Center, December 2017, https://rb.gy/a8kzin.

Appendix 3: Tips for Relocation Facilitators

1. See FEMA's fact sheet on hazard mitigation planning at https://www.fema.gov/emergency-managers/risk/hazard-mitigation-planning.

2. The toolkit is available at https://www.georgetownclimate.org/adaptation/toolkits/managed-retreat-toolkit/about-this-toolkit.html.

INDEX

Note: Entries in italics refer to images and illustrations.